Frozen Assets

Frozen Assets

How I lived Iceland's boom and bust

ARMANN THORVALDSSON

John Wiley & Sons, Ltd

Contents

Preface

Wednesday 8 October 2008, 10 a.m., Kaupthing Singer & Friedlander, London

In the cafeteria, I was talking to one of the girls from the Treasury desk. Half-heartedly, I was trying to explain our survival chances. Then I noticed that she was looking past me, started to shake uncontrollably and I saw tears streaming down her face. When I turned around, I saw why. Blazoned across the Bloomberg TV screen was the screaming headline 'Kaupthing collapses'. Shortly after, in a live broadcast from parliament, Alistair Darling, the Chancellor of the Exchequer, announced that he had sold the Kaupthing Singer & Friedlander deposits to ING Direct. He further said he had placed the bank into administration.

As the CEO of Kaupthing Singer & Friedlander (KSF), the news came as a slap in the face. Like everyone else, I knew there were difficulties, but had never been part of discussions with ING, or any other bank, about selling our deposits. The Treasury had invoked a law drafted in the aftermath of the collapse of Northern Rock in 2007, allowing them to remove the deposit base of any bank and replace it with a claim from the Treasury. I knew, though, that no law should have allowed Darling to place KSF in administration without my knowledge. In fact, we were still in discussions with the UK Financial Services Authority (FSA).

Glitnir, another leading Icelandic bank, had been clumsily nationalised a week earlier, precipitating a week of sleepless nights. Gradually but steadily, this had diminished confidence in the Icelandic banking sector – our funding base began to melt away. Over that weekend, we had worked hard on a detailed plan to shrink the business and generate the liquidity we so badly needed.

That Monday, we needed a decent market; a strong headwind. What we got was one of the worst days in the history of the London Stock Exchange. The FTSE index dropped by eight percent. We needed a signal of strong support from the Icelandic government. What we got was an address from the Icelandic Prime Minister announcing that an emergency law had been enacted, subordinating bondholders to depositors. The Prime Minister ended his address with 'God Bless Iceland'. So much for strength.

With both Glitnir and Landsbanki (the other major Icelandic banks) under the administration of the Icelandic FSA, the UK government used anti-terror laws to freeze the assets of Landsbanki in the UK. A fight started to brew over Landsbanki's Icesave deposit scheme, resulting in UK Icesave depositors being unable to access their funds. Icesave was the closest comparable product to our internet deposit accounts – Kaupthing Edge. This was bad news. The media coverage talked constantly of 'the Icelandic banks' – tarring us all with the same brush.

Almost all counterparties cut their lines to KSF. Then, that most dreaded event – a run on the bank. In a week, close to £1 billion evaporated. Under pressure, we managed to sell some assets and draw on lines with the parent bank. Further money from Iceland was being discussed when the ING deal with the Treasury was announced that Wednesday morning.

As the news flashed across the Bloomberg screen, I called my contact at the FSA in Canary Wharf. She seemed surprised. A few minutes later, she called back to tell me this wasn't right. If only the parent company back in Iceland could come up with £300 million more liquidity, we would still be a going concern. But the writing was on the wall. Darling's announcement made sure that Iceland wouldn't send any money, and that there would be an even greater run on the deposits. It was all over.

I sat alone at my desk, staring at the computer screen. I felt shattered. I had staggered on for a week, sleeping just a few hours each night, now I was running on empty. It was difficult to sort out the feelings. Years of work building up a business had come to an end. Hundreds of people would lose their jobs. People who had trusted us with their money would lose a part of it – how much I couldn't tell at the time.

But then the failure of KSF in the UK was almost overshadowed by the fact that Kaupthing as a whole had fallen. I had spent even more time, almost 15 years, building it with my colleagues and friends. Still, the failure of one bank seemed minor, compared to the fact that my country was in ruins.

I started to think about how all this had all happened. How Iceland – a tiny nation in the Atlantic – rose to the heights of international finance; how I was involved; and how and where it all went wrong. We had built up a bank from a floor of an office block in Reykjavik to beautiful offices in the world's financial capitals; from being worth less than $4 million to a market capitalisation of over $10 billion. We had travelled the world, changed the face of the high street and rubbed shoulders with celebrities.

I left the Kaupthing Singer & Friedlander building in Mayfair, and stepped into my chauffeur-driven car for the last time. I couldn't help but think back to when it had all started, and how my entrance at Kaupthing contrasted with my exit.

Chapter One

A Catalyst is Born

I had just turned 26 years old when I first arrived at the Kaupthing building in my Russian Lada, in the bitter snows of Boxing Day 1994. It wasn't a graceful entrance. My passenger door was held together by a piece of string, the temperature controls did the opposite of what you asked them and you had to switch the headlights on to get the windscreen wipers to work. I had bought it with money scraped together by organising a book market with a friend after six months of unemployment. I still remember the smell of the aftershave I was wearing as I walked through the doors of Kaupthing. It was probably because it was one of the first times I had actually worn aftershave. It was my first real job and I was seriously stressed. Although I had specialised in finance during my MBA, I had no practical experience. What I had learned in the United States applied to the biggest financial market in the world. How the tiny Icelandic financial market worked was a mystery to me.

***

I wasn't born to be a banker. The neighbourhood I grew up in, Breidholt, was Reykjavik's equivalent to Brixton in London. The son of two teachers, my ambition from an early age had been to follow in their footsteps. Initially I wanted to teach physical education because I loved sport. But though I could easily swing a racket, throw a handball or kick a football, it quickly became apparent that I hadn't a clue how to explain these skills to someone else. At the age of 21 I decided that academic subjects would be better, and I began studying history at the University of Iceland, intending to be a history teacher. I did well, although I never felt completely at ease there. I suspect the professors mainly remember me because I finished my studies in two years, while the standard was three years. Some of them didn't like the fact that I did it so quickly and one of them even admitted he had lowered my grade because of it. Evidently he didn't believe I showed the subject enough respect by rushing through it.

At the time, if someone had told me that my future career would be in business and finance, I would have laughed in their face.

Ever since I was a child I had been known for either losing or giving away any money that came into my possession. The only business initiative I had shown in my early years was when, at the age of nine, I had set up a cinema in my parents' garage and shown 8mm films to the neighbourhood kids. When my older brother saw the level of interest, he immediately took over the operation on the basis that he was the family's first born and could easily beat me up. Considerably more business savvy, he charged admission (which I hadn't thought of), bought popcorn and liquorice wholesale and sold it with a 100 percent margin to the appreciative and mostly illiterate audience. Under his management the garage cinema became an instant commercial success, not surprising given that he even charged me admission, although most of the films belonged to me.

During my college years I must have seemed like a bit of an introvert. I was shy, not particularly comfortable in my own skin. Most of my time was spent on sports, badminton in particular, which I played at an international level, and through which I met my wife, Thordis Edwald, who was the Icelandic champion. I didn't socialise much in college. I didn't drink until the age of 19 and without the confidence boost attached to drinking I wasn't comfortable going to parties or school dances until my final year. I couldn't even stand up in front of people without hyperventilating and sweating uncontrollably.

In my early twenties, however, all this rapidly changed. Over the next decade I gradually became the complete opposite of my college self. I socialised more and, boring as it sounds, I started to see myself working in an office. I didn't really think about what kind of office, or what kind of business I would be doing there. It was just the thought of working in a room full of people that attracted me. I had taken a few classes on economic history, and reading Adam Smith, John Locke, Frederick Hayek and Milton Friedman had fuelled my interest in the economy and business in general. What I didn't know was how to make the transition from history to business. If I were to commence business studies at the university from scratch, that would take another four years. That seemed a long time. When discussing this dilemma with a friend, he told me about the possibility of taking a Master's degree in Business Administration (MBA), which would take two years. You couldn't do that in Iceland at the time, but the degree was offered in various other countries. This was an ideal route for me to switch into business. I also fancied the idea of moving abroad, and quickly set my eyes on the United States of America, the Mecca of the business world. Thordis and I decided on Boston, based on the fact that it was closer to home than California. So in the summer of 1992 we and our newborn son, Bjarki, headed for Boston, where I was enrolled in the MBA programme at Boston University.

In Boston, we quickly felt the effect of being from a small country with a weak currency. My student loans were paid out in Icelandic krona, which meant that our financial status was very different in the first year compared to the second year. In the first year, the krona was very strong, so we were able to afford a good apartment in a nice neighbourhood close to Boston College. In our second year, however, the krona had devalued by more than 20 percent so we needed to move to Jamaica Plain, one of the worst areas of Boston, where we lived in a small bug infested apartment with a wolf parading outside our bedroom window. Despite that, we had fun in Boston. We made many friends, mainly international students and Icelanders studying in the area. A few of them would later join Kaupthing and others became clients when they moved back to Iceland. We had also made friends through playing badminton, which we mainly did to scrape together some money. Thordis did some coaching and we also travelled to tournaments, mainly to win prize money. Although it wasn't huge amounts of money, it made a considerable difference if we could earn a couple of hundred dollars from a tournament. That also enabled us to travel a bit around the east coast, although most of the sights we saw were the insides of various sports halls.

Living in a foreign city when you are a student is obviously very different from living there when you have an income. When we came back to Boston with some friends a few years later, they were massively unimpressed by our knowledge of the city. We had no idea about where the restaurants, bars and cultural highlights were. The two years we lived there, we had no money so we never ate out, unless it involved waiting in line to order and cleaning up after yourself. With a young child, the few times we went out were really just drinks at a friend's house. Much to my chagrin, I didn't even manage to go to see the Boston Celtics or the Red Sox while we lived there.

I enjoyed the MBA hugely. I had decided to specialise in finance even before the programme began. I did that without knowing what finance exactly was. My reasoning was that because my undergraduate studies were in a fluffy subject like history, I needed to specialise in something analytical to be taken seriously when entering the job market. That ruled out marketing and human resources. Accounting sounded boring, so I picked finance. As it turned out, I actually enjoyed finance very much and it became my favourite subject anyway. I found applying the rules of the market to real life problems fascinating. I was also still uncomfortable speaking in front of people so I found some of the management and marketing classes, where participation in discussions was very important, more uncomfortable. Burying my head in a book with only a calculator for company was more up my street at the time. Despite the 'fluffy' background I did very well in the programme, graduating somewhere close to the top ten percent of my class. At the end of my studies I briefly considered whether to seek employment in the USA but decided against it in the end. Because I didn't have any work experience before the MBA, which was unusual, it was difficult for me to find interesting work. Also I wanted to go back to Iceland. I've always been very attached to my home country, and at that stage, being abroad for two years felt like a long time.

Back in Iceland though, finding a job in finance, or in anything else for that matter, turned out to be a difficult task. The economy was not in great shape and my academic background wasn't winning me any favours. Headhunters suggested that I might be more suited to journalism than business, whilst recruiters at Icelandic banks looked at my MBA with a mixture of distrust and suspicion. At 26, I was unemployed, debt-ridden, with a wife, a young son and a baby due.

Luckily, my father had been on the lookout. In November, he had bumped into a cousin in an art gallery and discovered that he was an executive at a small brokerage firm called Kaupthing. The cousin agreed to see me, and asked me to work on a temporary assignment between Christmas and New Year, helping the back office to settle an Initial Public Offering (IPO) for a recently privatised pharmaceutical business. Later, colleagues used to joke that he had forgotten about me, so didn't ask me to leave until it was too late. But with only 28 employees working in Kaupthing at the time, that wasn't too likely.

Kaupthing had been founded as an advisory and securities firm in 1982. In Icelandic, the name means an exchange or marketplace. Its eight founders were young, well-educated idealists, interested in developing a financial market in Iceland. At that time, there wasn't even a stock market. In a tiny country with limited opportunities, survival depended on being a jack of all trades. A newspaper at the time described the operations of the new company as 'any kind of advisory and research services in the areas of macroeconomics and management, IT consulting and services, sales and marketing consultancy, investment advice, bond and equity brokerage, asset sales, asset management, real estate brokerage, sale of companies, aircraft and ship sales, and any services related to these businesses.' The business lines appeared to outnumber the staff.

Over the next decade the new company's focus narrowed and it aborted its consulting practice and real estate agency activities, becoming a more specialised securities house. When a stock market was established in the mid-eighties, Kaupthing quickly became an active participant. Its ownership and management changed a few times over this period. In the early nineties two financial groups jointly owned Kaupthing. One of them was the savings banks group and the other was Bunadarbanki, the agricultural bank of Iceland, owned by the government. At the time there were three major banks in Iceland: two of them were government owned, Landsbanki and Bunadarbanki, while the third Islandsbanki (later Glitnir) was publicly listed. They were all of fairly similar size, although Bunadarbanki was the smallest by most measures. All had purely domestic operations. Landsbanki had the largest equity base, amounting to just over £50 million. To us this was a massive amount, but to anyone outside of Iceland it was tiny. There were only four brokerage houses of any meaningful size, including Kaupthing. At the time, the commercial banks all owned separate brokerage houses. The banks focused on lending, while their brokerage subsidiaries specialised in brokerage, asset management and corporate finance activities. Capital and balance sheets were for the most part safely separated from the brokerage and advisory business. Investment banks were unheard of.

In 1994, then, the company was small by any standards, even Icelandic ones. We didn't have our own building, and rented one and a half floors, covering approximately 1000 square metres. There were only two divisions: asset management and what was called the securities division. The asset management division both operated mutual funds and managed money for private clients while the securities division did pretty much everything else. I joined the securities division in the beginning. We were involved in the broking and trading of both equities and bonds, but also corporate finance and foreign exchange and derivatives trading.

Chinese walls were as alien to us as, well, a wall from China would be in Iceland. That didn't mean, however, that ethical standards were low; on the contrary people were well aware that they were often privy to sensitive information and would place big emphasis on confidentiality. Staff's own trading was frowned upon and trading in unlisted shares was banned internally, although no such ban was forced upon us by the regulators. In a way, light regulation at that time probably made people take more ethical responsibility themselves.

As I walked through the office on my first day, I met the people who were to lead the company's meteoric rise over the next 13 years. The CEO at the time was Gudmundur Hauksson, but he would shortly leave his post. The other key people who would stay on were mostly fresh out of college and had recently joined. When the generation above us left over the next few years, we were ready to move into management, with big ambitions and unshakeable confidence.

Of all these people, Sigurdur Einarsson would probably do the most to influence the events of the next decade, not only for Kaupthing but for the whole financial market in Iceland. Ten years older than me, his prior experience at Islandsbanki and Danske Bank gave him prestige in the company. His fluent Danish also gave us an advantage later, when we expanded into the Nordic countries. He started as head of the securities division, but less than three years later he would be CEO. Short and stockily built, squint-eyed, with an ever-receding hairline, Sigurdur resembled nothing so much as a young Winston Churchill. He was tough too, but he kept his friends close. As I used to joke, he was like Russian toilet paper, rough on the edges, but definitely better than nothing when you're in need. Far from being a micro manager, he tended to give the younger people a lot of freedom and responsibility. Known to exaggerate numbers, he once famously answered the question 'how many people live in Iceland?' with 'less than a million' – the population was slightly more than 250,000 at the time. This bullish hyper-confidence set him apart from the rest of us – in the beginning, he was the only one of us who really did have a boundless imagination about what we could do.

Three other key players, Hreidar Sigurdsson, Magnus Gudmundsson and Ingolfur Helgason had also joined shortly before me. All were business graduates from the University of Iceland around my age, with little experience of the wider world.

Hreidar was an innovative thinker and fantastic dealmaker; he was behind some of the best-known deals we ever did. He was very thin with ears so big that we joked that his head looked like a trophy. As a child, an arrow had been shot into his right eye, partially blinding him and giving him a lazy eye. Every time a deal didn't go right, he claimed that he'd looked at it with his bad eye. Naturally hyperactive, the invention of the BlackBerry led to him develop the attention span of a squirrel. Yet Hreidar was a top student, and fantastically analytical. He could read through financial reports at the speed of light, quickly spotting the necessary information. His creative mind was naturally entrepreneurial; he thought like many of the big players we met along the way. He started out in asset management, but by 1998 he had become the deputy CEO. Subsequently he became more involved in our corporate finance and proprietary trading activities.

Ingolfur was short with blond hair, though like Sigurdur's his hair receded as Kaupthing grew. We had played badminton competitively together as children, making him the only one I knew before starting at Kaupthing. He became known as the 'fashion police' – he was such a neat dresser we always suspected him of ironing his jeans – he was relentless in advising the rest of us on what was and was not acceptable. But his down-to-earth common sense made him a vital asset with investors, who trusted him implicitly. He was crucial to our early attempts to raise capital in Iceland, for ourselves and our clients. In 2005, he was made CEO for Iceland.

What Ingolfur did for institutional clients, Magnus did for the private client business. Tall and athletic, he stood out in a crowd. He was a shrewd investor, always more at ease with numbers than languages. But he was also a great people person. He was chosen to spearhead our expansion overseas and moved to Luxembourg to set up our offshore banking services in 1998. He performed fantastically and customers loved him. One of his major clients even moved to his neighbourhood in Luxembourg to be near him. For some time, anyone with any money in Iceland banked with us in Luxembourg.

And me? In my first few years at Kaupthing, I moved around a lot, not quite settling in. Still quite shy at this point, I didn't bond quickly with people. The girls in the back office later told me they thought I was slightly backward because I spoke so rarely. The first time I had to make a small presentation to the management, I only barely avoided fainting and perspired so heavily that I had to go home and change shirts afterwards. Worst of all, only three weeks into the job I managed to make a serious faux pas at the first office party. Nervous, and surrounded by people I didn't really know, I drank quickly. When someone started to tell jokes late in the evening, I had enough Dutch courage to follow up with my own jokes. The first two went well, so I eagerly followed them up with a third, completely inappropriate one, involving a morgue and dubious sexual activities. Silence descended on the room. I was mortified and, out of the corner of my eye, I could see my cousin, who had recruited me, looking down at the floor in disgust. Permanent employment seemed highly unlikely. In the end, though, what seemed like a disaster turned out to be a blessing. Hreidar told me later that this was the first time he, or most other people, had noticed who I was.

I was involved in research, brokerage, foreign exchange, derivatives, and for a while I was responsible for the funding of the firm. Various activities that required contact with the world outside Iceland often found their way to my desk. The firm was small and it was helpful to be able to multitask. I was equally strong in languages and finance, which was probably the reason for the wide range of activities. As Kaupthing grew and became more specialised I eventually settled down as head of investment banking. That was the division that worked on mergers and acquisitions, arranged and underwrote equity offerings and IPOs. Success was based on building relationships with corporate clients and entrepreneurs, and over time I became quite good at it.

The culture that was formed in the early days was unique. We were young; we wanted to have fun, and that created a 'work hard, play hard' atmosphere that became Kaupthing's trademark. Internal competition was fierce, not only in terms of profitability, but also in terms of what division created the best comedy act at the Christmas party or who organised the most intellectually stimulating morning meeting. We met up for drinks after work, organised karaoke competitions and went camping at the weekends. Hierarchy was almost non-existent and reflected Iceland's classless society. It was common to see the janitor chatting to the CEO at an office party. Being part of a prominent family created no respect, unless it was accompanied by skill and intelligence. At Kaupthing it wasn't important who you were, what mattered was what you were capable of. The culture was fairly male dominated, as tends to be the case at brokerage companies and investment banks. The split between men and women was equal in total numbers, but in the front office men outnumbered women greatly, and the opposite was true in the back office. Applications for brokerage jobs was heavily skewed towards men and that was reflected in the recruitment numbers. Of course we still had a good number of women in the front office and I don't think anyone who worked there would have described the culture as sexist. Yet we still had the reputation for being a boys' club and there was some truth to that.

Our sense of humour was quite hard-hitting – we loved nothing more than a practical joke. Sometimes it all got a bit out of hand. One member of staff who was celebrating his 30th birthday secretly hired an actor to attend the party and give a speech. The actor pretended to be a client of Kaupthing whose life had been ruined by investment advice given by the birthday boy. He became more and more foul-mouthed and aggressive during the speech until the guests were in a state of complete shock. When a fight erupted between the guest and the host, the ninety year old grandfather of the birthday boy, a former supreme court justice, started to shake uncontrollably and had to be carried away. By the time it was finally revealed that people had been witnessing an act, the atmosphere had been destroyed and the party dissolved.

The newer members of staff bore the brunt more often than not. When the King of Sweden was on a formal visit to Iceland, a broker who had recently joined was told that the King would be visiting the trading floor. A water pipe under the hard wood floor had recently burst, causing the surface of the floor to swell slightly. The broker was told that he would have to stand on top of the bulge so the King wouldn't notice it. After half an hour later, with no sign of the King, the snickering on the trading floor became loud enough for the red faced broker to realise that he had been had. Unfortunately, the young broker took the ill-fated decision to get back at his tormentor. When an e-mail was sent round to all staff announcing drinks after work, the victim used a colleague's computer, to reply to all with the sentence: 'I will be there with a massive hard-on!' Unluckily for him, this was a violation of both e-mail policy and sexual harassment policy; after only a few weeks at the bank, he found himself out of a job.

Even our more senior people were not spared. Shortly after a new head of legal joined, I placed the first major transaction on his desk. One of the large fishing companies, located in Akureyri in northern Iceland, was considering a major takeover of a company in Denmark and they wanted us to advise on the transaction. The first thing they needed was a letter of intent they wanted to sign with the seller. Our man got cracking and after some dialogue with the CFO of the fishing company, he flew to Akureyri to meet with the company and the Danish lawyer representing the seller on a Friday afternoon. The CFO introduced our lawyer to the Danish lawyer, who turned out to be a beautiful blonde in her thirties, then swiftly left the room. As they started running through the letter of intent, our man started to notice some peculiarities in the young lawyer. For one her Danish accent sounded awfully Swedish. Also, although the girl was wearing a typical business suit, he had never seen anyone in business wearing open high heel sandals with carefully varnished toe nails. When she began to complain about the high temperature and unbutton her shirt, his suspicion grew. His suspicions were confirmed when a group of his closest friends and colleagues jumped into the room at the same time as the 'lawyer' (who turned out to be a Swedish exotic dancer) ripped off her shirt. Our new employee was getting married a couple of weeks later and we had done all this to trick him into a stag do in Akureyri.

Clients came to love the corporate culture at Kaupthing. In the early days, client entertainment was heavily scrutinised and done quietly, on a small scale, so it wasn't perceived as a sign of excess. It became clear though, that nothing was better for building up trust and relationships. We organised salmon fishing trips, invited clients on trips abroad to meet financial institutions, and set up seminars in Iceland. It wasn't so much the nature of the events that made us successful, but rather the atmosphere we created. We didn't spare them the wicked humour and the teasing that was a big part of the culture – and most took it in their stride. Of course, we sometimes overstepped the mark. On one fishing trip at a salmon river in Western Iceland, I noticed that one, very overweight, prospective client was sharing a tiny room with Sigurdur Einarsson, himself not a thin man. Looking at them and their bags, I innocently asked 'where are you two going to keep the luggage?' Not surprisingly, we didn't get much business from the client after that.

But we matched all this with a work ethic more akin to that of an American investment bank than anything that had come before in Iceland. We worked evenings and most weekends. If we were competing we never gave up. Once, one of the pension funds in Iceland was selecting an asset manager to run their portfolio of assets and decided on another firm without considering us. When we learnt of this, we harassed all their board members until they agreed to allow us to submit a proposal. Unfortunately the board meeting was the following day and we had no presentation or proposal ready. We worked through the night and until midday the following day to finish the presentation. Even though the board had already made up their mind and was really only humouring us by allowing our presentation, they were hugely impressed with our proposal. So they decided to split the portfolio in two and gave half of it to us to manage. I left the office at lunchtime the second day, after working 30 hours without stopping, only to find that our HR manager took off a half day's salary. She correctly pointed out that according to my agreement I didn't get paid overtime, and if I left early a deduction would be made from my salary!

Looking back, the numbers and amounts we were dealing with at the time sound very modest. The biggest asset management clients had the equivalent of £2–300,000 under management. To us this was a huge amount of money; one could only dream of ever building up that kind of wealth. The amounts involved in securities trading were in proportion to this. In my first year we frequently had days in the stock market where no shares changed hands. The profits were modest too. In 1994 profits were around £200,000 and in 1995 profits actually declined to £175,000. Still, these were considered fairly decent in Iceland at the time.

Salaries and remuneration were in line with the size of the company, but also the prevailing views on income distribution. The CEOs of the biggest companies in the country received around £100,000 annual compensation, but unlike in the US and the UK, by that time, it was unheard or for bankers or brokers of any kind to receive anything close to that amount. When I started out my basic salary was £15,000 and I couldn't believe how well I was getting paid. Two years after I started, Sigurdar put in place a long-term incentive plan. Previous attempts to allow employees to buy shares in the firm, or issue shares options to them, had come to nothing, blocked by the board. Increasingly, this was a problem, as Kaupthing grew and the staff became more and more sought after in the marketplace. Everyone liked working there so much that we practically never lost key personnel, but as increasing amounts were offered, the pressure mounted. Finally, Sigurdur came up with a long-term incentive plan. It was simple. Around ten of the key people in the business were promised a lump sum payment in three years, if they hadn't left by then. The amount we were promised was to me an amazing amount of money, as much as one million dollars would have sounded to an American investment banker. It was one million kronur, the equivalent of £8,500. One of my colleagues declined to be part of the plan, as he didn't want to be tied down for such a long time. When pointed out to him that of course he could leave at any time, even if he was part of the plan, it still didn't change his mind. Being a bit of a bohemian, he didn't want the prospect of such a huge amount of money clouding his mind. He ended up working for Kaupthing for another six years. Three years later, though, the amount looked puny, considering that in the intervening years, we had grown the value of the firm by approximately £50 million.

Beyond the numbers, Kaupthing was a small company. Shortly after I joined there was an uprising in the back office, due to what became known as the 'Big Switchboard Scandal'. The switchboard was managed by one person only and she was obviously entitled to her lunch and coffee breaks. We had a system of replacement, where the girls in the back office were asked to take turns in managing the switchboard during coffee breaks and lunches. This wasn't a popular task and one day the dissatisfaction erupted. The view of the back office workers' 'union' was that answering the telephone wasn't their job any more than it was the job of the brokers and traders. With the wisdom of Solomon, Gudmundur the CEO decided that all staff members, excluding himself, would now fill in on the switchboard.

Star traders sat sour-faced in reception with the headphones on while sniggering colleagues walked by. Naturally, the incoming calls were sometimes for the selfsame person who was on the switchboard at that time. More often than not that person would pretend to be someone else, calmly replying 'I will see if he is in', pressing mute and then unmute before answering as himself. A few weeks in, I became a victim.

At my brother-in-law's birthday party I had met our CEO's lawyer. We had spoken quite a bit at the party and discussed my job at Kaupthing. With each drink, the importance of my role at Kaupthing grew. Only a few days later the lawyer came to the office to see the CEO. As luck would have it I was wearing the headphones in reception. In my head, I quickly calibrated the options of trying to explain the switch board system or pretend I had never seen him before. I opted for the second choice and sent him through to our CEO without flinching. After a few weeks and a number of similar incidents, the system was abandoned and a second receptionist was hired for the switchboard.

Around Christmas time each year, Icelanders flocked to buy shares before year end. Tax incentives at the time allowed people to deduct a proportion of the shares they had bought from income tax. Of course, people could buy shares anytime during the year, but in typical Icelandic fashion they tended not to do anything until the last minute. This meant that in the week between Christmas and New Year, the volume of share buying was several times the amount traded in a normal week. There was no way the brokers and asset management staff could handle the volumes. People were queuing up outside our office and everyone, no matter what their job description was, would be given a desk to sell shares. This was done either over the phone or in person. Even the CEO would turn into a broker. Some of the elderly clients, coming to buy £1000 worth in Kaupthing's equity fund, almost had a heart attack when they were shown into the CEO's office to close the transaction.

The markets weren't that impressed by the changes at Kaupthing in 1994 and 1995. More experienced staff were leaving, and rumour had it that Kaupthing was in trouble. For a while, we did struggle a bit, but we soon learned the ropes. Although there was a mix of people, the culture that emerged reflected the things we all had in common.

Crucially, we were all outsiders in Icelandic business. None of us had any connections to the business establishment or political powers at the time. The sons of teachers, sailors and electricians, we had little regard for the establishment. It wasn't that we were out to shake the balance of power, it's simply that we didn't care whether we did or not. We were fiercely ambitious, and that ambition was focused purely on building the business and making profits. Whether we ruffled some feathers along the way was of no consequence to us. We were so small in the beginning that no one particularly noticed what was brewing within the walls of Kaupthing. Important changes that were taking place in Iceland would, however, create a very exciting platform for us to grow from. We were about to take full advantage of that opportunity.

Chapter Two

The Financial Caterpillar

In the mid-nineties Iceland was hardly buzzing. It was probably the last place on earth you would expect an exciting business environment to brew. The country was at the tail end of a six-year economic downturn. A 20 percent reduction in purchasing power had left many in a tight spot. The economy was a one trick pony at the time, far too dependent on fishing, which accounted for close to 70 percent of exports. A collapse in the cod stock in the eighties, followed by a sharp reduction in fish prices in the nineties, had hit the economy hard.

Still, the country had come a long way. Sitting isolated in the middle of the Atlantic Ocean, Iceland is barely habitable due to the rough terrain and unforgiving weather. It was settled mainly by Norwegians in the ninth and tenth centuries who fled their native land to escape heavy taxes, and regain autonomy from the Norwegian King, Harald Fairhair. Wind, rain and snowstorms were obviously preferable to the heavy duties that these tax-avoiding, freedom-seeking settlers were fleeing from. But over the course of a thousand years, the weather and volcanic activity regularly did their best to eliminate the population, and came close a few times. At the end of the eighteenth century the population was down to almost 30,000 people. Icelanders were nearly extinct.

In the early twentieth century the majority of the population still lived in mud huts. As late as at the beginning of World War II, Iceland was among the poorest nations in Europe. The country benefited financially from the war, however, and received Marshall Aid in the aftermath. In the second part of the twentieth century the position turned upside down. When I started working at Kaupthing, Iceland was already one of the richest nations in Europe by any measure.

How had this happened? Ironically, the wealth was created by leverage. Not by financial leverage – that would come later – but rather the leverage of vast natural resources compared to the size of the population. About one-and-a-half times the size of Ireland, Iceland has two important natural resources: generous fishing stocks and enormous energy, both geothermal and hydroelectric. Tourists also flock to see the spectacular volcanic landscape. Measured on a per capita basis, Iceland attracts more tourists than France. Like a Middle Eastern oil state, Iceland had a lot of resources for a small population, and started to use them efficiently.

Natural resources aside, Icelanders also like to work. Historically, unemployment has been almost non-existent. Over the last 30 years unemployment has typically ranged between 1 and 2 percent and the very highest rate was 5 percent – close to what many economists deem to be 'natural unemployment'. Working the system was almost unheard of. In many cases, even when people are unemployed, benefits are so frowned on that they remain uncollected – they are only ever a very last resort. But benefits are also relatively low, in stark contrast to the social democratic paradise offered by other Nordic countries.

Despite increased prosperity, Iceland was not a very liberal society when I was growing up. It was a bit backwards in many respects and its peculiarities caused raised eyebrows amongst foreign visitors. Private ownership of radio and television was banned until the mid-eighties. Instead, there was one state-owned TV station, and one state-owned radio station. The radio spent only two hours a week on two shows that played pop music. One was called 'Tunes for the teens' and the other was, extraordinarily, called 'Songs for the sick', in which people in hospital sent in to request particular songs. Not surprisingly, these tended towards the sentimental, filling the airwaves with 'I can't smile without you', 'Yesterday', and 'Stand by your man' The television was similarly conservative. To add insult to injury, the station did not broadcast on Thursdays or at all during July. Members of parliament even debated the need to broadcast television in colour.

Attitudes towards alcohol were also restrictive. For a long time people were not allowed to buy alcohol in restaurants and bars on Wednesdays, and beer wasn't allowed at all. As a replacement, people would drink what was called 'ersatz beer', a horrific blend of low alcoholic pilsner and vodka. All alcohol beverages were only sold in special purpose wine stores, owned and run by the government.

In the late eighties, however, a wave of liberalism washed over the island. Both privately owned radio and television stations were allowed and beer was made freely available in March 1989. The government television station even went with the flow and started to broadcast on Thursdays and in July. On the back of this wave a man who would change the landscape of Icelandic politics, re-energise the economy and give freedom to the capital markets was climbing to power. His name was David Oddsson.

Oddsson was a member of the Icelandic Independence Party, the biggest and most powerful in the country. Unlike other Nordic countries, where social democrats tended to be in power, in Iceland the leading party for the majority of the last century was centre-right, somewhat similar to the British Conservative Party. After being one of the most popular mayors Reykjavik ever had, Oddsson launched what you might call a hostile takeover bid to become the leader of the Independence Party. In 1991 he formed a government with the Social Democrats and became the Prime Minister of Iceland at the age of 43. He would hold the position for a record 13 consecutive years.

A relatively short, chubby man, Oddsson wouldn't catch your eye if it weren't for his unusual Afro-like hair. But, behind the modest exterior there was a brilliant and very determined mind. He became a super-man in Icelandic politics and, at his peak, he was undoubtedly one of the most powerful men the country had ever known. The source of his power was not just his position, but his intelligence, wit and ruthless-ness. He was a phenomenal orator – whether in parliamentary debate or in private arguments, he could be pretty sure of winning. Yet he was also a fiercely aggressive man, and so intensely well-connected that he knew everything about everyone. People desperately tried to avoid making him an enemy.

It was under Oddsson's leadership that Iceland went through such a massive change in the nineties and early 2000s. In 1994, Iceland joined the European Economic Area, resulting in the free flow of capital, goods, services and labour to and from the country. As international op-portunities opened up, the younger generation began looking overseas with great excitement.

At the same time Iceland went from being probably the least market-oriented of the Nordic countries, to the most. Taxes were lowered to a level not seen in any other Western European country apart from Ireland. Government influence was diminished and, in a Thatcherite privatisation effort, state-owned companies were placed in the hand of private individuals. The disposal of the government-owned banks fuelled the rapid growth of the financial system. In less than a decade, Iceland became a capitalist heaven. The flipside of this coin, though, was that the power and influence of politicians over the economy declined. Those that took the most advantage of the liberalisation were not the established businesses, but rather the younger generation. Ironically, as that happened, the man responsible for the development didn't like it at all.

***

The business environment was changing, and so were things at Kaupthing. The small business volumes in Iceland at the time meant that we would get involved in almost anything we could think of that generated revenues. This spurred innovative thinking and resourcefulness, which would become the hallmark of the firm. Indeed, many of the things we did genuinely broke new ground.

We created products that hadn't existed before. People were encouraged to be innovative and they were given freedom and responsibility to develop new opportunities, in large part as a result of Sigurdur's management style. I developed the first foreign exchange options on the Icelandic currency, the krona, in 1996. The options gave companies the opportunity to buy or sell krona at a fixed exchange in the future, making it possible for them to hedge against adverse currency movements. Sigurdur had been instrumental, while at Islandsbanki and before joining us, in making the first forward agreements on the krona, making a lot of money for Islandsbanki in the process. In early 1996 he mentioned to me that he thought there would be great demand for options on the krona if we could develop them. I had taken derivative classes during my MBA so I told him that I thought I could do it, much to his delight. When I started looking into it, I quickly found out that properly hedging any options would be a problem. We could partially hedge our exposures by trading in and out of the underlying currencies, but the only way to hedge against changes in volatility was to buy options and they didn't exist. We were still so keen to be able to offer the product that we concluded that we should accept a greater risk by charging for it through higher pricing. Fortunately, the options had limited commercial success, due to the high premiums we had to charge to compensate for liquidity and volatility risk. I was quite relieved – not a natural risk junkie, I didn't really fancy running a big option book that couldn't be hedged properly.

The swap products we developed on the krona were much more successful. These enabled investors to receive high interest rates in krona while paying lower rates in foreign currencies, a transaction often referred to as 'carry trades.' The idea for the instruments came during my trip with Hreidar to New York in 1996 where we had been pitching to investors to buy Icelandic Treasury Notes. Interest rates in Iceland were considerably higher than in most other countries and American investors could pick up a yield difference of six percent between the krona and US dollar. An investor needed to accept the foreign exchange risk, as any devaluation of the krona would cause him losses. Investors found the market small and illiquid. Flying back we discussed whether we couldn't somehow generate the yield difference between the krona and other currencies for Icelandic clients, who were willing to take the foreign exchange risk, and the idea for the krona currency swaps was born. What we intended to offer was a swap where they received high interest in krona and paid us in turn much lower interest rates in foreign currency. We wanted to offer a three-year trade with the sale pitch that if the exchange rate was at the same level at the end of the three years, the profits would be 20 percent of the nominal amount of the swap. The krona had been stable for a long period of time so we were pretty certain that there was investor appetite for the product. The problem we had was that there was no derivatives market available to hedge our exposure, which was the opposite of our investors.

What we did was to buy the underlying Treasury Notes, which paid the krona rate. We then borrowed the equivalent amount in a basket of currencies resembling the krona trade-weighted index from a German Landesbank by pledging the Treasury Notes to them. As we predicted, there was a big appetite among investors and we quickly sold swaps for £10 million, which was a very large amount at the time. The profit to us over the period of the swap was close to half a million pounds, a massive amount at the time. The trade was successful and at the end of the three-year period, investors reaped impressive profits. We felt like geniuses!

Innovation started to flow at Kaupthing. We were the first financial institution in Iceland to offer guaranteed products, securities that guarantee the investor repayment of the nominal amount they invested and additionally a percentage of the increase of, for instance, a stock exchange index. Early on we approached some of the foreign companies that had subsidiaries in Iceland and issued debt for them in Icelandic kronur to reduce their exposure to the krona.

One of our more innovative trades was a funding exercise for one of the larger fishing companies in Iceland and Shell Iceland, the oil distribution company. Both needed funds. The fishing company wanted to borrow in foreign currency as all of its sales were outside Iceland. Shell wanted to borrow in krona as all its sales were domestic. We had begun to build relationships with Scandinavian and German banks who were happy to consider lending to Icelandic companies. They, however, did not like lending to fishing companies. They weren't very familiar with the fishing industry and didn't like the volatility of earnings inherent in the sector due to the unpredictability of fish catches. They were, on the other hand, very happy to lend to an oil distribution company like Shell Iceland at very competitive terms. At the same time, the Icelandic corporate bond market was open to both companies and the market actually didn't price their risk very differently. Investors were both knowledgeable and comfortable with the fishing sector and put value on the fishing quotas held by the fishing companies. So, the solution we came up with was to underwrite a bond offering for the fishing company in krona and broker a loan to Shell Iceland from one of the German banks in foreign currency. This, of course, gave both companies exposure to the wrong currencies, so we created a swap between them that effectively turned Shell's exposure from foreign currency to kronur, and vice versa for the fishing company. The terms both companies got were considerably better than what they would have got by borrowing directly in their currency of choice. In turn, we made money by receiving a fee for underwriting the bond issue and for being the intermediary for the loan, plus we charged fees on the swap. Everyone was happy.

Necessity was also sometimes the mother of innovation; our best ideas sometimes came from the need to get ourselves or our clients out of trouble. One of the local authorities for whom we had brokered a foreign loan makes a good example. As well as getting a US dollar loan for them from a German bank, we had recommended that they swap half of the loan from dollars to yen to diversify their foreign currency exposure. When the dollar significantly devalued, they suddenly had a large loss on the swap. The mayor who had made the decision on the loan and swap came under heavy attack in the local community.

We essentially offered to turn back time by simultaneously entering into two agreements with the local authority. One was a foreign exchange contract where the dollar/euro exchange rate at the time of the granting of the loan was used to reverse all the currency losses on the initial swap. The other was an interest rate swap, where the local authority agreed to pay a fixed interest rate for the term of the loan at the rate that had been prevailing when it was granted. Because that rate was higher than the prevailing rate, the gains we made on that contract more than offset the losses we incurred on reversing the foreign exchange losses. They mayor was delighted. He had got rid of all the foreign exchange losses on the initial swap and the fixed interest rates he was paying were anyway the same as the short-term rates he had previously been paying, as the yield curve was downward sloping. He thought we were either some kind of magicians or that we had simply taken the losses on our own books. But everyone was a winner, he got out of his dilemma while we were able to help out a client, and actually made some money on it.

***

Despite being a small, isolated country, Icelanders have always sought fame and fortune abroad. There are several theories about why this is. The small population probably shapes the national character in this regard. We are used to hearing jokes about the size of the population. One story goes that on a visit to China, ex-president Vigdis Finnbogadottir met with the Chinese president who, upon hearing the population size, asked: 'why didn't you bring them all with you!?' Ignorance about our tiny country is also common. When shopping in a mall in Boston, my wife Thordis was asked by a woman where she had bought the shoes she was wearing. Upon responding 'in Iceland,' the puzzled shopper asked 'is that on fourth floor?' Because of these regular insults, we Icelanders feel we have to prove that we matter abroad. We even have a saying that goes 'recognition comes from abroad.' The Beatle Ringo Starr came to visit Iceland for the first time in 1984. Journalists were waiting when his private jet landed in Reykjavik airport. As he was walking down the steps from his aircraft an eager reporter anxiously asked 'How do you like Iceland?' Starr of course calmly pointed out that his feet hadn't even touched Icelandic ground. The question became a humorous saying in Iceland, but the story gives a good insight into Icelanders' yearning for approval from foreigners.

The United States Naval Air Station in Keflavik, built during World War II and operational until 2006, had a major impact on Icelandic culture. From the outset Icelandic women showed a very strong interest in the US personnel (and vice versa), and attempts were made to restrict interaction (hence the alcohol ban on Wednesdays, the only day soldiers were allowed to leave the navy base). Even so the influence was noticeable. The first ever radio and television signals in Iceland came from the naval base before Icelandic state-owned broadcast media. In the seventies, the signal from the television station at the base was blocked, to avoid too much American influence on Icelandic culture. The radio station broadcast continued until it was closed down a few years ago, although its popularity decreased over time, as the variety of Icelandic stations increased. Yet exposure to American culture through the media made people more aware of what was happening abroad. Even as Icelandic media took over, American and English programming was abundant; many children learned English just from watching television.

The disproportionate number of flights to and from Iceland also made the country far less isolated than might be expected. In the late fifties, Loftleidir (the predecessor to the current Icelandair) became effectively the world's first low-cost carrier, using Iceland as a hub between America and Europe. Their pricing gave them a competitive edge, as they bought old aircraft to keep costs down, using the slightly dubious marketing slogan 'We're slower, but we're lower!' In the sixties, they were nicknamed Hippie Air. Whilst studying in Boston I met a number of Americans who had flown via Iceland – two of its most renowned passengers at the time were a youthful Bill and Hillary Clinton. All these flights meant that, even before the advent of the Internet, contact with the outside world was easier than one might imagine.

We took advantage of all this as the need to generate funding led us quite quickly to set our sights outside our own small borders. Many of my initial tasks revolved around transactions with an international flavour; one of the first tasks I took on after joining was to work on the bond issues we organised for international companies with Icelandic subsidiaries. That market quickly dried up since there were only a handful of those companies, so we started to look at acting as an intermediary for loans from mainly Scandinavian and German banks to our clientele. The first deal we managed to close was a loan from a regional Danish bank to a small municipality outside Reykjavik. Sigurdur was the one responsible for the deal, not surprisingly given that he was the only one that knew any banks outside of Iceland. He was, however, not particularly interested in the finer details of the transaction, so when it came to reading over the loan documents for the client it was handed to me.

The problem was, I had never seen a loan agreement before. No bank had been reckless enough to lend me any money and in any case Icelandic loan agreements at the time tended to be written on one page. This agreement on the other hand was 75 pages and written in a language I could barely recognise as English. Sigurdur, enjoying the sight of me squirm, refused to give me a helping hand and told me to liaise with the Danish bank on any items of the agreement I didn't understand or found strange. I duly obliged and the result was a 17 page letter with questions and comments such as 'what is LIBOR?' and 'what constitutes an act of God?' Needless to say, the Danish bankers had never seen such magnitude of questions about standard items in a loan agreement, but fortunately they had the patience to go through everything with me; I learned a lot very quickly.

Gradually we built up very good contacts with banks abroad. Later we would use these contacts when we began to raise debt funding to finance acquisitions for our corporate clients. This business of brokering loans to Iceland became a good source of income and created competition and more options for lenders in Iceland. But we didn't just source funding for our clients. Kaupthing was always on the lookout for funding itself and keen to agree foreign exchange lines with international banks.

When I had joined Kaupthing in 1994 the funding of the company was solely Icelandic. As the balance sheet was tiny, people hadn't seen the need to explore other avenues. Sigurdur, however, had more ambitious plans and in 1996 wanted to start building relationships with international financial institutions with the aim of getting funding, foreign exchange and money market lines to expand the business. Again, because of my experience studying abroad (the closest thing to having actual experience in working abroad!) he felt I was the person to work on this project with him and we began preparing for a trip to London to build contacts.

To start with, though, we didn't really have any proper contacts outside Iceland to build on. I certainly had none. Sigurdur's solution to that problem was to throw on my desk his folder of business cards that he had collected in his previous employment and *The Bankers' Almanac* – essentially the Yellow Pages of the banking world. With no concrete knowledge or experience I took a scattergun approach, contacting everyone ranging from tiny brokerage houses to the likes of Barclays and Royal Bank of Scotland (RBS). I would then send letters and faxes to these firms asking for meetings, sometimes addressed to particular people (when using Sigurdur's business cards) but most of the time addressed to 'banking departments' that usually didn't exist. Many of the letters got lost. Even with this approach – and despite the fact that many of Sigurdur's contacts had moved on – through sheer perseverance I put together a 2–3 day trip to London filled with meetings.

Some of these encounters were quite funny. Most of the people we met didn't have a clue who or what Kaupthing was, except that it was a financial institution from Iceland. If they had known, they probably wouldn't have agreed to a meeting because we were absolutely tiny. The thing was, I didn't realise quite how small we were in an international context so was usually confident about presenting the firm. When asked about the equity base of Kaupthing I would say with pride 'two *million* dollars' expecting the people across the table to reach for the phone to call the CEO of the bank to meet these important Icelandic guests. They were obviously more minded to call security to have us thrown out. Although we were, in most cases, courteously dismissed on these first trips we had some surprising successes and were able to get some credit lines set up for Kaupthing. Usually the lines were with the branches of German or Italian banks which hadn't been very successful in pinching customers from the UK banks. They probably concluded that having these weird and strangely confident Icelanders as clients was better than having none. We continued these trips on a regular basis and gradually we built up more credibility and managed to establish more and more lines of business from outside Iceland. In the early years we pretty much doubled the size of the firm every year and, as it grew bigger, more and more of our foreign counterparts became interested in doing business with us, which in turn fuelled more growth.

We were also keen to get investors from abroad to invest in Icelandic equities and bonds. Along with the Icelandic embassies, we regularly hosted seminars in London, New York and Copenhagen to increase investor interest in Icelandic securities. At the time the total market value of the Iceland Stock Exchange was around £600 million so, needless to say, it turned out to be very difficult for us to gather interest from global investors. Most memorably, Hreidar and I went to New York in February 1996, ostensibly for an investor seminar organised by the Icelandic-American chamber of commerce, but with the intention of using the opportunity to set up meetings with investors. We did that with the assistance of a company call Auerbach Grayson that specialised in giving overseas brokerage houses access to US investors. They managed to set up a fairly large number of meetings in New York although most of the investors had little clue about the Icelandic market. When they learned more about the market in our meeting, their interest quickly faded.

I particularly remember one meeting on the top floor in one of New York's skyscrapers with a manager of a sizeable fixed-income fund. Hreidar and I were pitching the idea to him of investing in Icelandic krona Treasury Bonds that were yielding around five percent higher than he was getting on his US Treasury Bonds. We felt we were making good progress as the manager was very impressed with the high credit rating of Iceland, the stability of the currency in recent years and the big interest differential he would be getting. That is until he thought of asking how many people lived in the country. We replied that the population was slightly above 250,000. He stood up and walked to the nearest window. He pointed over to Brooklyn, looked at us and said: 'Are you telling me that your population is around one tenth of this neighbourhood!? Am I on Candid Camera?' We never heard from him again.

Institutional investors first ventured overseas at around the same time as Kaupthing. Until then, institutional investors in Iceland were first and foremost the pension funds. Employers and unions in Iceland had jointly agreed in 1968 to build a pension fund system, which by the mid-nineties was one of the strongest in the world with assets of

65 percent of GDP. A decade later the assets would exceed the GDP. Until Iceland entered into the agreement on the European Economic Area, capital movements had been severely restricted and investments made by the pension funds were mainly in government bonds. This was now changed and the funds were suddenly free to explore investments abroad within certain limits.

Unfortunately, there was almost no experience in portfolio management within the funds. The Icelandic market was in its infancy and people were just getting accustomed to investing there, when the vast global markets opened up to them. This was a brave new world for the fund managers just as it was for us. As a result, with hindsight, many of the investment strategies they took seemed quite strange. A small part of the overall funds managed within the pension funds was allocated to international investments. Although a sizeable part of that was placed in funds managed by professional money managers with the big global investment banks, a surprisingly large amount was being placed in more exotic investments. The man most influential in attracting Icelandic pension fund capital into these investments was an Icelandic broker called Benjamin[1].

At the time, he was really the only noteworthy Icelandic stockbroker working outside the country and was very successful in building relationships with institutional investors in Iceland. Benjamin was a fascinating character and countless stories about him float around in Iceland. In many ways he was the stereotype that people have of stockbrokers. Very slick, he looked like a black-haired Gordon Gekko.

My favourite story involving Benjamin happened when he was visiting my colleagues at Kaupthing in Luxembourg. They took him out for dinner at a Mexican restaurant. Following dinner the plan was to go to Hotel Le Royal, Luxembourg's poshest hotel to meet the chairman of Kaupthing Luxembourg, and introduce him to Benjamin. At the restaurant a traditional Mexican guitar trio was playing for the guests; Benjamin absolutely loved it. After the dinner and a number

---

[1]   Not his real name

of drinks, my colleagues were getting uneasy, not wanting to keep the chairman waiting. Benjamin, however, dreaded the thought of having to go to the hotel where the greatest source of excitement was if the pianist hit a wrong note while playing 'Strangers in the night.' So, to add interest to his evening he paid the Mexican trio to join him. They squeezed into a cab with their oversized guitars and drove to the Royal. There, Benjamin paid the resident pianist to make himself scarce, placed the band on the stage, sat down at the table with the dumbstruck chairman and shouted at the terrified band 'play "Money, Money, Money" for me!'

Not surprisingly Benjamin's recommended investments were sometimes as adventurous as his antics. Those included investments in gold mines in Eastern Europe, seed capital for restaurant chains and exotic private equity investments. One of the most speculative investments for which he attracted funds was a fast food seafood chain by the name of Captain Smollett's[2]. There he was backing a management team led by an American who had written a thesis at business school on how to run a fast food business. When one Icelandic fund manager, considering the investment in Smollett's came to New York, the American walked to him, shook his hand while looking firmly in his eyes and said 'I am going to make you so rich!' Unfortunately, the American was long on promise and short on delivery. Captain Smollett's never made any money and would gradually run into trouble. In a bizarre move to capitalise on the dot com hype, the company announced in February 2000 that it was moving into 'web design, web consulting and content creation services, and will seek to acquire, invest and form joint ventures with web design, web consulting and digital content companies.' It was left to anyone's guess what the logic and synergies were in web design and serving fish and chips. Not surprisingly this signalled the end of both the dot com boom and shortly thereafter the company itself.

***

2   Not real name

In 1996, when both innovation and the international side of the business were really taking off, a big shift took place in management, and the newcomers properly took over. Gudmundur Hauksson, who had been the CEO, was offered the same position at the Savings Bank of Reykjavik (SPRON) in 1996. At the time, this was considered a big promotion; SPRON was many times the size of Kaupthing. That would quickly change but, at the time, few doubted that this was a big step upwards for Gudmundur. I still questioned his decision. I couldn't predict the meteoric rise of Kaupthing, but I could tell that, in terms of the momentum of the business and the quality of the people, it felt like a more exciting place to work. But Gudmundur's key legacy at Kaupthing would be to pick the team to take things forward. Though he missed out on some of the rise, he came back as Chairman of the board of Kaupthing (SPRON was the largest shareholder).

Gudmundur's immediate replacement was Bjarni Armannsson, who ran the Asset Management division at the time. His tenure was, however, short-lived. Less than a year into the job at Kaupthing he was offered the job of CEO at FBA, a bank that had been formed with the merger of three government loan funds that were key lenders to the fishing and industrial sectors. FBA, or The Icelandic Investment Bank, became the biggest in Iceland in terms of equity and the move was considered a big step up.

When Bjarni left in 1997, Sigurdur, who had been his deputy, replaced him. The role of deputy CEO was up for grabs. Hreidar and I were the main candidates, but for various reasons, it seemed like Hreidar was the right man for the job, and he was duly appointed. For a short period of time I was used as a replacement CEO when both Sigurdur and Hreidar were away, but after I had staff break out beers and nachos on a couple of Friday afternoons to increase my popularity, I was silently removed from the post.

Sigurdur made some other organisational changes, which resulted in me taking over the Investment Banking division, Ingolfur running Capital Markets and Magnus in charge of Asset Management and

Private Banking. All (except Sigurdur) in our late twenties with just three years' work experience, we were now firmly established as the management team at Kaupthing.

It might well seem extraordinary that such a young team came to manage the premier securities firm in the country. The thing was, though, that there weren't many people with more experience of any relevance. Ten years earlier the stock market didn't even exist. The market had developed so rapidly that experience from more than a few years ago just wasn't that relevant.

Under Sigurdur's leadership the direction of the firm became clearer. The cornerstones of his strategy were to build financial strength, promote cross-selling between the different divisions of the firm, co-invest with key clients, and to look for growth beyond the Icelandic borders.

The firm had grown impressively over three years. The number of employees was now approaching 100 people. In late 1997 we had been granted a license to operate as an investment bank. To get the licence we had received an equity injection of £4 million from our owners, the savings banks, creating a capital base of close to £10 million. This was our niche, and properly set us apart from our competitors, the bank-owned brokerage houses. We had built up some financial strength they didn't have, and although our capital wasn't enormous it was growing.

All the key people were in place and we were gaining market share in all areas of the business. Our name was synonymous with innovation and the profitability was higher than we had ever seen. There was no doubt Kaupthing was the up-and-coming player in the financial market. Everyone took great pride in working for the firm, and it in turn demanded loyalty from people. If you wanted to work in finance, Kaupthing was the place to be. And we were ready to take it to the next level.

Chapter Three

Rattling the Cage

Hreidar and I exchanged nervous glances. We were sitting alone in what seemed, at the time, like an enormous office, laden with mahogany. It was as if we were suddenly school boys again and had been summoned to the head teacher's office for a serious telling-off.

But this wasn't the head's office, and although we were young, we were no longer at school. When the door to the office finally opened, it wasn't a teacher that stepped in, but the CEO of Eimskip, by far the most prominent public company in Iceland. And we hadn't been pulling the girls' hair in the playground or throwing stones at the school windows. Our mischief was that we had accumulated a five percent stake in Eimskip, which meant that we were now the third largest shareholder in the company. Kaupthing was not particularly welcome as a shareholder, but perhaps more importantly, the man entering the room was concerned about who we might sell our stake to. We were in the midst of what became known as the first 'greenmail' transaction in Iceland. Greenmail is a term describing the situation where a company is forced into buying back its own shares from unwanted shareholders who are threatening to make a bid for the company or gain influence over it. It was a term that became known in the eighties when used in the United States by a number of corporate raiders.

Eimskip was the biggest listed company in Iceland at the time. It was a shipping company, established in 1914 while Iceland was still under Danish rule, and was regarded as a national treasure and lifeline, due to its initial importance in maintaining transportation between the island and the rest of the world. Eimskip was *the* blue chip company in Iceland and had strong political ties with the omnipotent Independence Party. In addition to its own operations, it was the cornerstone of a power bloc, ominously referred to as 'The Octopus.' Its tentacles were wrapped around Sjova, the largest insurer in Iceland, Shell Iceland, a number of the biggest fishing companies and Icelandair, the national airline. These companies were interconnected in various ways, through family ties and cross holdings. As a major shareholder in this large group, Eimskip was very much the powerhouse of corporate Iceland and therefore of great interest to a number of people. In a highly diversified list of shareholders, Sjova, the insurance company, stood out in the crowd as the only company that held a significantly sizeable stake.

Hreidar was the man who, in 1999, spotted the great opportunities this situation presented. First of all, he didn't believe that the market was correctly valuing the portfolio of the controlling shareholdings Eimskip held in the various companies. Secondly, because of the diversity of the shareholder list, he believed that if we could accumulate a sizeable stake in Eimskip, we could lay claim to a board seat and greater influence in a company that many would be interested in. So we gradually started to buy up shares in Eimskip and, by Christmas Eve, were already in a position to flag that we controlled five percent of the company's shares. The news created some jitters in the market and a lot of speculation about the nature of our interest. We had started to buy when the stock price was around 7.7 kronur, but the price had steadily climbed up to 13.5 kronur by the end of the year, as we continued to buy and others in the market followed suit.

By mid-January, a few investors had already contacted us to express an interest in the shares, while at the same time, the board and management of Eimskip were starting to feel very uneasy about our shareholding. We had announced that we weren't going to ask for a board seat, but they knew that we were on the lookout for someone to buy the stake. Many of the people who were rumoured to be interested were people they were very keen to avoid having on the board. There were two entrepreneurs in particular who had separately shown great interest in the stake. One was Jon Olafsson, the country's leading media mogul, and the other was Jon Asgeir Johannesson, the retail king of Iceland. They were both among the wealthiest businessmen in Iceland at the time and also among the most controversial. They were both stigmatised as outsiders by the establishment, and neither was likely to get a warm welcome as new major shareholders by the incumbent management and board of Eimskip. Keenly aware of their unpopularity, we made no secret of the fact that we were entertaining discussions with them on a possible sale of our stake. We figured this could only help to whet the appetites of other potential buyers. And we were right. Hreidar eventually got a call from Eimskip's CEO, Hordur Sigurgestsson, requesting a meeting with him that evening. Hreidar asked me to join him for support, although I hadn't really been involved in the transaction, and that was how we had ended up sitting in this mahogany heaven like two mischievous pupils.

Fortunately for us Eimskip couldn't just confiscate our shares, give us a good hiding and send us back to the schoolyard. The only way to ensure that we didn't sell our shares to the likes of Jon Olafsson and Jon Asgeir Johannesson – the barbarians at the gates – was to buy the shares back from us. And that is exactly what they did. That evening they made us an offer for the shares, which we accepted. It meant that in just over three months Hreidar's trade had made us around £4 million, which to a company with an equity of around £15 million and an operating income of the same amount in 1999 was an astronomical amount of money. The trade was widely recognised in the market and the press as the country's first case of 'greenmail'. To some the trade was a sign of our innovative thinking, which was to be admired; to others it was an example of an aggressiveness that was not to be encouraged. The timing of the sale was very good for us, since just a few months later, the dot com bubble burst and the market fell. By the end of 2000, the share price of Eimskip had fallen drastically.

The significance of this trade was not only measured in the money we made. It was also a clear sign that the balance of power in the Icelandic business world was shifting. Kaupthing had gradually built up considerable financial strength and was now a force to be reckoned with. The fact that we had been able to build up a stake of this size was the living proof of that. What was also noteworthy was that it was probably the subtle threat of us handing over our stake to 'unwanted' entrepreneurs that had prompted Eimskip to react.

Gradually, and without any strategic intention to do so, we had become the bank of choice for many of the high net worth individuals that were becoming increasingly influential in Iceland. It wasn't that we didn't try to work with the blue chip companies. On the contrary. We made numerous attempts to build relationships with them, but with very limited success. They preferred to deal with the established commercial banks and were slightly suspicious of this fast-growing and aggressive investment bank. One of the major differences between us was that these companies were more out to preserve wealth and the status quo, whereas we were out to change things and create wealth. Another factor was the simple lack of personal chemistry between us. These were companies that had a long history behind them and were run by people from a different generation to ours. We were thirty-somethings, whereas most of the CEOs of the blue chip companies were in their fifties. They might have known our parents, and we often knew their children, but we didn't know each other.

But we were gradually finding a niche clientele that we could collaborate with in a way that was to radically change the Icelandic business landscape. Eventually it would also form the basis for the dramatic expansion of Icelandic businesses overseas. We had found a way of tapping in to the up-and-coming entrepreneurs of the country, people who belonged to our generation and had, in most cases, founded and built up their own business successfully. These entrepreneurs were open to new opportunities, both domestically and abroad. Their businesses were usually sizeable, but they were looking for someone to help them get to the next level. And that someone was Kaupthing.

***

The man who was to become the face of the Icelandic business community abroad was Jon Asgeir Johannesson. Jon Asgeir had recently turned 30 when our paths crossed. With his rugged good looks, he would soon be portrayed in the foreign press as the seductive playboy from the north with glacier eyes. One newspaper in the UK was unable to refrain from describing him as 'devastatingly handsome'. When I first met him, he hadn't yet developed that shoulder-length hair that Danish journalists would later refer to as the 'Bundesliga haircut', much to his dismay. But he was already wearing his trademark leather jackets and had a slight 'bad boy' aura about him that followed him wherever he went. Jon Asgeir is a complex character; you could ask ten different people who know him to describe him and they would all give you different answers. To people that didn't know him, he came across as a very timid person. He could be so reserved, in fact, that his shyness could occasionally be interpreted as rudeness. Sometimes Jon Asgeir wouldn't even greet people when he entered a room. It took me the best part of two years to figure out whether his behaviour towards me was dictated by the fact that he was shy or he simply didn't like me (it was the former!). If he didn't know people, he could grow very quiet, but as soon as the conversation shifted to business and deals, he got very animated. Most of the people who did business with him in the UK found him very charming. No one doubted his flair for business and ability to structure deals, skills he had developed from a very early age. At the age of only six, he had already started to help out his father at the store he was managing, stacking the coolers with Coke. During his school years, he always had his own business going on the side, selling popcorn through special stands he set up in shopping malls. He created his first big break after his father, Johannes Jonsson, was sacked as store manager. Jon Asgeir responded by quitting school so that the two of them could establish the first low-price supermarket in Iceland, called Bonus, in 1989. They sold groceries at the most competitive prices consumers had ever seen, by refusing to accept credit cards and paying cash directly to their suppliers. They were also groundbreaking in their use of barcodes and IT systems. The business was an overnight success and, in a matter of years, Jon Asgeir and his father grew the business into the second largest retailer in the country. For years it was also the most popular company in the country.

When Jon Asgeir approached us in the summer of 1998, it was to seek our financial assistance and advice on a bid he was preparing for Hagkaup, the largest retailer in Iceland. A few years earlier, the Hagkaup family had bought 50 percent of Bonus from Jon Asgeir's family. Following this, the relationship between the two dynasties soon started to resemble a plot from the soap opera *Dallas*. The Hagkaup family was controlled by the children of its founder, Palmi Jonsson. Those were his two sons, Sigurdur Gisli and Jon Palmason, and his daughters, Ingibjorg and Lilja. Initially, the two brothers and Jon Asgeir really seemed to hit it off. They started spending a lot of time together, sharing their common interest in business and outdoor activities. But the first cracks in the relationship began to appear when, in early 1998, the two brothers approached Jon Asgeir with the aim of acquiring the remaining 50 percent of Bonus to form by far the largest retailer in Iceland. Jon Asgeir, however, had other plans. He suggested that he would buy them out, which is why he was now approaching us to provide the financing. The deal, combined with the fact that Jon Asgeir had started a love affair with one of the sisters, Ingibjorg, who he later married, quickly soured the relationship between Jon Asgeir and the brothers. Tensions were so high in the final stages of the deal that Jon Asgeir couldn't even park outside our headquarters. The brothers refused to enter the building if they knew he was in the building as well. This sequence of events also created a rift between the sisters, Lilja and Ingibjorg, on one hand and the brothers on the other. Fortunately, some time later the rift was mended and the relationship between the siblings and Jon Asgeir improved.

The acquisition of Hagkaup by Bonus created a company that was baptised as Baugur – a name that was to become synonymous with the Icelandic expansion. The deal was obviously huge by Icelandic standards, with an enterprise value of more than £60 million. It was also unusual in that the business was first split into an operating company and a real estate company, with the Hagkaup family holding on to most of the property, but selling the operating company. Initially Kaupthing and one of the other Icelandic banks, FBA, would hold 37.5 percent each of the newly founded Baugur. Gaumur, the holding company owned by Jon Asgeir's family, held 25 percent. Over time he would acquire a bigger stake.

Neither we nor FBA had any intention of holding on to those shares in the long term. Once the deal was closed, the plan was to sell our shares down quickly to institutional investors in Iceland, mainly the pension funds. Subsequently we intended to list the company on the stock exchange. However, we had underestimated two things. One was the sceptical reaction to the fact that we just bought the operating company, and not the property. This was unusual and prompted many people to claim that Jon Asgeir had just bought some shelves and a bunch of shopping carts for an exorbitant amount of money. The transaction was featured in the business section of one the papers as the 'sale of the year', implying that the sellers had got the best part of the deal. The other factor we had underestimated was how Jon Asgeir would be perceived by the institutional investors. With his bad boy looks, he never conformed to the image of a typical businessman, and many people treated him with a degree of suspicion.

The combined effect of these two factors resulted in the complete failure of the placing of the shares in the autumn of 1998. We couldn't sell a single share, as investors reached a general consensus that the deal just wasn't worth doing. This was a major blow to us. We were convinced that these negative factors would pale into insignificance because there would be so much interest in having a stake in a company that was by far the biggest retailer in the country. We faced a big problem; we had stretched ourselves to the limit to close the deal, and the stake we held was enormous in relation to our size – more than £10 million. We felt like a small rowing boat that a killer whale had jumped into and was slowly sinking. There were rumours that Kaupthing was going bust and the deal was looked upon as a complete and utter failure. We hadn't got a clue of how to dispose of the stake.

Our saviour came in the form of Norway's largest retailer, Odd Reitan, the owner of Reitangruppen. Odd was a good friend of Johannes', and he and Jon Asgeir were able to convince him to take on a 20 percent stake in Baugur, which would be bought from Kaupthing and FBA. Both FBA and we were ecstatic, since it both relieved us of a very big part of our stake and, equally important, gave the transaction the validation it so greatly needed. Reitangruppen's acquisition of a 20 percent stake in the company was perceived as a stamp of approval. When we sat down in Reykjavik to map out the details of the deal with Odd, we were so nervous he wouldn't go through with it, that some of us were visibly shaking. He was the only buyer, we had no other options, and if he had walked away, we would have been left in dire straits. Fortunately, he didn't. Moreover, he made no attempt to use his advantage to squeeze us. The only issue he raised was the interest rate applied to his purchase price from the time of signing until he concluded the payment, which was a couple of months later. We suggested seven percent. He only wanted to pay six percent. This was of absolutely no consequence to us, but in order not to seem too eager, we faked having to break up the meeting to discuss the issue amongst ourselves. So we broke for half an hour, which was spent toasting our imminent success with glasses of sparkling water, until we returned and duly accepted. We toasted with champagne later that evening to celebrate. In the wake of Reitangruppen's investment, a few other

Icelandic investors followed suit and finally, half a year later, we floated the company on the stock exchange and sold our remaining shares in the IPO. When all was done and dusted, we had made millions of pounds on the transaction, which more than made up for the sleepless nights earlier on.

The formation of Baugur established Jon Asgeir as one of the most powerful businessmen in Iceland. Prior to the deal, few people knew of his existence, despite the success of Bonus. His father was the face of Bonus and was an incredibly popular figure, thanks to the low prices he offered consumers. Jon Asgeir, on the other hand, had remained in the shadows. This was all about to change. The face of Bonus, represented by the benign white bearded Santa Claus-like Johannes, was no more. In its place came the face of Baugur in the form of the dark, long-haired Jon Asgeir, wrapped in a leather jacket.

At around the same time that we were working on the Baugur transaction, our paths crossed with two brothers who we immediately took a liking to. Agust and Lydur Gudmundsson had founded a seafood business in 1986, focused on the processing of fish roe. They had built the business from out of their garage and the back of their van. They drove around the country in the van to buy roe from the independent fishermen in the small fishing villages along the coast. The side of the van read 'If you have roe in store – call Bakkavor!'

I first met Agust and Lydur at their Annual General Meeting, shortly after we had concluded a £5 million refinancing for them. One of the first things that struck me when I met them was how very different they looked, considering they were brothers. Agust was relatively tall and thin and looked a bit like the Scottish actor John Hannah, while Lydur was rather short and stockily built. Their facial features didn't seem to have much in common either. Apart from both being shy, they were quite different characters, but they complemented each other perfectly. Lydur was the finance man, while Agust focused on strategy and marketing. I don't think I ever saw them argue. If they did, it must have been behind closed doors. When travelling they were so money conscious that they were even known to share the same bed. Notoriously stingy, a trademark not often associated with Icelanders, they were a complete nightmare to travel with. We quickly learned not to allow them to organise the accommodation on trips. If we did, they would book us into shady youth hostels, where you slept with your back against the wall – that's if you could sleep at all. Of course, their thriftiness reflected the way they ran their business. Expenditure was kept to a minimum and they were very efficient operators.

The brothers were already starting to look beyond Iceland for opportunities. They had set up a business in France and were also selling their roe products to various other countries. Despite the fact that the meeting was a very small one by any standards, with no more than a handful of people present in the room, it was quite memorable. As I listened to Agust's presentation of their vision for the company's future, I started to wonder whether the brothers were completely sane. They were running a small chilled prepared seafood business in Iceland, with a modest turnover of about £6 million. Yet their plan was to build one of the largest food companies in the world in a matter of years. Although I was used to ambitious people, this sounded completely crazy.

Not long after this first meeting, the brothers came back to us and we made our first transaction together. They had set their sights on a Swedish company – fairly sizeable by their standards – which they needed our help to acquire. The company, Lysekils Havsdelikatesser, was a specialised producer of herring and caviar. This was an opportunity for us to further strengthen our ties with Bakkavor and, as part of the transaction, we invested equity in the company and became a shareholder. It wasn't a huge transaction compared to the ones that would follow, but it did strengthen Bakkavor significantly. It took a couple of years to digest the Swedish company, but they would soon be ready to move on to even bigger things with our help.

There were many other companies and individuals with whom we developed strong contacts, and which generated deal flow. We established ourselves firmly as the bank of choice for companies that wanted to make things happen. Our placing power when it came to raising capital or debt from the market was second to none. Ingolfur had built a great capital markets team. In some cases we used the contacts we were rapidly establishing abroad to obtain debt funding for our clients. On the advisory side, we were also perceived as the ones that offered the highest quality people. What really set us apart from other financial institutions, however, was our ability and willingness to put equity into deals we liked. No other institution was doing that, whether it be brokerage houses or banks. Some of the brokerage houses would probably have liked to have been able to do it, but they didn't have the capital. The banks had the capital, but had no interest in using it this way.

Of course, not all the investments we made were successful, but we tended to be resourceful in getting value out of them, even when they went bad. One of our biggest private equity investments in those days was made when we facilitated the creation of Iceland's biggest media company, Northern Lights. This was a project we had worked on with Jon Olafsson, a somewhat controversial character. Tall, thin and fair, Jon was slightly older than the rest of us, and was in his forties when we got to know him. His was a classic rags-to-riches story. Deserted by his father, he raised by his grandparents because his mother was too young to care for him and he had a rough childhood. In his early years he had been the prime suspect for just about every misdemeanour that had been committed in his hometown, Keflavik. But fortunately his entrepreneurial spirit eventually found a more commercial direction and he acquired a reputation as a successful band manager. That was his way into the music and media business. Step by step, through organic growth and acquisitions, he built what was to become the biggest media company in Iceland. He had acquired partners along the way, but fallen out with many of them, who claimed he was a ruthless businessman.

I got to know Jon quite well through our business dealings. Despite having dropped out of school very early, it was clear to me that Jon was very smart and incredibly good with numbers. One of his business partners once told me that when Jon claimed he didn't remember a particular number or amount, you knew he was bluffing – he always remembered figures when they suited him!

Jon approached us because he wanted to create a single, big, media and entertainment company out of various independent companies, most of which were either partly or wholly owned by him. These were the leading companies in television, radio, music distribution and retailing, and cinema in Iceland. The new company, Northern Lights, would also be a major shareholder in Tal, a successful mobile phone operator in Iceland. The debt funding was underwritten by a consortium led by JP Morgan Chase and the Dutch bank NIBC. We provided the equity and became one of the three biggest shareholders, together with Jon and Joni Sighvatsson. Joni, with whom we also did other business, was Iceland's most successful movie producer. His greatest claim to fame was to have established Propaganda Films, which for a period was one of the biggest producers of commercials in the US, and music videos for superstars like Madonna. He had also produced David Lynch's *Wild at Heart*, the winner of the Palme d'Or at the 1990 Cannes film festival.

This was a big and highly publicised deal in Iceland. The banks provided a large amount of credit, and many critics felt that the company would struggle with the debt burden. But we and the banks felt that the company's cash flow, which had been very stable for a long time, justified the leverage. From a very early stage, it looked as if the investment would be the most successful one we had ever made. Shortly after the deal was closed, the Scandinavian Broadcasting Group (usually called SBS) entered into negotiations with Jon to acquire Northern Lights. The proposed purchase price meant that we were about to double our investment. We were ecstatic. However, this was the point when we discovered why people got frustrated with Jon. He was leading the negotiations and it took him ages to negotiate the price and close all the necessary details that would enable us to proceed to due diligence. To complicate matters even further, as part of the deal, he was going to join SBS as a director. His remuneration was therefore part of the negotiation, which did not make things any easier.

The negotiations dragged on and on. We became very frustrated with him, and even more so with the unfolding of events that eventually resulted in SBS pulling out of the deal. Essentially the company began to struggle. A rival private television company had just been established, cutting deeply into the licensing and advertisement revenues, the most important income generator of the firm. At the same time, the economy was sliding into a downturn, which further decreased revenues. With the downturn came the sharp depreciation of the krona, which hurt the company, as a large part of its loans were denominated in foreign currency. The company was therefore left struggling heavily, as SBS walked away. Moreover, we soon realised that the value of our equity had been lost. This was a considerable amount for Kaupthing. Hreidar and I, who had put the deal together and had been very cocky when it looked like we were on the point of tripling our investment, suddenly went from heroes to zeros. With our tails between our legs, we embarked on long, protracted negotiations with the banks to see if we could find ways of salvaging part or all of our investment. And we got there in the end. Through a series of moves that involved buying some of the senior debt at a discount, selling off the mobile operator, and finally disposing of the company, we managed to recoup pretty much all of our investment.

Naturally there was no shortage of entrepreneurs looking for funding in the second half of the nineties, when the dot com bubble was growing. Iceland was infected by the same kind of enthusiasm for technology and biotech companies that had gripped most other countries. Having the biggest placing power, Kaupthing was the obvious place to go to. We were bombarded with proposals to finance or raise capital for various endeavours of mixed potential. Icelanders are entrepreneurial by nature and that, coupled with an inherent optimism, created a flood of new ventures.

One company was raising money for computer generated animation films that they believed could compete with the likes of Pixar. Its founder had apparently bought software that enabled him to create an animated film. The fact that he hadn't actually used the software to create anything and had no experience whatsoever in movie making of any kind didn't seem to bother him in the least. One tech company that asked us to raise money for it claimed the share price was 13 kronur. When queried, the director we spoke to admitted that the only shares traded at that price had been exchanged for a used car. Even conventional businesses got caught in the excitement and felt they were almost priceless. The owner of a small taxi company called us and wanted to list the company. When we asked what he thought it was worth, he replied 'I am not greedy, maybe just 30 times earnings.'

But many companies, that didn't seem to make any sense were getting very high valuations from respectable investors. One night I was working late with one of my colleagues and we were ridiculing the valuation of a company called letsbuyit.com, which was part-owned by Icelanders. It was a platform for people to team up and bulk buy particular products. We were laughing ourselves senseless looking at their webpage where a small number of people were jointly buying Christmas trees or electric drills, only to wake up the following morning with an announcement from the company that BSkyB had invested £10 million in the company, valuing it at £100 million. Less than a year later it was bankrupt.

Of course, there were also good companies with realistic ideas every now and then, but they were few and far between. We were also inherently sceptical and well aware of the many things that could go wrong with a start-up. We were very wary of offering these kind of investments to general investors. In fact, we only raised money through public placings for two early stage companies during this period. Both are noteworthy, one for its eventual success, the other for the fact that it is the only company that I know of that was actually delighted to have gone bust. The company was called Bepaid and had developed a technology that enabled companies to get in contact with users on the internet and pay them to watch their ad – hence the name Bepaid. We knew the people behind the business, who were actually sensible guys, and we successfully raised some start-up capital for them. They opened up offices in the US very quickly. But the idea didn't work and, in less than a year, the company ran out of money, went into administration and closed down its office in the summer of 2001. The office was on the 84th floor of the south tower of the World Trade Center in New York. When the list of occupants was distributed in September, shortly after the aircraft crashed into the towers, Bepaid's name was still on the list.

The other company was – and still is – CCP, which was developing an online computer game called EVE. We raised a fair amount of funding for them in 1999, and after a few more rounds of capital raisings, the company launched EVE Online in 2003. It was a runaway success and has grown into one of the most successful multiplayer games in the world today, with over 300,000 subscribers.

The most famous company in Iceland to have benefited from investors' appetite for tech companies, which were short on cash flow but supposedly long on future profits, was the biotech company deCODE Generics. The company's CEO had founded it in 1996 with the backing of venture funds in the US. His name was Dr Kari Stefansson, a truly unique character, both in appearance and behaviour. A former professor at Harvard Medical School, Kari was in his late forties, almost two metres tall and built more like a track and field athlete than a typical academic. He had long grey hair and a grey beard that made him look like a ninth-century Viking who had stepped into a time machine and been catapulted into the 21st century, landing on the Harvard campus.

When I met him back in Iceland some years later, he hadn't changed much. Despite his quirks, he was undoubtedly quite brilliant, a charismatic speaker with an odd sense of humour. Many remember the speech he made when deCODE formally opened its new headquarters next to the University of Iceland. Stefansson had been arguing with the university about the height of the building, off which the university wanted to shave 10 inches. Stefansson felt they were stingy to be quibbling over such a small difference. As he was describing the argument to his audience, Stefansson, never one to shy away from shocking people, told them a story from his student days. He had been driving around the country with two of his friends, when they began to argue about which one of them was the best endowed. So they stopped the car and stepped out to measure. 'In that competition, 10 inches would have made a difference,' he said to the stunned audience.

The idea behind deCODE was an interesting one. Essentially it was going to use Iceland's unique gene pool to identify and isolate disease genes. Compared to most countries, Icelanders are fairly homogenous, making them an ideal sample population on which to conduct genealogical studies. Moreover, family ties are documented hundreds of years back in time. What Stefansson wanted to do was build a central database of family ties, medical records and blood samples containing each individual's pattern of genes. This was a revolutionary idea, which, of course, triggered off a lively debate. The most contentious issue was the rights of privacy and also whether a database of this kind, if it were to be allowed, should be in the hands of a private company.

I suspect that there aren't many countries in the world that would have authorised the creation of such a database. It was bound to contain incredibly sensitive information. Not only health information, but also information on whether individuals were correctly fathered and cases of incest would be revealed. But Stefansson probably had the only ally who could really push this legislation through parliament – none other than the Prime Minister, David Oddsson himself. They had been classmates in high school and Oddsson had become a fervent believer in the ideas behind deCODE. He saw this as an opportunity to build a sizeable biotech business in Iceland that would create high-paying jobs and produce job opportunities for Icelandic scientists – a great diversification from fishing and power-intensive industry. Nothing would deter him from this goal. At the time, he was so powerful that his support effectively guaranteed the passing of the legislation, which was enacted in 1998. And his support for deCODE didn't end there. A few years later, amazingly, he pushed another bill through parliament that allowed the government to guarantee an enormous $200 million bond issue for the company. No one but Oddsson could have done something like this.

Despite both of these bills being passed, neither of them actually came to fruition. In the end, deCODE opted out of creating the database because of the costs involved and the government guarantee was aborted, following objections raised by the EFTA Surveillance Authority, which generally doesn't allow government subsidies. deCODE was – and is – a proper company, and it has been widely credited for its contribution to genetic research. The commercial viability of the venture has, however, always been debated. Since its foundation, more than ten years ago, it has never returned a profit. Its notoriety is, however, mainly linked to the gold rush that was created around its unlisted shares, shortly after it was founded.

Intoxicated by the hype and optimism that characterised the dot com era, Icelanders flocked to buy shares in this highly publicised venture. The shares were unlisted, but nevertheless traded actively on the un-regulated 'grey market' where they kept on climbing in value between 1996 and 2000. I had friends coming to me asking whether to buy, when the shares were at $6. The valuation of the company, given the uncertainty, seemed excessively high so I advised them not to buy. They bought anyway and came back to me a year later when the price was

$15 and asked me if they should sell. I told them to take the money and run – it was all hype. They didn't, and came back a year later when the price was $40. This time I suspect they were mainly bragging, although they did ask me whether they should sell. I was wavering, but still told them to sell. By the time the price reached $60 I had lost faith in my own analysis. The country was full of institutional and retail investors buying the shares hand over fist. People mortgaged their houses to fund share purchases. Some invested their disability payments in deCODE. One local authority gambled half of its cash on it – and then actually got out and made money. The shares were eventually listed in July 2000 on Nasdaq, but the hype died with the dot com bubble. It opened at $18, and climbed in the months to follow up to nearly $29. Then it began to fall just as quickly. At the year end the shares closed at around $10 – now they trade at less than a dollar. Speculating in these shares even bankrupted some people. Critics claimed that the company, created to save lives, was actually destroying them.

The transaction that pushed the new generation of business people into the limelight more than any other was the privatisation of our partners in the Baugur transaction, FBA – the Icelandic Investment Bank. Not surprisingly, Kaupthing played a key role.

Although the privatisation process had started in the early nineties, it was initially focused on the smaller, state-owned enterprises. That included Icelandic Pharmaceuticals, The Icelandic Drilling Company (a specialised geothermal drilling firm) and the government-owned IT company Skyrr. But these were all relatively small companies and the most valuable state assets were, by far, the banks, Iceland telecom and the power company Landsvirkjun.

The first step towards privatising the banks was taken in 1998 with the stock market listing and IPO of Bjarni Armannsson's FBA – it was the easiest bank to privatise, since it was not a retail bank and people looked on this IPO as a test of the privatisation effort. Our involvement would go down in history and is probably a good example of the aggressiveness and innovation of Kaupthing at the time. It would also eventually result in turning the most powerful man in the country, the Prime Minister himself, against us. Something that would haunt us in the years that followed.

The IPO took place in the early part of November. The intention was to sell 49 percent of the bank to retail investors and to ensure a proper diversification of the shareholder base; no individual was allowed to subscribe to more than the equivalent of £26,000 or 3 million krona at the share price of 1.4 kronur. The size of the offering was huge by Icelandic standards at the time – the equivalent of £40 million.

As the offer period came to a close, a debate was taking place within the walls of Kaupthing. Always out to make money, Hreidar saw an opportunity to profit immensely if we could somehow gain control of a large stake in the bank and subsequently sell it to someone who would be interested in it. Thus the idea of offering a price of 1.45 to anyone who subscribed to the offering (at 1.40) was born. The problem was that, by the time we had decided to go ahead and accumulate subscriptions, there were only four hours left before the offering closed. Everyone immediately pounced on their phones, calling clients, friends and family to enquire whether they were interested in making money without any risk. Within four hours, we had managed to buy subscriptions from thousands of people and build a 14 percent stake in FBA. Subsequently, at the end of 1998, the Savings Banks acquired the stake, which by then had risen to 22 percent, and placed it in an investment company, called Scandinavian Holding, which Kaupthing also held shares in. The aim was to pursue the goal of merging FBA and Kaupthing.

By early August 1999, however, Jon Asgeir Johannesson had begun the task of forming a consortium of four well-known and somewhat idiosyncratic businessmen, and bought the shareholding from Scandinavian Holding. The consortium was named Orca. When a press conference was announced, it was known that Scandinavian Holding had sold the FBA stake, but the identity of the buyers remained a mystery. When the journalists showed up at the conference, the four investors behind Orca sat in the panel. It was an odd and amusing sight, and many Icelanders will remember the pictures from this press conference. The famous four didn't really look anything like the image people had of businessmen. Thorsteinn Baldvinsson, founder of the largest trawler company in Iceland (he would later become the Chairman of Glitnir Bank) was a thorough seaman and never wore a tie, Jon Olafsson, media mogul, was the spitting image of Jonathan Pryce as the Bond villain Elliot Carver, and Jon Asgeir showed up in his signature leather jacket – as if he was about to inaugurate a Harley Davidson rally and not a banking consortium. Eyjolfur Sveinsson, who had made his name in publishing, admittedly wore a tie, but it was a black tie against a black shirt and a black suit, so he looked like he was attending a mob funeral rather than a press conference. If you wanted a picture that captured the generation shift that was taking place on the Icelandic business scene, this was it.

Following the press conference the shit really hit the fan. Prime Minister Oddsson went ballistic. Even though he was probably already starting to dislike Jon Asgeir, it was Jon Olafsson's involvement that infuriated him the most. Jon had attempted to gain some influence in the Independence Party early on in his career. But there were many people in the party who disliked him. Oddsson had a particular antipathy for him and made sure that he was not welcomed in the party. Eventually he was chased away and subsequently became a supporter of the Social Democrats party, using his wealth and media muscle to promote their cause. That made him immensely unpopular with Oddsson, who seems to have seen Jon as one of his main political adversaries. So when he realised that Jon had just become one of the key shareholders in the country's largest bank, he was not a happy man. And his anger wasn't only directed at Jon Olafsson – he was angry with him already – but the firm he saw as the facilitator that had enabled Jon and his co-investors to gain this position, Kaupthing.

Even though the sale had been announced publicly, it still had to be ratified by the board of Scandinavian Holding a few days later. This had initially been considered a mere formality, since the shareholders of Scandinavian Holding were very keen to sell the stake. We hadn't, however, anticipated the political turmoil we created. The board consisted of Sigurdur and the managers of four savings banks. Three of them had strong affiliations with the Independence Party and, in the days leading up to the board meeting, came under immense pressure not to ratify the deal. The Prime Minister summoned them to his office for a meeting and was fuming.

Oddsson seems to have been fairly confident, after the meeting, that the majority of the board of Scandinavian Holding had been convinced to vote against the sale. Shortly before the board meeting, the editor of *Morgunbladid* told Sigurdur Einarsson that he would not get the deal approved. Three of the board members had told him personally that they would be voting against it. However, despite heated debates at the board meeting, Sigurdur was successful in the end and the deal was approved. This outcome was heavily influenced by the fact that the savings banks, which the board members represented, were making an absolute killing on the transactions. Some of them were struggling and they simply couldn't afford to refuse the deal, despite all the pressure they were under. After the meeting, once he had overcome his initial surprise at the outcome, the editor philosophically told Sigurdur, 'If you guys weren't making so much money for the savings banks, you would have been fired ages ago!' That was very close to the truth, since many of the managers that represented the savings banks on the board of Kaupthing didn't really like Kaupthing and the people that worked there. But we had made so much money for them that it was impossible for them to justify getting rid of the management.

So the Orca group became the key shareholder of FBA and suddenly this unconventional group of businessmen could throw their weight around the country's largest bank. That effectively put a halt to the sale of the rest of the government's stake in FBA, which ended up being placed with institutional investors a couple of years later. The Orca group was influential for a while and was still a key shareholder when FBA merged with Islandsbanki in 2001, creating a bank that would later become known as Glitnir. Eventually internal clashes would dissolve the Orca group, and the fabulous four parted ways as business partners.

As the end of the nineties approached, this new generation of businessmen had firmly established themselves in Iceland. They had grown in strength, and so had Kaupthing. By the time champagne corks began popping to usher in the new millennium, the bank had £16.5 million of capital, a balance sheet of £200 million and was more profitable than ever. We had already begun to dip our toes into international markets, and were now ready to step on the accelerator in moving overseas. Our clients were actively looking for opportunities to expand beyond Iceland, and we were on the brink of some groundbreaking transactions abroad.

Chapter Four

The Grand Master Syndrome

Back in 1972 the Cold War was at its peak. That July, Reykjavik staged an event that channelled these Cold War frustrations, and thrust it into the global media spotlight. The US chess wonder boy Bobby Fischer competed in the World Chess Championships against the Russian champion, Boris Spassky. Oddly, looking back, it's an event that explains a huge amount about the way the Icelandic psyche works and why Iceland went global.

The match took almost two months. It was the first time since 1948 that a player from outside the Soviet Union was competing for the championship title. Fischer's bizarre behaviour also upped the ante. He wouldn't attend the opening ceremony, and only flew to Iceland when the prize money was raised substantially. He forfeited the second match by not showing up at all. He insisted that the camera crew was replaced. Spassky even followed suit and demanded the Icelandic police sweep the match area for electronic devices – although the only bugs they found were a couple of dead flies in the lighting system. Eventually Fischer won, with 12.5 points to Spassky's 8.5. After that, he became something of an Icelandic national hero – even gaining Icelandic citizenship more than 20 years later in a bizarre twist of events.

In Iceland, where TV was still a bit of a rarity, every man, woman and child was hooked. Children everywhere wanted to learn to play chess.

During school intervals, they would flock to break-out areas where chess boards were available. Established chess clubs were flooded with new members, and many new clubs were founded. By competing and learning from each other, many graduated to the international arena. By 1986, there were six Icelandic chess grand masters (the highest title a chess player can obtain), an absurdly high number for such a small country, At the time there were ten UK-born grand masters, and twelve from the US.

Similarly, in other sports people would compare themselves to larger nations. Success was only success if you were beating one of the big guys – winning against Malta or Cyprus was little better than losing. When I won gold medals in badminton in the Island games, my friends simply laughed and asked if I had beaten Robinson Crusoe in the final. Iceland has a disproportionate number of professional footballers, three Miss Worlds and eight World's Strongest Man titles. If ever you need proof that ambition counts, you need look no further than Iceland.

That's the context in which my generation grew up – with ambitions that bore no relation to what might realistically be achievable from a tiny, remote Arctic island. As we got older, people would be asking not how Icelanders got so good at chess, but how we came to form part of the world's business elite. Like the chess players, we learned that by co-operating, competing and aiming for the stars, the limit to what you can achieve is much higher than you might think.

***

By the late 1990s Kaupthing had built up a reputation as Iceland's most dynamic financial firm. If you wanted to do something groundbreaking, we were your first port of call. That meant we were at the hub of Iceland's international expansion. Of course, that didn't mean that we were consummate professionals by this stage – far from it. With each big deal we were feeling our way, but what we did well was using the knowledge and contacts we made, building them up and transferring them from one client to another. The deal that broke new ground and opened peoples' eyes about what was possible wasn't itself a big deal, and came from a sector not known for generating high returns for investors.

On the 9 October 1999, Icelanders everywhere were hooked on what *Morgunbladid* called 'one of the highlights of Icelandic football history'. At the Stade de France, Iceland was playing the world champions France on their home turf, in the last game of the European Championship qualifiers. The Icelandic team captain scored from a 30-metre free kick. Another goal followed just a few minutes later. A couple of the Icelandic players had cleverly broken down the French defence. What a great moment in Icelandic sporting history.

The only problem was that we lost the game. France scored a decider in the final minutes. It is the curse of a small nation, even one that punches above its weight, that a game you lose can seriously be considered a highlight. The performance of the football team at the glamorous Stade de France was still impressive, bearing in mind we were playing the world champions. We had drawn with them at home, and had come close to qualifying for the European finals. The team coach became a national hero. His name was Gudjon Thordarson and his coaching career up to this point had been very impressive. He had previously taken a team from Akranes, a town of 3000 people, and made it practically unbeatable in Iceland. This small team had even managed to beat Feyenoord, the Dutch champions, in the European Cup. But Thordarson had an ego to match. His temper was notorious. When he wasn't happy with his players' performance he'd give them what they called the 'blow-dry' treatment. He would stand so close to their faces and shout with such force that their hair would stand on end. He once jokingly shouted at one of his players during half time, 'If you don't get out there and perform, I'll go and shag your wife! Again!'

Thordarson believed he was destined for greater things than Iceland. Towards the end of 1999, he approached his nephew, who was working at Kaupthing, with the idea of forming a consortium to buy the second oldest football club in England, Stoke City. He believed Stoke was an ideal acquisition. It had recently been relegated to the English second division, but it had an impressive history, a brand new stadium and enthusiastic supporters. The plan was to buy the club, instate Thordarson as coach, and get into the Premiership, which he estimated would take him three or four years.

It was pretty clear from the start that the only way of making any money from a football club was by getting it into the Premiership. Despite this being a high-risk investment, we quickly concluded that there would be considerable interest in backing the venture, given Thordarson's track record and popularity. We were right. Putting together an investor consortium, largely made up of millionaires from the fishing sector, didn't prove to be a difficult task. One journalist told me that at no time had the mindless optimism of the dot com years risen higher than when Icelanders decided to teach the English how to play football.

Thordarson was the selling point – our business pitch consisted of just putting him in front of investors. He was as effective in the meeting rooms as he was in the locker rooms. He was charismatic, absolutely loved football, and had very firm ideas about how to manage a team. He believed most of the managers in the English league were unsophisticated in their coaching methods and mainly focused on working the players so hard they coughed up blood. When describing the English approach, he stood up and placed his face up against one of the investors, saying '… and if a player questions why the coach is asking them to do stupid things he will say …' He then slammed his fist so forcefully on the meeting room table that the coffee cup jumped in the air and broke into pieces, as he shouted in 'blow-dry' style, 'because I fucking said so!'.

The consortium quickly came together. The next task was to approach Peter Coates, the owner of the club, to see if it was for sale. Coates was unpopular with the fans because of the lacklustre performance of the team, and it didn't take too much convincing before he was ready to sell. This was the first real negotiation we had done for a client outside of Iceland. Our team of advisors was far smaller. It was really just a single Liverpool-based lawyer whom we got hold of through a friend. This simple approach at least ensured the transaction went smoothly, since the number of advisors capable of complicating things was limited.

In November 1999 an agreement was reached and the transaction was announced. The amounts were not large, even by Icelandic standards. The consortium bought 66 percent of the shares for £6.6 million and put an amount into the club to buy players. Even so, the acquisition was huge news in Iceland. Icelandic companies had bought businesses abroad before, but previous transactions had mainly been in the fishing sector and passed largely unnoticed. Now, everyone knew Stoke City and, at the time, it felt unreal to people that such a well-known club could be owned by Icelanders. For us, it really changed what people felt was possible.

Like most investments in football, this one didn't bring a large fortune for any of its backers. Thordarson still performed during his reign at the club. In his first year, the club won the Auto Windshield Cup, the lower league cup competition, which was celebrated widely by the people of Stoke-on-Trent. In the second year they narrowly missed a promotion to the first division, but got it the following year. In the last year though, Thordarson's relationship with the chairman deteriorated rapidly, ending in so much animosity that the club wasn't big enough for both of them. Paradoxically, Thordarson was sacked just after the referee blew the whistle at the end of the game with Brentford that secured the first division place.

Stoke City did eventually secure their seat in the Premiership, in 2008, but that was two years after Peter Coates had bought the club back from the Icelandic consortium. In the end, the Icelandic investors lost around 30 percent of what they put in. The losses could have been greater, but fortunately they had put a clause in the agreement they made with Coates, which stipulated that on promotion to the Premier League, and if Stoke stayed in the league, they would receive additional payments.

The Stoke City takeover wasn't so remarkable in itself, but the thing about it was the wave of acquisitions that it triggered, each one bigger than the one before. Soon we were making aquisitions in everything from prosthetics to high street fashion.

***

Ossur Kristinsson had been born with a deformed right foot. He left Iceland to study prosthetics in Sweden, then on his return in the early seventies, founded his own company, Ossur. Ossur's real claim to fame in the prosthetics industry was its invention of a silicon lining, used to attach an artificial leg to a residual limb. The liners became the industry standard. In 1999 Kaupthing listed the firm on the Iceland Stock Exchange in a very well-received IPO, by which time the company had been grown to a £15 million business.

By that time, Ossur himself had stepped down from running the company, and the CEO was Jon Sigurdsson. The prosthetic industry was very fragmented, and Sigurdsson saw an opportunity to turn Ossur into a consolidator. After the listing, they had access to capital, which gave them an advantage over their competitors. In early 2000 Sigurdsson had identified a target company that he saw as an ideal addition to his, and approached Kaupthing for assistance. The target was California-based Flex Foot, another innovator in the field, known for its creation of the carbon-fibre foot.

The value of the company was over $70 million, making it the biggest cross-border acquisition made by an Icelandic company. To make the transaction possible we needed to raise almost $50 million worth of equity from the stock market. This would be the biggest capital raising ever done for a listed company. We liked the deal, and could see that the transaction would transform Ossur into one of the biggest players in the industry. In our minds there was little doubt that a placement would be well received by Icelandic investors. The problem, however, was that the sellers of Flex Foot did not want to sign any deal without being certain of receiving payment. Any deal subject to us being able to raise capital for Ossur was a no-go. The only way to close the deal was if we were willing to provide a hard underwriting of the equity offering. This meant that if we were unable to sell the shares to investors, we would have to buy them ourselves. The amount to be underwritten was two times Kaupthing's capital, an enormous amount for a company of our size. If we failed, Kaupthing would essentially have been turned into a part bank, part prosthetics firm. The synergies were hard to spot.

Because of the money at stake Sigurdur Einarsson was heavily involved in the deal. Toti Palsson, who would later head up our research department, worked with Sigurdur on the transaction and spent countless hours with him in California to close the deal. The founder and main owner of Flex Foot was a keen promoter of healthy living and, during the deal negotiations, he was curious to know why there were so few instances of modern society diseases in Iceland. As he ate his vegetarian meal during one of the lunch breaks, he looked across the table at Sigurdur and Toti, who were both heavily overweight, and asked if it was true that Icelanders didn't eat junk food. Toti looked down at his own belly and across at Sigurdur's and quickly replied 'how do you think we achieved this shape? Eating bananas?!'

The seller needed some convincing that an underwriting from a bank the size of Kaupthing was worth the paper it was written on. Sigurdur fortunately managed to convince the sellers of the financial strength of the bank. This he mainly did by only referring to Kaupthing in the context of the biggest financial conglomerate in Iceland, the savings banks group. All the numbers he cited were the combined amounts of the entire savings banks system in Iceland. This presentation of the financial strength of Kaupthing was something of a stretch, as we were a lone subsidiary of the savings bank group.

Anyway, the strategy worked and the sellers were persuaded by the might of Kaupthing's financial empire, as described by Sigurdur, to stand behind the underwriting. This created another problem, which was that we weren't in a position to underwrite such a large amount on our own. Sigurdur therefore had to actually go to our owners and convince them to back the deal by sub-underwriting the bulk of it. Fortunately, he was successful and we managed to close the deal in March 2000. The share offering went like magic. Toti tirelessly ran between the brokers, making the case for the bright prospects of the merged companies. He jokingly argued about the advantages of having a titanium leg instead of a real one, regularly asking the brokers if they were still strutting around on their outdated 'flesh legs.' The size of the offering and the risk we took resulted in the biggest fee we had ever seen, close to £2 million – a dizzying amount at the time. Kaupthing had evolved at such a pace that we were now making more money on one deal than we had made in total profits three years earlier.

The acquisition established Ossur as one of the main players in the prosthetics industry. They were one of our most valuable clients over the next decade, and we did numerous equity raisings and debt financing for them. Within two years of their listing on the exchange their turnover had grown to almost $70 million. Later on they expanded into the wider field of orthopaedics. By the end of 2008, Ossur had grown to $350 million in sales and $80 million of operating profits.

***

The next big deal fell into our lap from Eastern Europe. Bjorgolfur Thor Bjorgolfsson, was someone you don't easily forget. I had met him years ago, at a friend's birthday party. I'd just seen him listed in a bizarre tabloid survey as one of Reykjavik's best lovers. His rare self-confidence made him stand out. He was immensely physically strong and bench pressed over 450 pounds. He was an entrepreneur from early on, and by the age of 11 he was delivering newspapers in the early hours of the morning. A year later he was a delivery boy at the University of

Iceland and, at 13, was running his own home video delivery service. While still in high school, he was running a nightclub in Reykjavik and organised the first Oktoberfest beer festival in Iceland. After high school, he studied business in New York. Fluent in several languages, and with an unusual ability to both blend in and stand out, he embodied Iceland's internationalism.

My friend, at whose party we had met, told me that he had seen Bjorgolfur Thor at the airport in Iceland where, by a strange coincidence, they were both going to Russia. My friend was on his way to Kamchatka to lay lino in a swimming pool for an Icelandic fishing company that was operating there. Bjorgolfur Thor, having recently finished his business studies in New York, was going to St Petersburg to set up a beverage business, using old equipment from a bankrupt Pepsi bottling plant in Iceland. It was such a farfetched plan that our friend recalled feeling sorry for him, because he was sure it was doomed to failure, whereas he had been guaranteed the grand sum of £10,000 for the six weeks it would take him to work on the swimming pool. Graciously, he offered Bjorgolfur Thor the chance to join him and his lino laying team in Kamchatcka. Fortunately, Bjorgolfur Thor declined and subsequently made his fortune in Russia.

The business he set up in 1993 in St Petersburg was originally called Baltic Bottling Plant (BBP) and was owned by various British, Russian and Icelandic shareholders. His first years in St Petersburg were extremely tough. The food was terrible so he survived on Snickers bars and Pepsi. The initial years of BBP were characterised by disputes and litigation between the shareholders. In 1997, Bjorgolfur Thor and his father, Bjorgolfur Gudmundsson, and their partner Magnus Thorsteinsson finally sold the bottling plant to Pepsi and set up a new business called Bravo Holding.

Initially they produced soft drinks and alcopops, which turned out to be a huge success. But it wasn't until the company entered into beer brewing that its fortunes really started to take off. Russians gradually developed a taste for premium beer at the expense of dry vodka. Bravo built a large bottling plant in St Petersburg that, by 2002, was already budgeted to produce 535 million litres of beer with an annual turnover of more than $200 million. Completed in only 18 months, it was the sixth largest bottling plant in Europe and a major achievement for Bjorgolfur Thor and his partners. The brand name was Botchkarov and it gradually gained a sizeable market share, particularly in St Petersburg.

The timing of the expansion into the beer sector was perfect. The market grew by 20 percent every year, and soon whetted big multinational beer companies' appetites for a slice of the action. In October 2001 Bjorgolfur Thor and his partners hired Merrill Lynch to manage an auction of the business, which attracted a lot of interest. In early 2002 Bravo Holding was sold for $350 million to Heineken. Bjorgolfur Thor and his partners had struck a goldmine.

The deal that Bjorgolfur Thor brought us in for mid-2000 was not in the beverage sector, however. In Russia, he and his partners kept a low profile while building up the Bravo business. When they realised that it was becoming a success, they started to invest elsewhere. In 1999, he and his father teamed up with Deutsche Bank and Pharmaco, the largest pharmaceutical distributor in Iceland. They acquired the state-owned generic drug manufacturer Balkanpharma in Bulgaria. The deal he approached us to work on was a reverse takeover, whereby Pharmaco acquired Balkanpharma through a share swap.

Previously we had listed Pharmaco on the stock exchange and, at the time, it was a stable but fairly boring pharmaceutical distributor, turning over close to £30 million. Bjorgolfur Thor's intention, however, was to use the listing of Pharmaco to push the company into overdrive. The reverse takeover would establish him as the controlling shareholder in Pharmaco, but we now needed to place the bulk of Deutsche Bank's shares with institutional investors. Deutsche had not intended to exit the Balkanpharma transaction through a listing in Iceland and wanted to be taken out. We needed to place £24 million worth of shares, a large amount at the time. All potential investors were taken on a trip to Bulgaria to see the Balkanpharma operations. The Icelandic investors were treated like royalty. Police cars escorted our buses through traffic. At the end of the trip, we went out on the town, visiting the coolest bars. Lines of A-list party people were moved aside, while Icelandic suits were ushered through the door. Luckily, Eastern Europeans can drink like Icelanders, although after everyone had downed their 20th shot of tequila, things got a bit messy. The share offering was not an easy task, following the deterioration of equity markets in the aftermath of the collapse of the dot com bubble, but in the end we pulled it off, and the placement was a great success.

We learned a lot from this offering, not least because Deutsche Bank made numerous presentations to Kaupthing when we were debating the valuation of the business. The methods they used to analyse and evaluate businesses was quite developed compared to what we were used to at the time. Like sponges, we sucked in all the knowledge from those presentations and then used it when selling the offering to our investors. The professionalism of the pitch books was way superior to what was the standard in Iceland and, of course, we borrowed all the ideas and templates we came across. Later on, when we met with different people from Deutsche Bank in other transactions, they commented that our presentations looked incredibly similar to their own. We just smiled innocently.

As with Ossur, this transaction created a platform for Pharmaco to grow from. Shortly after the Balkanpharma transaction, they merged with Delta, a very successful generic drug manufacturer in Iceland, and subsequently went on an acquisition spree all over the world. It changed its name to Actavis along the way and, when Bjorgolfur Thor's investment fund Novator took the business private with the help of Deutsche Bank in the summer of 2007, it was the third largest generic pharmaceutical business in the world.

***

Our invasion of the UK high street began in the summer of 2000, when I flew to London to meet Kevin Stanford and Karen Millen, founders of the eponymous fashion chain. Karen had been the design force behind the company, but it was Kevin who had built up the business. They founded the company in 1981 by borrowing £100 to buy material. Karen designed clothing that they subsequently sold to their friends, and it was only in 1983 that they opened the first proper store in Kent. The business grew from there, and when I met with them in 2000, they were operating over 60 stores across the UK and were already expanding into other countries. It was highly profitable, if somewhat volatile.

The meeting had been set up by two Icelanders, Magnus Armann and Sigurdur Bollason, who worked for Karen Millen's franchise partner in Iceland. They had approached me to ask if we could put together an investor consortium to buy a significant shareholding in Karen Millen. Bollason had befriended Kevin through their partnership, and knew he was open to selling part of the business. I knew the brand and was interested in the business, so I went to Kent to find out more.

Kevin was likeable with a great sense of humour. He had a background in engineering and combined an impressive eye for design with a firm operational mind. He was a demanding employer and respected by his staff. He enjoyed having people around him and often played the host. When we met, he had just bought and was refurbishing a house in Kent, which was amazing to visit. There was clay pigeon shooting on the lawn and you could fish trout in a small lake. The kids loved going there. When the local fire department got a new fire engine, he bought the old one so they could drive it around the property, usually with the siren on at full volume. The estate was also packed with exotic animals, from peacocks to midget ponies. At one point he had all but shipped a herd of wallabies from Australia when he realised that the walls around his garden were so low that the wallabies could easily have jumped over them. Alarmed by the prospect of seeing tiny marsupials skipping on the roads of Kent, he cancelled the shipment.

Karen and I also became good friends. Like Kevin, she was very good looking and stylish, but less outgoing. Despite the glamour surrounding her name and her A-list status, she was actually quite shy and reserved. When we met she had largely withdrawn from the business to spend more time with their three children. She also began to spend most of her time on charity projects, but her flair for design was still obvious – her house and apartment were among the most beautiful living spaces I have ever seen.

When we met, Karen and Kevin were splitting up, although remaining business partners. After some discussion, we agreed with Kevin and Karen that they would be willing to sell half of the business to the consortium, which we would put together, for a sum of £25 million. In putting together the deal, we capitalised on the experience with Stoke City. Initially we recruited the services of our lawyer from Liverpool. Our experience with him had been very good, so we saw no reason why we wouldn't use him again. That is, until we had the first meeting with Kevin and Karen's team of lawyers. They were being represented by a London City firm and we immediately knew we had to rethink our legal strategy. We were conscious of the fact that we were inexperienced and young, so we came to the conclusion that the way to compensate for that was to hire a team of lawyers to make up for our shortcomings. We went all the way and retained Slaughter and May, one of the most prestigious 'magic circle' law firms in the City of London, and they would be our lawyers of choice for the coming years.

When an agreement in principle was reached with the sellers, the next step for me was to approach investors to join Kaupthing and the two investors, Bollason and Armann, to buy the 50 percent in the business. We began to present the case to investors in the late summer of 2000 and got a very good reaction. After a few weeks we had lined up a mixture of institutional investors and high net worth individuals to form the consortium. In early 2001, we had reached an agreement on heads of terms with the sellers and commenced our due diligence work. As that was progressing, however, various things started to go wrong. As the downturn in the stock market extended its run after the dot com crash, a growing number of investors were losing money, and some of those that we had lined up for the transaction began to waver. To make matters worse, the company began to underperform so the numbers started to look less appealing. Months of renegotiating the deal with the sellers followed, as well as trying to re-patch the investor group.

Finally, at the end of summer 2001, we managed to close the deal, and the group bought 46 percent of Karen Millen. Kaupthing needed to take a bigger stake than had been initially intended, which didn't go down too well because the firm was having a difficult year and there was a significant liquidity squeeze in the Icelandic market. I had to put my head on the block to persuade Sigurdur to agree to the investment, which I was convinced would be a great one. Eventually, when he could take no more of my begging and pleading, he reluctantly agreed, shouting at me: 'and if we lose money on this, I'll have you digging ditches for the rest of your life!'

Thankfully for me, the investment was a great success and we all got our money back many times. The Karen Millen transaction was not huge, but it was still one of the most important ones we did. A few years later, we would co-operate with Baugur in creating one of the UK's biggest fashion retailers, where Karen Millen played a big part. Because the name was well known, it was also a well-publicised example in Iceland of what Kaupthing could put together with its clients.

The new millennium seemed to have sparked our investors' interest in looking abroad. Towards the end of 2000, Jon Asgeir came to us with an idea that subsequently culminated in a deal that was to springboard him into the UK high street. A year earlier he had become a franchisee of the UK clothing giant Arcadia, the owner of brands such as Topshop, Burton's and Dorothy Perkins. He opened up a Topshop in the centre of Reykjavik, but his attention quickly turned to the brand owner.

Arcadia was the second largest clothing retailer in the UK, after Marks & Spencer. The company had been struggling for a while. It had a large number of brands in its stable, but didn't seem able to run them effectively. Profitability was suffering and the share price was spiralling downwards. When Jon Asgeir approached us, it was only around 40 pence, substantially down from its historic high. The British retail impresario Stuart Rose had recently taken over the helm, and Jon Asgeir was convinced that his turnaround strategy was bearing fruit. If Rose was able to change the fortunes of the struggling retailer, buying the shares at or around 40p was a steal. Jon Asgeir's idea was to acquire a ten percent stake in Arcadia and become involved with the company. He believed the younger brands, Topshop in particular, had great growth potential. Even with the low share price, a ten percent stake in Arcadia was worth over £20 million. It was too big a bite for Baugur to swallow alone. A consortium was needed and Jon Asgeir initially tried to pull one together himself. He invited a group of bankers and investors to London to look at the Arcadia shops and to discuss the proposed deal.

My deputy head of Investment Banking, Helgi Bergs, went with the other investors and Baugur on this trip. Helgi was solidly built and didn't frequent the gym. Spas were closer to his heart. He also didn't drink so he didn't really socialise much. Helgi was not particularly known for building client contacts, but he had many other qualities and we complemented each other very well. He was very determined, famous for closing every deal he started. Stubborn as hell, he sometimes got on the clients' nerves, but always reached the finish line. So we became a tag team – I got the clients in and he closed the deal. It worked like a charm.

On the London trip, Helgi quickly came to the conclusion that Jon Asgeir's method of trying to assemble a consortium himself wouldn't work. Jon Asgeir wasn't exactly known for his organisational skills and he didn't have the experience to pull it off. So, after the London trip, Helgi fired off an e-mail telling Jon Asgeir that Kaupthing was not prepared to participate in the transaction purely as an investor, but that we were willing to advise him on the stake building, form the consortium for him and participate as well. On those conditions we would be interested and would be charging half a million pounds for our advisory work.

The e-mail Helgi got back from Jon Asgeir was characteristically short but to the point. It went something like this: 'No way am I paying you that fee. Won't work with you. Will find another bank.' Two weeks later Helgi got another e-mail, even shorter than the previous one, saying, 'Couldn't find anyone else. You're hired.' For transactions of this kind, there was no one but us. Although by most standards we were inexperienced in international deal making, we were experienced compared to the other Icelandic players. We had already advised on transactions in the UK, and had built up a useful relationship with Deutsche Bank through the Balkanpharma transaction, which we could use to execute the Arcadia stake building. On top of that we were willing to co-invest with clients if the opportunity was right, and that gave further credibility to trades such as the Arcadia deal.

We formed a special purpose vehicle called A Holding, got the funds in from the investors, signed Deutsche Bank on as broker, and before year end, A Holding had accumulated a three percent stake at an average price of 38p. By spring 2001, the stake had grown to ten percent. And the investment had been a success. Rose was making good progress in turning the ailing retailer around and the share price steadily rose. Not surprisingly, this caught the attention of the UK press and the management of the company. What did the Icelanders really want? That's exactly the question Rose asked when he met with Jon Asgeir and Baugur's chairman Hreinn Loftsson in Arcadia's headquarters in London for the first time. Loftsson answered in clumsy English, 'We want to work with you.' A surprised Rose responded with 'What? Here in the office?'

In the summer, Baugur bought out the other investors, including Kaupthing, by offering them shares in Baugur. The conversion price for the Arcadia shares was 191p, while the average purchase price had been less than half that. We sold the shares we received in Baugur shortly after that, and more than doubled our money. Despite having sold our shares in Arcadia, we were very much involved in the ongoing dealings Baugur had with the company. Shortly after they had acquired the whole stake, Jon Asgeir began discussions with Rose to buy Topshop out of Arcadia. We were working with him on getting bank financing for the deal, but then September 11 struck, and things were put on ice.

The Arcadia shares began to fall, and the idea of trying to take over the whole company surfaced. It was, of course, incredibly ambitious. The total enterprise value would likely be in excess of £600 million, while the market value of Baugur was slightly more than £100 million. But it seemed like a once-in-a-lifetime opportunity. Hreidar was now spending a lot of time working with Helgi on the transaction, and when they did their analysis with Baugur, we could hardly believe the low valuation. They figured out that, by selling the in-house credit card business and the properties Arcadia owned, we would be buying the operating business at less than one times earnings before interest, tax, depreciation and amortization (commonly referred to as EBITDA). A fantastically low price. We spoke to Deutsche Bank and RBS to close the financing gap. The banks could see this was a great opportunity, but understandably were a bit uncertain of what to make of the small Icelandic retailer they were backing.

Discussions about the takeover had been confidential, but at the end of October 2001, Arcadia's advisors accidentally sent a fax containing information about the discussions to the wrong number, and the *Daily Mail* made the news public. Baugur was forced to declare its intentions and decided to announce publicly that it was looking to bid for the whole company. By this time, the price of the company had skyrocketed sixfold from the time we began negotiations and the announced takeover price was 280–300p.

Yet, despite our desperate attempts, we were simply unable to pull the financing together. We were too small. Discussions with possible equity partners, including the private equity arm of Deutsche Bank and Philip Green, came to nothing. Jon Asgeir even met with Amancio Ortega, the founder and main owner of Zara, which required an interpreter, to investigate his interest. In the end, everything proved to be fruitless, and we pulled out of negotiations in early 2002.

That spring, Baugur considered selling the stake, as the price had reached around 400p. The shares had performed fantastically, following a string of good results. But over the summer the shares started falling again, and Jon Asgeir began to reconsider a takeover. This time he decided not to go it alone and began discussions with Philip Green. Green was highly respected after his successful takeover of British Home Stores and famous for his attempted takeover bid of Marks & Spencer. I wasn't involved in the negotiations on Arcadia, so I didn't meet him as part of that deal. Despite his fantastic success, he could be quite unfriendly, although he seemed to take a liking to Hreidar. He often made snide remarks about the size of Kaupthing; he once quipped 'I like you, you've got balls – but no money!'

Eventually, Green and Jon Asgeir reached an agreement. The plan was for Green to bid for the whole of Arcadia, but immediately sell four of the brands to Baugur: Topshop, TopMan, Miss Selfridge and Wallis. Halifax Bank of Scotland (HBOS) and Kaupthing were by then committed to financing Baugur's acquisition of these brands. This would have been a fantastic deal for Baugur, as Jon Asgeir had rightly spotted that Topshop would create massive value. The bid was made public in mid August, the price being 382p. It was rejected by the board, but after a couple of weeks of haggling between Green and Stuart Rose, they agreed on a price of 408p. The deal was as good as closed, the champagne corks were about to pop, when the unimaginable happened.

As the final touches were being added at Green's offices on Marylebone Road, Jon Asgeir received a phone call. A voice at the other end of the line informed him that the fraud unit of the National Commissioner of the Icelandic Police had raided the headquarters of Baugur in Reykjavik. One of Jon Asgeir's disgruntled former business partners, Jon Gerald Sullenberger, was accusing him of embezzlement. Sullenberger claimed that Jon Asgeir had made Baugur pay costs of his personal yacht, *Thee Viking*, in Miami. He had given the police invoices to back up his claim, and they had raided the Baugur offices three days after Sullenberger first approached them.

By this time, Prime Minister Oddsson had developed a strong dislike for Baugur and Jon Asgeir. It seems he felt Jon Asgeir was becoming too powerful in Iceland, and after the FBA episode, he became very hostile towards Baugur. Jon Asgeir saw the actions of the police in the light of this. The storyline, later revealed when various private e-mails found their way to the media, could have been invented by the writers of *The Bold and the Beautiful*. Sullenberger owned a struggling import company, which had imported goods from the US to Baugur in Iceland. Baugur and Jon Asgeir had declined to support the business, and Sullenberger turned subsequently bitter. He later claimed that what prompted him to take actions against Baugur had been when he learned that Jon Asgeir had made a pass at his wife at a party in Reykjavik, though this story was unfounded. One of Sullenberger's friends, who had previously had connections with Jon Asgeir's family, put him in touch with a lawyer, who advised him to go straight to the police, which then resulted in the raid. Yet the charges also implicated Sullenberger who had issued what he now claimed were fraudulent invoices. The raid sparked a three-year investigation by the police and when charges were finally brought, it would affect another large deal.

When Reuters published the news of the raid the following morning, Rose immediately called Green. Initially Green thought Rose was lying.

How could this have happened without him knowing, when Jon Asgeir had sat in his office at the time of the raid, putting the takeover bid together. But then he suddenly remembered that Jon Asgeir had taken a long call from Iceland the previous day. When Green had asked him if something was wrong, Jon Asgeir had said no. He was just dealing with some petty problems, nothing to worry about. Green went ballistic that Jon Asgeir hadn't told him what was happening and that he had to learn about it from the media.

The raid threw the whole bid into jeopardy. The board of Arcadia declined to accept any bid that was contingent upon Baugur in any way. Green quickly made the decision to go it alone and put pressure on Jon Asgeir to drop out of the race and simply sell Baugur's 20 percent share to him. But to Jon Asgeir and Hreidar, buying the young fashion brands was still the ultimate prize, and they fought tooth and nail to somehow keep Baugur in the bid. Kaupthing's incentive in the deal was almost as big as Baugur's. We were going to invest a vast amount and had also lined up a few of our clients to take some of the equity as well. They proposed that Green should enter into a forward agreement, whereby he would sell the young fashion brands to Baugur at some point in time in the future. Green refused and eventually Jon Asgeir had to throw in the towel.

I later told Green, at a charity dinner, that the police raid had been the best thing that could have happened to him, as it enabled him to buy the whole company. Topshop in particular was a fantastic performer and created hundreds of millions of pounds for Green in the space of a few years. His response was that he had taken a very big risk by deciding to take on the whole bid himself; he didn't even have time to do a proper due diligence. I suspect that was a fair comment, and it is also questionable whether Topshop would have fared as well under Baugur's ownership as it did under Green's. Whatever one thought of Green, there was little doubt he was a great operator.

The board of Arcadia accepted Green's bid of 408p, which meant the total value of the company was now over £850 million. Green commented to the media that Jon Asgeir couldn't complain about the deal. 'I made him a rich man, what more could he ask for?!' Baugur's stakebuilding in Arcadia, was undeniably a massive success. The takeover price was ten times higher than the prevailing price when we began to buy up the shares. The average purchase price that Baugur paid was, of course, considerably higher, but they had still more than doubled the money they put in. The value of their shares, when Green bought the company, was over £165 million. The cash gave Baugur a fantastic war chest.

Our inroads into the UK were not limited to the retail sector. In early 2001, the two owners of the seafood company Bakkavor, Agust and Lydur Gudmundssons, came to ask Kaupthing for assistance in acquiring a London-based business that would be their launch pad into the UK market. Agust and Lydur had been strategically reviewing their business and had come to the conclusion that the company needed to change course. They saw that the future of food production would very much be focused on fresh food and ready-made meals. That was the fastest growing market with the highest margins, and they wanted to be part of it. That meant they needed to go more into private labelling and move away from building their own brands, as the big supermarket chains sold most of that produce under their own name. The most developed market in the world for fresh food and ready-made meals was the UK.

In 2000, they had identified a small business in Birmingham, called Wine and Dine, a supplier of dips and dressings to supermarkets. Bakkavor supplied Wine and Dine's roe, and knew the family that owned it. We assisted them in acquiring the Birmingham-based business in late 2000 for just short of £8 million.

Wine and Dine was owned and run by a Greek Cypriot. Through him, the brothers got to know another family, originally from Cyprus, who had built up a substantially bigger food company in London. The business was called Katsouris Fresh Foods and was a very successful producer of various fresh food, ready meals, and dips for the big supermarkets, Tesco in particular. This was a fantastic business, very fast-growing with high margins and exceptionally strong cash flow. Because everything they made was fresh, the raw material was sold almost as soon as it was bought, resulting in practically no cash being used to fund inventories. It was the ideal platform for Bakkavor in the UK. The family was also interested in discussing the takeover, as the CEO was getting close to retirement and didn't have any children to take over from him. They didn't particularly fancy selling out to a bigger competitor or a private equity fund, so when they took a liking to the brothers, a sale to them felt like the optimal solution. The tiny fly in the ointment was the same as in most of our initial transactions abroad, namely that Katsouris was many times the size of Bakkavor. While the latter had a market value of around £20 million, Katsouris was worth slightly over £100 million. At the time there had never been a corporate takeover of that size in Iceland. But, as with Jon Asgeir and Arcadia, the brothers saw this as a once-in-a-lifetime opportunity which they couldn't let slip between their fingers. The only way they would be able to do this was with the help of Kaupthing. And even if we wanted to help, this was a huge stretch.

When the brothers approached us, asking whether we could help them put the transaction together, we were baffled by the size. It wasn't hard to see why they were interested in the company, it was a fantastic operation and the valuation was very low, given the growth and high cash-flow generation. The amounts involved, for a company the size of Bakkavor, were staggering, however. The timing for raising financing was also horrendous. The dot com bubble had recently burst and many investors were burned.

Hreidar and Sigurdur were very doubtful about the prospects of being able to finance a deal of this size. Helgi and I were given the task of dealing with the brothers. This was a deal we desperately wanted to do, so we discussed various ways in which we could close it. It was obvious that there was no way we could raise anything close to a hundred million pounds of equity for Bakkavor. The size was humongous for the Icelandic market and investors had little appetite for new issues. After some consideration, we came to the conclusion that the only way for Bakkavor to acquire Katsouris was if we were able to debt finance a considerable part of the deal. Since Katsouris didn't have any meaningful assets they could pledge, we needed to provide financing against the strong cash flows of the company; effectively do a leveraged buyout. But even if we were able to do that, we would always have to raise a considerable amount of equity and, at the time, we couldn't see that we could raise that much in Iceland. Despite the various obstacles to closing any transaction, we still entered into an agreement with Bakkavor to advise and structure the financing of the deal. Because of the difficulty in achieving the final goal, we demanded very high success fees if our work resulted in an acquisition of Katsouris. The brothers, uncharacteristically, agreed to all our fee proposals without haggling. Later they told me they knew that the only way they could close this transaction was by giving us a huge incentive to close it. They knew we'd move heaven and earth to achieve it and it therefore wasn't in their interest to quibble about our success fee.

And they were right – we were going to try everything to close the transaction. Essentially we were working on three things simultaneously: negotiations with the Katsouris family, finding debt for the acquisition and raising the additional equity needed. Negotiating with the seller was the easy part. Financing the transactions was tricky to say the least. It took us almost a year to close it, and during that time the goalposts shifted constantly, much to our frustration. We were constantly celebrating important milestones, when they fell apart and we were back to the drawing board.

Our knowledge about international debt structuring was academic at best. We didn't know how the leverage debt market would structure a transaction like this and we didn't know any bankers involved in leverage finance. We began by putting together a proposal on what we thought was a realistic financing structure, split between debt and equity. This we did by making cash-flow projections with the brothers and using that to come up with the right quantum of debt that the cash flow could service interest on and gradually pay down. By this time we had made good headway with the sellers in the negotiations and a purchase price of around £100 million was agreed.

Endless Excel cash-flow projections showed that the business should be able to take on around £70 million of debt if one was aggressive. Having come to that conclusion, the next step was to approach banks likely to be interested. It didn't take us long to eliminate the Icelandic banks. They didn't have any experience to speak of in organising leverage debt, and the size of the financing was too big for them. The logical step was to speak to banks in London, where we managed to get meetings with two banks. One was the incumbent bank to Katsouris, RBS. After the first meeting, it was clear they were not willing to provide as much debt financing as we felt we needed. The next bank we spoke to was Commerzbank in London. I'd known them since I started handling the financing of Kaupthing and had good contacts there. As it turned out, they were quite keen to increase their exposures to leverage finance in the UK. After brief discussions, we received heads of terms from them, whereby they agreed in principle to provide the required debt. The champagne came out big-time. But the bank still needed to do its due diligence on both Katsouris and Bakkavor. Three months of intensive analysis had only just begun.

As part of the due diligence, we arranged a meeting between Commerzbank and the Bakkavor brothers and management. At lunch, Bakkavor products were brought out, to give the bankers a taste of what they were financing. As we ate, my throat started to swell up. I turned white, overcome by nausea. Eventually I had no choice but to run to the bathroom. It wasn't a great moment to discover I was allergic to caviar.

Whether or not this had anything to do with it or not, we began to experience problems with Commerzbank in the autumn of 2001. After spending 16 weeks on due diligence, they started getting signals from Frankfurt that headquarters wanted to decrease leverage in the deals they did. This resulted in us having to completely rethink the financing structure. Kaupthing decided to put in a subordinated bond that could be converted into equity in order to replace some of the debt Commerzbank was providing. After this round of negotiations with the bank, we again thought that we had now concluded the debt financing. Again corks popped and champagne flowed. And again the celebrations proved to be premature. When the restructured deal got to Frankfurt for final approval, it was swiftly rejected. The bank even had a policy of not revealing to its clients its reasons for bowing out of a transaction. After almost four months of work, we suddenly had no loan financing in place and no clue as to why they had backed out. To make matters worse, we were experiencing problems on the equity side as well.

Despite counting on the Commerzbank debt funding, we still had to raise an enormous amount of equity for Bakkavor to enable them to conclude the acquisition. The amount we needed, based on the loan financing we were negotiating with the Germans, was in the order of £50 million. We couldn't raise that sum in the Icelandic market – it was simply too much.

Once more our focus shifted away from the domestic market. We concluded that our best chance would be to list Bakkavor in Stockholm and raise capital there. At the time, Bakkavor's biggest operations were in Sweden, after the acquisition of Lysekils Havsdelikatesser, so there was a rationale for a listing there. This would require some co-operation with a Swedish institution and, of course, we had no contacts with the brokerage companies and investment banks there. I used some of my old contacts from my fund-raising days to get a number of meetings with some of the key players. Eventually that led us to Handelsbanken's

Capital Markets team. They liked Bakkavor and the pending transaction, and were keen to work with us on raising capital for them. They concluded, however, that the best exchange to be listed on was the Norwegian one, and on the back of that, they could raise capital from all the Nordic markets. The reason why they liked the Norwegian market was because of the large number of food companies listed there and the high valuation they enjoyed. In the summer of 2001, we had signed a term sheet with Handelsbanken and the equity financing seemed all but certain. Another crate of champagne was the order of the day.

In early autumn of 2001, the Norwegian market crashed, in particular the largest food companies. Many of them were fish producers and when the price of salmon dropped significantly in the summer, so did the shares in the companies that made money selling it. Suddenly the attitude of investors changed and, as a result, so did the attitude of Handelsbanken. In response to the swing in market sentiment, they pulled their support and the proposed listing in Norway, and pan-Nordic equity raising evaporated. We were depressed when leaving the offices of Handelsbanken in Oslo, after they had informed us that the offering was off. Trying to push the door's exit button, Lydur accidentally turned off the lights in the reception of the bank. 'Just as well,' he exclaimed. 'There is nothing happening here anyway.'

So there we were in the autumn of 2001, on the brink of closing the acquisition, when both our debt funding and equity funding disappeared. Half a year's work down the drain and back to square one again. There was still no way we were going to give up and Helgi and I went back to the drawing board with the brothers. Bakkavor had built up some contacts in Birmingham, thanks to their earlier acquisition of Wine and Dine and, through them, managed to get in touch with the Birmingham branches of a few of the big UK banks. They moved incredibly fast, and formed a consortium led by HBOS to provide the debt financing. However, the quantum of debt was lower than we had originally planned for, so the equity gap was even bigger than before. To close the gap, we agreed with the Katsouris family to invest a part of their consideration back into Bakkavor. Kaupthing agreed to increase the size of its convertible bond, and we also decided to change course and raise £20 million of equity in Iceland. Despite the poor market conditions, we believed that this was such a fantastic deal that we would be able to convince investors at home to support it. Again we needed to underwrite the offering to close the deal with the sellers, and again that risk paid off.

The offering in Iceland was very successful and we managed to get it considerably oversubscribed, despite the large amount we were placing. The amount we were going to sell to retail investors was £5 million and we knew that was going to be tricky. Retail investors, like other investors, had been badly burned in the dot com crash, and their participation in the stock market had all but disappeared when we approached them with the Bakkavor offering. There were situations like these that brought out the best in Kaupthing, and during the retail sales we managed to energise the whole firm to promote the offering to private investors. This time, I put my head on the line and told people that this was a share offering they could recommend to their grandmother to take a small part in (which I did myself!) which carried meaningful weight. We even promised the employee with the most subscriptions champagne and a spa day at one of the hotels in Reykjavik. That wouldn't have got a big reaction in an American investment bank, but it worked well in Iceland at the time. I knew people were really stretching themselves with their friends and family, when I overheard the eventual winner of the competition start his pitch something like this:

'Hi Jon. This is Gunnar Pall.
(pause)
Gunnar Pall Tryggvason!
(pause)
Karen's husband!
(pause)
Your niece Karen?'

So, by the end of 2001, we had concluded the largest acquisition in Icelandic history and made Bakkavor one of the five biggest companies in the country. This time we pounced on the champagne bottles without any reservations. The acquisition was a fantastic success, and the new entity over-performed for many years. The price in the offering had been at 6.8 kronur, and five years later it had multiplied more than eightfold. The debt to the UK banks was repaid within three years and when we eventually converted our bond into shares and exited the investment in 2006, the value of our £20 million investment had swollen to almost £200 million. Again our fees for the transaction were astronomical and helped to make sure that 2001, which was otherwise very difficult for Kaupthing, was another record year. The transaction revolutionised Bakkavor and established them as a major producer in the UK. It gave them a platform that they would subsequently use to grow and multiply.

*****

There was an 18-month period during 2000 and 2001 where we really did break new international ground. This was the beginning of the Icelandic international expansion. The work we did during this period was amongst the most enjoyable of my career at Kaupthing. With practically no experience and limited contacts, and in an incredibly difficult period when investors were burned and liquidity was scarce, we helped our clients achieve unbelievable things. It was a case of growing in adversity. The deals were enormous by comparison to our clients and gave them fantastic platforms to grow from. But the deals weren't only large. Stoke City apart, they were all very successful.

The people behind these transactions knew their sectors, they were buying good companies and at sensible valuations. This was achieved before the world was flooded with liquidity. The privatisation of the commercial banks in Iceland had not taken place yet and they played practically no role in the successful execution of these transactions. The funding came mainly from equity investors and UK banks, and we had to fight hard to get it. As tends to be the case when money is scarce, reason prevails, and the capital employed in these acquisitions would multiply in the coming years. The value creation from a total invested equity of just over £100 million in 18 months would be many hundreds of millions in the next few years. The equity created would form the core building blocks of the Icelandic incursion into the UK and Scandinavia. With the ample debt funding that would subsequently become available, the purchasing power would be counted in billions of pounds.

We didn't just get money from these deals. We also got experience to die for. We structured and managed international acquisitions. We began to understand the murky world of leverage finance. We became far more professional, and built up a fantastic network of contacts with banks and brokerage houses abroad. We took all this on board and used it to finance the new grand masters of Icelandic business. Kaupthing was now the nerve centre behind the sheer brawn of the new Icelandic business world. We were about to make bigger waves.

Chapter Five

Empire-Building

'Follow that car!' Henrik Gustafsson shouted through the window at the cab driver waiting outside Arlanda airport in Stockholm. He jumped into the car, his heart thumping, acutely aware that he must have sounded like someone who had watched one too many cop thrillers. But, just like in the movies, the stakes were high for Kaupthing.

It was the middle of June 2004, and we were in the final stages of acquiring the Danish bank FIH. The takeover would double the size of Kaupthing, making us the eighth largest bank in the Nordic area, and by far the largest bank in Iceland. The people in the cab Henrik was chasing were the management team of Landsbanki, our biggest competitor in Iceland. They had suddenly appeared on the scene as a potential buyer for FIH, and now seemed likely to outbid us at the very last minute. Henrik had noticed the group on the plane over from Iceland and saw them circulating documents, which he knew were related to FIH. Until that moment we had believed we were just about to clinch the acquisition. He now needed to confirm that they were really so advanced that they were negotiating with the sellers. Our response to the sellers would be based on that information.

Henrik chased the Landsbanki cab through the streets of Stockholm until it finally pulled over in front of a big building on Norrmalms Square in the centre of the city. He immediately recognised it. It was the offices of the Mannheimer Swartling law firm, the lawyers who were representing the sellers of FIH. The deal we had been working on day and night for almost two months was going to be snatched from under our noses at the very last minute.

***

FIH was to be the final step in a four-year Nordic expansion spree, during which time we opened in all the Nordic countries, as well as expanding aggressively in Iceland. To take the story back a bit, though, our first steps outside Iceland weren't taken in Scandinavia. Not long after I joined Kaupthing, it was already looking beyond Iceland's coast. Early on, Sigurdur had set his sights on Luxemburg, which had a similar population to Iceland and had an even less exciting domestic market. It did, however, have historical links with Iceland. When Loftleidir, Icelandair's predecessor, started their low cost route from the US to Europe, Luxembourg became the European hub. Loftleidir also became a founding shareholder in Cargolux, which later became one of the largest cargo airline in the world. This led to the formation of a small Icelandic community there. There were also other reasons why Luxemburg was an interesting outpost for Kaupthing.

We began our foray into Luxemburg in 1996, when we established our first international mutual funds there. These were funds, which were invested in a variety of global bonds and stocks, managed from Iceland. Initially we didn't place any staff in Luxembourg, but shortly after the establishment of the fund company, we began to contemplate launching a full-service securities firm there.

The attraction of Luxembourg was primarily its status as one of the world's most advanced offshore banking centres. At the time Iceland didn't have offshore banking services but we believed there would be considerable demand from wealthy Icelanders for their money to be managed offshore. For many clients it was simply a question of privacy. Iceland is a small country and some people didn't have a lot of faith in banking secrecy there, often for good reason. A friend of mine – the daughter of a well-known businessman – was once sitting in a coffee shop when she overheard the cashier from her bank discussing how much she spent on expensive clothes on her Visa card. The tax treaties in place between Iceland and Luxembourg, also meant that it could be advantageous to set up holding companies in Luxembourg for investments in Iceland and other countries.

We founded the securities firm Kaupthing Luxembourg SA in 1998. Magnus Gudmundsson was moved to Luxembourg to run it – the joke went that for our first office abroad it would be appropriate to send the one executive who didn't speak English properly. Prior to moving, Magnus was actually sent on a week's crash course in English. It was like a band-aid on a bullet wound. The real reason for choosing Magnus was that our Luxembourg operation was a private client business, and no one was better qualified to run it.

Initially he was joined by two others. One of them was Halldor Thorsteinsson, one of our key brokers who later moved on to New York when we opened our office there. The other one was a Dane, Nils Johansen, who had lived in Luxembourg for a long period and whom Sigurdur had identified through some Danish friends. Danes are renowned for their thriftiness and the Almighty had been particularly generous with Nils when he was handing out frugality. When Magnus asked where he could buy a mobile phone, Nils sorted it out, by driving to Belgium where he knew there was a sale on second-hand phones. He drove to France to buy coffee cups and saucers for the office at a factory sale. After that, Magnus hurried to the local supermarket to buy coffee before Nils jumped on a plane to Brazil. Although Nils left us shortly after, the office in Luxembourg had a very Danish feel, as we later hired a Danish banker and long-standing friend of Sigurdur's, Johnie Brogger, as Magnus' co-CEO.

It was a fairly big event when our offices in Luxembourg opened that June. To mark the occasion, we invited the managers of the 27 Icelandic savings banks, our owners, and some other members of the 'Saving Banks family' to a celebration in Luxembourg. Many of them weren't used to being invited abroad, or even going out of the country at all. Several forgot to take their passports, complaining that they hadn't been mentioned in the travel itinerary. The whole event had the air of a high-school trip, despite the fact that most guests were close to retirement age. At the opening cocktail party, the champagne flowed. The guests, however, didn't consider that a real drink, so sent waiters back to the kitchen again and again for gin and tonic. The guest of honour was the finance minister, Geir Haarde, who later became Prime Minister. In his speech he said he hoped that this would be only the beginning of the expansion of the Icelandic financial companies into international markets. His wish more than came true.

The Luxembourg office was almost an instant success, and grew rapidly and profitably. In the beginning the clientele was almost solely Icelandic, either living in Iceland or abroad. That would change over time and gradually the vast majority of clients came from other countries, mainly the UK and Scandinavia. Most of the clients had some kind of offshore status, so the setting up and managing of holding companies was an important part of the business.

In 2000 we applied for and were granted a banking licence for our subsidiary, which became known as Kaupthing Bank Luxembourg. There was another celebration in Luxembourg with a large group of investors and shareholders. The President of Iceland formally opened the bank. The inauguration was followed by a dinner at one of Luxembourg's best restaurants. The day after, when Magnus went to settle the bill, the owner told him off for not informing him that the President of Iceland would be attending – he wanted to have his picture taken with him. Magnus was surprised, and reminded him that he had actually told him that the president would be there. 'Yes,' replied the owner, 'but I always assumed it was the president of the bank, it never occurred to me that the president of a country would attend a bank opening!' It is sometimes good to come from a small country.

By 2004, the Luxembourg operation had grown to almost 100 people, and made up over 10 percent of the total revenues of the group.

It was already bigger than the parent company had been when it was founded in 1998. At one point it was one of the top ten taxpayers in Luxembourg.

I had started to get to know a lot of high net worth individuals in the UK as part of our investment banking work. As these people sold their businesses to our Icelandic clients or others, we often built up a very good relationship with them – that was always one of Kaupthing's strengths. These people often later came on board as private banking clients in Luxembourg. For me, it was an easy sell, I had such faith in Magnus' team, that recommending them came naturally.

***

Private banking clients in Luxembourg also came from the other start-ing point in our worldwide adventure – the Nordic area. Although we had set up a small brokerage unit in New York in 2000, the main focus was on the Nordic countries: Sweden, Denmark, Finland and Norway. These are the nations we consider our closest relations and, having been under both Norwegian and Danish rule at different periods, there is obviously a common history. Icelanders learn Danish at school (until 1997 it was the second language, ahead of English), which means that most people have a rudimentary understanding of Danish, Norwegian and Swedish, which are all very similar. Finnish, however, is completely unrelated.

As in all families though, there are tensions. Soon after we expanded into Scandinavia, I began to doubt our logic in doing so. Many multi-nationals, including Kaupthing at the time, viewed the Nordic market as a single entitiy. Looking at the region from that perspective, it seems like an appealing place to do business. With a combined population of over 20 million highly educated and entrepreneurial people, it has an established and sound legal framework with reliable institutions. The problem, however, is that it isn't really one market area, but rather four (excluding Iceland and the Faroe Islands from the equation) independ-ent, if somewhat related, countries that don't particularly like one another. The Finns don't like the Swedes, who dislike the Danes, who in turn make fun of the Norwegians. Individually, each of these markets is small, but still overcrowded and very competitive.

In the UK we were looked upon as Scandinavians, and people didn't really distinguish much between the various Nordic countries. In Scandinavia, however, we were looked down upon as a precocious little brother. The linguistic barrier was also bigger than it seemed, and communicating in English wasn't really the same. Even though I had spent some time in Norway when I was younger, and was therefore comparatively good in 'Scandinavian', speaking it in business situations was a nightmare. I would nod my head in a fake sign of understanding or agreement, which I invariably had to retract when someone later explained what I'd actually agreed to.

Anyway, at the start of the millennium we were unaware of this, and seriously pondered various expansions. Sweden was the obvious place to start, being the key market in the region. Sweden is really the big brother in Scandinavia, and this is reflected in its relationship with the other Nordic countries. The Finns, Norwegians and Danes all have their own brand of jokes about the Swedes, which seem to be tinged with envy. Swedes, on the other hand, rarely make fun of the other countries, and have a more benevolent attitude towards their smaller neighbours – which the others sometimes see as a sign of arrogance.

A Dane once told me that if Denmark were playing an important football match against a non-Nordic country, Swedes would genuinely support Denmark. If, however, Sweden were in that same position, the Danes would generally hope to see them lose. The jokes and criticism of the Swedes are usually centred around them being formal and stodgy. They have a reputation for having endless debates and a grinding need for full consensus on everything. A popular joke tells of a Norwegian, a Dane and a Swede lost in the desert or a jungle, exhausted and about to die, when a genie appears and grants them each a wish. The Norwegian and Dane quickly request to be sent to some fantastic place, leaving the Swede behind. He can't make up his mind, so he uses his wish to summon the other two back so that he can consult with them. There is an element of truth in this. The Swedes seem hardwired to deliberate and reach a consensus, in stark contrast with the American model of decision-making where the buck stops with the strong leader. Yet the business, sporting and musical success of the Swedes is pretty hard to argue with.

We set up an office in Stockholm in early 2000. With only four people, the intention was really to get to understand the market a bit better without too much cost. We entered the market just as the dot com bubble was about to burst. Naturally, Stockholm – which was sometimes dubbed the Silicon Valley of Europe – was badly hit. The OMX stock index in Stockholm crashed, dropping by an amazing 70 percent, and the share price in the country's largest company, Ericsson, almost disappeared. It dropped by more than 95 percent from its high, and the joke went that investors would have been better off if they had bought beer rather than investing their money in the telecoms firm. The deposit received from returning the empty bottles was enough to beat the return on the shares. We thus had a very small operation in a very difficult market, resulting in little activity. The market got weaker and weaker, and an increasing number of brokerage houses and investment banks began to suffer considerable losses.

Sigurdur, who was now spending a considerable part of his time in Sweden, believed there would be opportunities in acquiring one of the established players in the market without too much cost. The first opportunity arose in early 2002, when Kaupthing acquired a relatively small brokerage and asset management firm called Aragon. The agreed price was the equivalent of SEK 230 million (£15 million), which we paid with shares in Kaupthing, giving the Swedish shareholders of Aragon, who were institutional investors, an 11 percent stake in the combined business. We had recently listed Kaupthing in Iceland, and this was one of the first of a small number of acquisitions we made in the Nordic region by using our shares as payment.

But Aragon wasn't doing well, and the only way to return it to profitability was to increase scale and cut costs. That meant consolidation, and only a few months after the acquisition, we entered into negotiations with an investment bank called JP Nordiska. In June, we reached an agreement with them, whereby JP Nordiska acquired Aragon from Kaupthing in exchange for a 28 percent share in the stock market listed JP Nordiska. But Sigurdur had greater ambitions than being a minority shareholder in the Swedish investment bank. Only a few days after the acquisition was announced, he negotiated a deal with Lars Magnusson, the second largest shareholder of JP Nordiska, which gave Kaupthing the right to acquire his 12.8 percent stake at a specific price before 15 January 2003. This meant that if we exercised this option, our stake would exceed 40 percent and we would be forced to make a takeover bid. Sigurdur took a seat on the board of JP Nordiska. Initially, the relationship between him and the other board members was good. That quickly changed. Merging Aragon with JP Nordiska elevated the scale of operations, but the combined company was still losing money. Sigurdur saw a dire need to cut costs, and wanted to take the number of employees from almost 300 to less than 200. The majority of the board was content with the actions that had already been taken and did not want to do more, as they expected the market to recover quickly.

An incredibly fierce fight and dramatic takeover bid followed. The chairman of the board was Bjorn Wolrath, the former CEO of Skandia, Sweden's largest insurance company. He and his colleagues on the board were part of the establishment. We were outsiders. That might have softened Sigurdur's approach, but then he was never known for his diplomatic touch. He was once asked in a Q&A session with staff whether the bank had an HR policy. His response was: 'Yes. If you don't like it here, you can leave.' He dealt with the distinguished board of JP Nordiska in a similar way – it was his way or the highway. He began by making a takeover bid for 100 percent of the shareholdings of JP Nordiska, offering shares in Kaupthing at a price which essentially meant that the Swedish shareholders were getting a 40 percent premium to the current market price of JP Nordiska. This was done without seeking the recommendation of the board and thus by definition a hostile takeover. When asked by a journalist why Kaupthing had gone hostile, however, Sigurdur responded 'this is not hostile. This is a friendly takeover – for the shareholders!' Sigurdur's approach became notorious in Sweden, especially after a bulldog-like image of him was splashed across the country's most popular business magazine, with the headline reading something like 'the terror of the City'.

In the midst of this takeover bid, he asked the chairman to fire the CEO, Lage Jonason. When Wolrath declined, Sigurdur turned around and requested an extra general meeting of shareholders, where he ousted the board. By then, the Swedish insurance group Lansforsakringer, who had become a shareholder in Kaupthing after our takeover of Aragon, had bought 11.5 percent of JP Nordiska. They supported Sigurdur, and with their support Kaupthing controlled around 58 percent of the shareholdings. The new board began by firing the CEO Jonason and hiring Christer Villard, who had been the CEO of Aragon, as a replacement.

The CEO and the ousted board did not take Kaupthing's aggressiveness quietly. Rumours and negativity about Kaupthing spread like wildfire in the markets and in the press. Many of the newspapers in Sweden wrote incredibly negative articles about Kaupthing. The shareholders' association in Sweden, Aktiespararna, went on a crusade against our bid. They filed charges on our takeover approach with the Swedish takeover committee, and recommended that shareholders in JP Nordiska should not accept the takeover bid despite the premium paid. The head of Aktiespararna furiously told a journalist that Kaupthing couldn't treat the venerable Swedish stock market like a 'fish market.' Their efforts were in vain, however. The takeover panel determined that Kaupthing had adhered to all applicable rules and regulations, and before the end of the year, over 90 percent of the shareholders in JP Nordiska had accepted our bid. Five years later the value of the

Kaupthing shares given to the JP Nordiska shareholders was ten times the value of the shares they had held previously.

Throughout this whole process, Sigurdur was incredibly driven, working day and night towards achieving his goal of building a prominent business in Sweden. What was supposed to be a fairly straightforward transaction had taken months in the making. A lawyer from our investment banking team had joined Sigurdur in the transaction, flying over to Stockholm for what was supposed to be two days' work with just his computer bag. Four weeks later he returned to his wife and newborn son after staying at ten different places (accommodation being scarce as Stockholm was celebrating its 750-year anniversary). In the hot summer months of 2002 he could be spotted wandering around Stockholm from one meeting to the other, looking like a Mormon handing out bibles, in the one black suit he had brought with him. Every other day he would visit Hennes and Mauritz to buy new socks and underwear. Eventually he ended up in an apartment on the outskirts of Stockholm rented from the daughter of Jan Fock, the Chairman of Aragon. The nametag on the house bell read Lotta Fock, but nothing could be further from the activities taking place in Sweden during those hectic summer weeks.

In January 2003, the name of JP Nordiska was changed to Kaupthing Bank Sverige. Although successful, all this proved a massive drain on management, Sigurdur in particular. The negative press we got during the process was also very damaging, and it didn't end there. Bad press lives forever, and when we entered other markets in the following years, the negative articles from Sweden would be regularly resurrected and translated. In hindsight, although we had legitimate reasons to seek a new leadership and course for the Swedish bank, more diplomacy might have produced better results. In any case it taught us to follow a more cautious route in the years to come. The takeover battle also had a very serious consequence, which only came to light a few months after we secured the acquisition of JP Nordiska.

On 27 May 2003, the Economic Crime Unit of the Swedish police orchestrated a multinational house search in co-operation with local police in Sweden, England, Luxembourg, Germany and Iceland. The actions were targeted at six individuals, five Icelandic and one Swedish, whom the Swedish police suspected of insider trading in relation to Kaupthing's takeover of JP Nordiska. The case was big news, especially in Sweden and Iceland, and Robert Engstedt, the Swedish prosecutor running the investigation, did nothing to play down its scale and importance. He was quoted as saying that the profits resulting from the alleged criminal activities were estimated at around SEK 4–5 million (£3–400,000), which, if proven, would make it the biggest case of its kind in Sweden's history, adding that the suspects could be sentenced to up to four years in jail.

Of the suspects, the best known were the Bakkavor brothers, Agust and Lýdur Gudmundsson, and Lars Magnusson, who had been JP Nordiska's second largest shareholder. Essentially the case revolved around the fact that the individuals had been big buyers of shares in JP Nordiska, after Kaupthing had acquired the initial 28 percent stake and entered into the agreement with Magnusson, which secured a further 12.8 percent. When Kaupthing published its takeover bid for the Swedish bank a few months later, the individuals made considerable gains. Not surprisingly, it had been the former CEO and board of JP Nordiska that had alerted the Swedish FSA, which subsequently referred the matter to the Swedish Police. The case, to be fair, looked compelling. The individuals had actually bought over 90 percent of all available shares in the bank during a two-and-a-half-month period and, shortly after that, a takeover bid appeared which resulted in a profit for the investors.

The truth, however, was less exciting. In Iceland it was practically assumed that Kaupthing would make a bid for JP Nordiska, after it had secured more than a 40 percent stake in the bank in June 2002. *Morgunbladid* had even created a pro forma balance sheet for the combined bank, Kaupthing and JP Nordiska, days after the deal with Magnusson was made. Everyone expected a bid of some sort, and that was what the investors had acted on. As the Bakkavor brothers pointed out in a statement after the house search was made public, Kaupthing would be forced to make a takeover bid when they utilised the agreement with Magnusson and acquired more than 40 percent of JP Nordiska. They commented that they were only surprised that more people hadn't bought shares in the Swedish bank, when this was made public.

For people in Sweden, where Kaupthing was virtually unknown, it was less obvious what the intentions of the Icelanders were. Therefore the trading in the shares looked suspect and resulted in the aggressive investigation. In any case, the police investigation revealed nothing and, in June 2004, it was abandoned. The police didn't even bother to call the suspects to tell them the investigation was closed. They had to read that in the papers. When the Bakkavor brothers called the police to ask them to confirm the media reports, they were told that everyone on the case was on holiday. In an ironic twist, Kaupthing a few years later gave information to the Swedish police that led to the biggest insider trading scandal in Sweden – and that time it was real.

In the end, the timing of the takeover of JP Nordiska was quite good, and after significant cost cutting, the bank was returned to profitability. Over five years its assets grew from SEK 2 billion to 20 billion and the staff went from 175 to 417. In September 2004, both Sigurdur and Hreidar received a kommandor medal from the King and Queen of Sweden.

***

From Sweden we moved to cover all the Nordic countries in just over two years. We opened offices in both the Faroe Islands and Denmark in 2000. In both cases this was in partnership with the Faroese Savings Bank, with whom we had built up a good relationship. Initially, when we had approached the Faroe Bank – the biggest bank in the Faroe Islands – the Danish CEO of the bank was very blunt and told Sigurdur 'Go away – there are enough banks on the islands!' To be fair, he was probably right. The population was tiny, less than 50,000 people, and activity levels were very low. We still believed that a stock market could develop there like in Iceland, and opened the first Faroese securities house under our name. The good news was that we got very good people to run the firm and the fact that we had 100 percent market share. The bad news was that 100 percent of almost nothing is not much. The business was still relatively successful, although the amounts in the end were so small we couldn't justify the effort to build the business. A few years later we sold the business to the Faroese Savings Bank.

Before the triumph of FIH, we entered Denmark on a small scale, with a bank we set up in late 2000 and owned 75 percent of, against the 25 percent share of our Faroese partners. Considering the historical ties between Denmark and Iceland, the two countries couldn't be further apart in terms of character. A punishing tax regime means that Danes aren't keen to do overtime, whilst Icelanders often think nothing of working right through the night. Whilst Icelanders can't spend money fast enough, the Danes are incredibly thrifty. A girl I knew used to have a Danish boyfriend whom she eventually gave up on because he would charge her if she asked him for a cigarette, or if she made a phone call from his apartment. Where Icelanders jostle to get ahead, the Danes go by the informal law of 'Jante loven', dictating that no one should think himself or herself better than anyone else. When investors from their former fishing colony up in the North began to make inroads into Danish business, feathers were understandably ruffled.

The small bank in Denmark did reasonably well in the years we managed it, but never took off. When we acquired FIH, we sold our shares. With that acquisition, Denmark became one of the most important operations of the group. Sweden was also sizeable, but the other Nordic offices were less important. Through a couple of small acquisitions and hiring teams from other banks and brokers, we built a business in Norway that was never successful.

More effort went into the Finnish market, where we bought a midsize brokerage called Sofi in 2001, again using our shares as payment. We grew that business considerably and later on got a banking licence. Finding the right management there turned out to be tough. The first CEO of the Finnish business was the slowest speaker I had ever come across. To make things worse, he actually liked to talk and could be very long-winded. This meant that it took him about ten times as long to get his point across as a normal person. Putting him and Sigurdur in the same room for deliberations was worth charging admission for. Sigurdur, who liked to get straight to the point and could be very impatient, was visibly steaming in those meetings. His replacement as CEO was even more unusual. An avid reader of all kinds of management books, he could be really original in getting his point across. At an all staff meeting in Finland, he described how the journey of Kaupthing could be compared to the journey of Vikings. To drive the metaphor home, he threw himself on the floor face up and placed a metre-high pole-shaped prop from the stage between his legs. This was his imitation of a Viking ship where he was the boat, and the pole was the sail. Unfortunately he only looked like a large fertility icon that had fallen over. It wasn't until 2007 we found the right person to lead the business in Lauri Rosendahl who, after his stint at Kaupthing, became the CEO of the Helsinki Stock Exchange.

***

While we were building our little Nordic empire, we weren't exactly standing still in Iceland. In October 2000, the company was listed on the Iceland Stock Exchange. Thus we ceased to be a subsidiary of the savings banks group, although some of them would continue to be sizeable shareholders for a number of years. Both retail investors and institutional investors joined the shareholder group and, for the first time, employees could buy shares in Kaupthing. Key personnel were also granted stock options, although the amounts were quite small by international standards. The initial public offering was very well received, and heavily oversubscribed, as many investors had been waiting for the opportunity to buy shares in Kaupthing. The value we

had created for our shareholders in the previous years hadn't gone unnoticed, and was quite impressive by any measure. The IPO price was
10.25 kronur, but at the end of the first trading day it closed at 15 kronur
which meant that the market valued Kaupthing at £82 million before
the floatation and £118 million after it. When the savings banks had
acquired the whole company from Bunadarbanki in 1996, the valuation
had been £3 million. We had thus multiplied the value of the business
almost 30 times in less than five years. During that time our owners had
put in additional equity of around £5 million, so their total investment
in Kaupthing had multiplied 16 times.

The importance of the listing was mainly the access it gave us to
capital. Prior to the IPO, we were constrained by the willingness and
the ability of the savings banks to increase the capital of the bank
and, because we were rapidly outgrowing our owners, further capital
increases would have become problematic. Now we had access to
institutional investors and other shareholders when we needed to raise
capital. Almost equally important, we could now use shares in the bank
as payment for businesses we acquired, which we used extensively.

Prior to the public listing, the growth of Kaupthing had first and
foremost been organic. That was about to change. The organic growth
was still there, but with easier access to capital it could be accompanied
by acquisitive growth, which enabled the bank to continue its meteoric
rise. A lot of our efforts were focused on expanding abroad, but the
board was still looking at opportunities in Iceland and, shortly after
our listing, one arose that dramatically changed the size and the nature
of the bank.

After the listing of FBA on the stock exchange, the government
still owned two commercial banks, Landsbanki and Bunadarbanki, the
former being slightly larger. At the end of 1998, the government took
the initial step of listing both banks on the stock exchange, but with the
majority holding still in state hands. At the beginning of the new millennium, the government decided to fully privatise both banks. The initial
plan was to find an international strategic shareholder to buy all or most

of the government's stake. The most likely acquirers were thought to be some of the Scandinavian banks. After considerable efforts, by the end of 2001, it was clear that no interested parties had been found. Not a single bid was generated out of the process. Realistically, it was always going to be difficult to get international banks interested in the Icelandic banks because of the small home market. Many Icelanders, including the government and the people managing the privatisation process, didn't quite realise this. The sentiment was that the banks were a fantastic asset that people would fight for. So they made it even less appealing for potential buyers, by listing the banks first and only selling a controlling stake, rather than the whole bank. The timing of the sale was also bad. The market conditions were poor in the aftermath of the dot com crash, and international banks and investors had other things on their minds.

After this experience, the privatisation committee and the government went back to the drawing board and re-emerged in the summer of 2002, to offer anyone the chance to bid for the government's stake in Bunadarbanki and Landsbanki. The process and the decision making, however, was very political. Essentially it had been decided that groups close to the two political parties in power would be the favoured bidders, one bank for each group. One member of the privatisation committee resigned in protest at the dubious nature of the process. We, of course, were very distant from being favoured by anyone. Prime Minister Oddsson was the final decision maker and there was no way he would want Kaupthing as a bidder for either bank. Following the FBA episode, he made no attempt to conceal his contempt for us. Even though the board of Kaupthing saw a great opportunity in acquiring Bunadarbanki, people didn't even discuss it seriously. We talked about putting in a bid for Bunadarbanki, but that talk was followed by laughter, because we looked on it as a joke. The board of Kaupthing and the management were seriously worried about the possibility of public mudslinging and even police raids if we put a bid in for either bank. This was shortly after the police had raided the offices of Baugur and a bizarre atmosphere of paranoia and suspicion prevailed.

In the end the government's 45.6 percent stake in Landsbanki was sold to Bjorgolfur Thor, his father Bjorgolfur Gudmundsson, and their partner from St Petersburg, Magnus Thorsteinsson. The father, Gudmundsson, had strong ties with the Independence party and they were Oddsson's favoured buyers. Their offer was the third highest out of four, but was still the one they went for. This trio had shortly before sold their Russian brewing business, and formed an investment company called Samson, which was the acquirer of the shares in Landsbanki.

Bunadarbanki subsequently went to another investor group called the S-Group, favourable to the other half of the government, the Progressive Party. The leading figure of that investor group was Olafur Olafsson, another entrepreneur who had built up the second largest shipping company in Iceland, and was also the main shareholder in one of the three oil distribution companies.

Looking back, the privatisation of the two banks turned out to be a big mistake. With it, the government put its blessing over private individuals becoming controlling shareholders in the banks, which in hindsight was not a good thing. More importantly the buyers were allowed to heavily debt fund their shareholdings. Samson had no more than 30 percent equity ratio when it bought the shares in Landsbanki. The FSA in Iceland was not happy with this, but eventually caved under pressure, and approved the new shareholders. This should not have been allowed.

Although practically absent from the entire privatisation process, as soon as the sale of the two banks was done and dusted, Kaupthing became the centre of attention. The new owners of both Landsbanki and Bunadarbanki were keen to be part of the consolidation in the banking sector that everyone envisaged. They both turned their eyes towards Kaupthing.

It was assumed there would be competition issues in merging any of the three commercial banks. In any other country in the world, three commercial banks and 27 savings banks would be considered massive overbanking, but Icelanders always think big and the consensus was that there was too little competition. Despite the reality check of the privatisation process, people still wondered why international banks didn't enter the market.

More importantly, people approached Kaupthing because they liked the management team, and we had the most experience from abroad. Both owner groups saw that the future growth of their banks lay abroad, and were very keen to discuss mergers with Kaupthing. Sigurdur and Hreidar suddenly became the prettiest girls on the dance floor and were showered with attention. In the end they could effectively choose which route to go down and, although there were various considerations, my feeling was that they selected the route that suited them best. Tying up with Landsbanki meant that Bjorgolfur Thor and his colleagues would become the leading shareholders in the combined bank. We had a good relationship with Bjorgolfur Thor, but it was pretty clear that he would be a hands-on owner. Olafsson and his group, however, were much more likely to be less active as shareholders, which would enable Sigurdur and Hreidar, together with the rest of us, to run the show as before. Kaupthing had always very much been a management run bank. That didn't mean, of course, that the board didn't have a say, but because of the amazing success of the bank, Sigurdur and Hreidar had so much clout that their proposals were rarely turned down.

Discussions took place with Olafsson, even as he was negotiating the deal with the government, and shortly after the S-Group acquired the Bunadarbanki stake, discussions on a merger between Kaupthing and Bunadarbanki commenced. The merger was agreed in April 2003 and an almost equal value was put on the two entities. The combined market value was £500 million compared with Islandsbanki's £375 million, and Landsbanki's £225 million market capitalisation. We were now the largest bank in Iceland.

Two weeks before the merger was being finalised, we were sponsoring a seminar in Reykjavik where Jack Welch, the famous CEO of GE, was the guest speaker. He received a question relating to a merger GE had been a part of. 'There's no such thing as a merger,' he quipped, 'it's always one acquiring the other.' It was an apt comment and one that applied very well to the Bunadarbanki and Kaupthing situation.

From the beginning, everyone knew who was going to lead the new bank. Sigurdur had instigated a strategic change at Kaupthing, shortly before merger talks commenced, whereby he became the executive chairman and Hreidar took over as CEO. This was purposely done to gain an upper hand when the organisation chart of the new bank was negotiated and, in the end, it was agreed that Sigurdur would be the executive chairman and Hreidar would be co-CEO with one of the CEO's of Bunadarbanki, who was close to retirement. It was already clear from a mere glance at this new set up that the Kaupthing management would run the show. However, in some bizarre scheme to make everyone happy, other senior positions were split between people from Bunadarbanki and Kaupthing. It didn't affect me directly, since I was always going to run the combined investment banking unit, but I couldn't help feeling it was a feeble start for the new bank. In many cases, less qualified managers were obviously being picked to run divisions simply to keep quotas equal. Fortunately, however, the core of the management team at Bunarbanki had realised that the Kaupthing people were calling the shots.

Led by Sigurjon Arnason, around 50 employees, mostly managers from the Bundarbanki side, left and joined Landsbanki. Sigurjon had graduated in engineering from the University of Iceland with one of the highest grades in the university's history. He had been very good looking, a bit like a young Elvis, but unfortunately his physique developed like the King's. He sometimes 'double lunched', but he was as obsessed with work as he was keen on food and, even though he wasn't one of the two CEOs at Bunadarbanki, many believed he was the most influential man at the bank. At Landsbanki, Sigurjon became the co-CEO and other Bunadarbanki people moved into top positions there. This was the best thing that could happen for our merger and the Kaupthing people swiftly took over almost all divisions of the new bank. The new bank was initially called KB banki, which was its brand name in Iceland for a while. Abroad, however, we continued to use Kaupthing and, a couple of years later, the KB banki name disappeared and Kaupthing endured.

The consolidation of the two banks was undoubtedly a success. Costs were cut substantially, but revenues were also increased markedly, as Kaupthing products continued to develop and prosper, thanks to the access it had gained to Bunadarbanki's corporate and retail client base. The combined bank was massive in Icelandic terms. At the end of 2003, it had a balance sheet of £4.5 billion and equity of £375 million. The total number of staff was over 1200 and we now had operations in ten countries: all the Nordic countries, UK, US, Luxembourg and Switzerland. The shareholder structure had taken the shape it was to keep until the end. The merger with Bunadarbanki established Egla, the investment company controlled by Olafur Olafsson, as the second largest shareholder. The pension funds in Iceland were collectively a very sizeable shareholder as well, but the largest shareholder in the bank was a company called Meidur; but as no foreigner could pronounce that word, it would shortly become known as Exista.

Probably the most significant change the merger with Bunadarbanki brought to us was the access it gave us to funding. Whereas Kaupthing did not have a credit rating, an essential prerequisite to have proper access to international bond markets, Bunadarbanki had a comparatively strong A3 rating. Following the successful merger, Moody's upgraded the rating of the combined bank to A2. This strong credit rating completely changed how we funded the bank. Without a credit rating, we couldn't issue bonds in the international markets and needed to rely on bilateral and syndicated bank loans. Now, we suddenly had almost limitless ways of issuing debt abroad. For one it meant we could now consider much larger acquisition targets than before. Not long after the merger, the FIH opportunity showed itself.

***

FIH had been founded in the late fifties by the Danish State to provide loans to Danish industry. In 2004 it was essentially a wholesale lender to small and medium sized corporates in Denmark. It was majority owned by the Swedish bank, Swedbank, who had decided that it wasn't the right strategic fit for them and decided to sell it. Sigurdur had learnt through our Danish colleagues that FIH was up for sale and he discovered that the American Investment Bank, Morgan Stanley, was managing the auction process. They hadn't thought of contacting Kaupthing, or any of the other Icelandic banks, as they figured the size of the acquisition would be way too big for us. The likely price for FIH was in the area of 8–10 billion Danish kronur (£700–900 million) while Kaupthing's market capitalisation was slightly more than £1 billion. To us, as always, this seeming impossibility was irresistible. It would give us a strong foothold we needed in Denmark. FIH was a high-quality operation and we saw various possibilities in expanding its business, both by adding new services to the Danish clientele and by using FIH as a platform to consolidate our Nordic operations. The size of the takeover was undeniably huge for a bank of our size. When Sigurdur called me to assign the task of running the FIH process for the bank, I immediately questioned whether it wasn't unrealistic for us to go after such a big target.

The amount of equity that we needed to raise meant that our offering would be the biggest share offering in Iceland by a long shot. We could raise a meaningful amount of subordinated debt from the international bond markets, which by this time were by far our biggest source of new funding. The equity offering would still need to be in the neighbourhood of £500 million, a staggering amount considering it would be raised in small Iceland. At the time, the biggest initial public equity offering in the history of the US stock market was the AT&T Wireless offering in 2000, where $10.6 billion was raised. On a per capita basis, the offering we needed to take on would be the equivalent of almost $1 trillion for the US. Sigurdur still believed we would be able to raise the amount needed. When we approached the shareholders, he turned out to be right. The wealth of our key shareholders had grown rapidly over a short period of time, their access to capital and funding was easier than ever before, and they were enormously supportive to the management team that had increased the share price of the bank fourfold since its flotation four years earlier.

Henrik Gustafsson managed the bidding process for Kaupthing with me. He was Swedish and had been one of the first people we had hired when we entered the UK, and we became good friends. Before Kaupthing, Henrik had worked at Credit Suisse First Boston and then Lehman Brothers. I had persuaded him to leave Lehman after his department had been cut down from forty-two to six people and morale was low. Tall, handsome and with a smile that implied he had something to be happy about, Henrik was very popular with women.

A self-proclaimed salsa expert, on a dance floor he seemed to attract the most beautiful women in the club almost magnetically. Of course, he sometimes got it wrong, as I witnessed once at Cuckoo Club, one of London's best nightclubs. He had won the attention of a gorgeous French girl on the dance floor with his impressive dance routine and decided to take it up a notch. Michael Jackson would have been proud of the sharp 360 degree turn he did, which ended with him pointing his left hand at the ceiling and throwing his right hand back. Unfortunately, he had misjudged the distance between him and his dance partner, and his right elbow flew gracefully into the French girl's face. The sound of her nose breaking could almost be heard over the loud music. Blood splattered across the dance floor and people flew in all directions. The bouncers were rapidly on the scene and quickly came to the conclusion that Henrik had intentionally hit the girl, so they grabbed his arms and legs, and literally threw him out of the club. The French girl, trying to correct the misunderstanding, followed him out. The rest of the night was spent less glamorously at the hospital.

Like so many at Kaupthing, Henrik loved working almost as much as he loved partying. He was one of our hardest workers – quite an achievement in a bank which acted as a magnet for workaholics. He repeatedly cancelled his holidays because he couldn't leave a deal he was working on. For a period of time, we almost spent more on refunding his holidays than we paid him in his salary. We couldn't have assigned a better man to work on the FIH deal, which if successful, would revolutionise Kaupthing.

After the initial call from Sigurdur, I asked Henrik to find out who at Morgan Stanley was handling the sale process. We didn't know anyone on their Financial Institutions team, but we knew various other people at the bank, and quickly got in touch with the correct people. In the beginning we struggled to get them to take us seriously, but they soon realised we were dead serious. When we finally got over that first hurdle, we were lagging slightly behind in the process. Other buyers had already been analysing information on FIH for some time. No strangers to swift action, we quickly got going and assembled both an advisory team in Denmark and an internal team to work with us on the due diligence. We worked day and night to collect information, and analyse and prepare an initial bid for the bank, which we managed to do by the deadline at the end of April.

Our initial bid of DKK 8–8.5 billion (£700–750 million) was enough to get us through to the second round of the auction process, although we knew we were not the highest bidder at the time. Following that, we had a number of meetings with the management of FIH. We gradually discovered that they were very keen for us to buy the bank. Most of the other likely buyers were the Danish banks, which would be focused on synergies and cost-cutting, as they were mostly after the assets of FIH. We, however, were intent on building and growing FIH with the management that was in place.

Later on, Lars Johansen, the CEO of FIH, told us that the winning factor had been the personal chemistry between us. He had come to the conclusion that we were the right people after taking a few of us out to dinner and realising that we shared the same sense of humour. But I suspect Kaupthing's desire to grow the bank was actually more important. The management of FIH had wanted to expand its operations for some time, but had so far been blocked by Swedbank.

Our strategy during the second round was to gain an advantage over our competitors by doing more work than they in the first round of due diligence, so that we could put forward a bid that only needed a small amount of confirmatory due diligence if the sellers accepted. This meant that we needed to work longer hours, involve more people and spend more money on advisors than the others. We pulled more than ten of the senior managers of the bank out of their daily routine to work on analysing and performing due diligence on the various parts of FIH. For almost a month we had people working on the deal for 20 hours a day.

A manager I knew well at one of the banks bidding against us later told me that his surprised colleagues had asked him how we had managed to conclude the process so much more quickly than they had. Having known Kaupthing for a long time, he responded 'when you're sleeping, these guys are working!' The strategy paid off. While we had performed the due diligence, Sigurdur and Ingolfur Helgason had been working with the shareholder base in Iceland and got unilateral support for the transaction, which was important for us to demonstrate we could finance the acquisition.

In early June we submitted a bid for FIH for DKK 8.3 billion (£730 million). I had spent some time arguing with Hreidar and Sigurdur on what to bid. They were incredibly keen on the deal and wanted to bid considerably higher in order not to risk being thrown out of the process. Being closer to the process, I was convinced that we didn't need to stretch too much on the pricing as we were by now in a position to close a transaction faster than anyone else.

Morgan Stanley came to meet me and Henrik the day following our bid, and told us that if we could raise the bid slightly the deal was ours. After brief negotiations we agreed to bid DKK 8.5 billion (£750 million) and we shook hands on the deal, agreeing that we would aim to conclude all documentation within a week. We shook hands on a Tuesday, and were aiming to sign on the following weekend, so we could announce the deal before the markets opened on the Monday. Henrik and I spent the rest of the week in Stockholm together with our advisors, and by Friday we had all but finished all the details of the documentation. We then flew over to Reykjavik to attend a management seminar.

On Saturday afternoon, I got a phone call from Petter Sternby at Morgan Stanley who was in charge of the sales process. I could tell from the sound of his voice that something had changed. He informed me that they had unexpectedly received an offer, substantially higher than ours, from a party he couldn't name. The offer on the table, according to Petter, was close to DKK 10 billion (£900 million), more than 15 percent higher than our bid. If we wanted to do the deal, we would need to up our bid considerably. Initially I wasn't sure if he was telling me the truth or if this was an attempt to squeeze more money out of us, so I told him that this was a no-go. I pointed out that we had made a verbal agreement and that, from our point of view, it would be highly unethical for them to go back on that.

His point of view was that the board of Swedbank, which still had to ratify the deal, would not be doing their job if they didn't take the highest bid for their shareholders. He was, of course, right, but I was still furious and disappointed. Also, although I believed there was another offer on the table I still wasn't convinced that they were taking it seriously. If they wanted to go after another bidder, it would delay the process by at least a week and increase the likelihood of failure, and I knew the seller was keen to do a quick and smooth sale. We thus decided as a tactic to reject any possibility of increasing our offer and we didn't call the Morgan Stanley bankers back on the Saturday.

When they made no attempt to get hold of us, we became uneasy, and it was decided that Henrik would fly to Stockholm on the Sunday morning, to be close to the seller and his advisors. It was on that flight that he noticed the group of Icelanders rifling through documents with the name DAVOS written all over them. Davos was Morgan Stanley's codename for FIH. When he landed he began his car chase, and called me. It didn't take me long to conclude that the group was from Landsbanki.

This made the other offer very real and urgent. We now needed to decide whether we were willing to increase ours. I still thought we shouldn't have to overbid the Landsbanki offer, given that we offered more certainty. After some discussion with Sigurdur and Hreidar and calls with members of the board of Kaupthing, however, it was agreed that we could stretch a bit further. Sigurdur and I flew to Stockholm in the afternoon of the Sunday. After some phone calls with Morgan Stanley and Jan Liden, the CEO of Swedbank, we managed to get a meeting with them at midnight. Things became clear at that meeting. Essentially, Liden and Morgan Stanley were prepared to recommend our bid if we would increase it up to DKK 9.5 billion (£850 million). It was slightly lower than what Landsbanki was offering, which reflected the seller's view that we were a more certain option. I later found out that the board had debated that considerably and some wanted to go with Landsbanki's higher offer.

We asked for a break and called Hreidar, who was on holiday in Florida, fuming at not being able to be in Stockholm for the deal. Even before we spoke, I knew what he would think. Earlier he had been more than happy to go higher – he really wanted FIH. The fact that Landsbanki was the other bidder just confirmed this. 'Take it!' he shouted down the phone.

We shook on the deal with Jan Liden in the early hours of June 14. The following morning the board of Swedbank agreed to our offer. To say we were overjoyed would be an understatement. It shouldn't have made any difference, but snatching the deal back from Landsbanki made the victory even sweeter. Henrik overheard the conversation when the Morgan Stanley people called Sigurjon Arnason, the CEO of Landsbanki, to inform him that Swedbank had gone with another bidder. Disappointed, Sigurjon asked who was the successful bidder. When he was informed it was Kaupthing, Henrik could hear him yelling, 'Kaupthing! Is it Kaupthing?!' Until then we had assumed they knew about our interest in FIH.

I later found out from one of the Landsbanki board members that, although they initially suspected that Kaupthing was in the race, they had come to the conclusion that it couldn't be us. They knew Hreidar was on holiday in Florida, and Sigurdur had been seen at an airport when he was coming back from a short holiday only days before the deal was concluding. They figured there was no chance Sigurdur and Hreidar would both be on holiday when such a monstrous deal was in its final stages.

It wasn't without reason that we were keen on the acquisition of FIH. Size-wise, it elevated us into a league of our own in Iceland. The balance sheet of the Kaupthing group now exceeded €18 billion. It was a very significant step in our plans to expand outside of Iceland and meant that we had now diversified to such an extent that 70 percent of our income was being generated outside of Iceland. This was well received by the rating agencies; Moody's increased our rating from A2 to A1, which had a material positive effect on our costs and access to funding. FIH was also a great bank. It performed very well in the years following our takeover. With our support, they also expanded into capital markets activities and investment banking, where they were particularly successful.

In hindsight, the take-over of FIH was a mixed blessing. The bank had no deposits, and was financed via the international bond markets. Our dependance on wholesale funding thus increased which would prove to be a significant weakness when liquidity became scarcer a few years later. The bank's shareholders also borrowed part of the capital needed to inject into Kaupthing, which increased their leverage and made them weaker.

In the summer of 2004, however, no one could foresee the looming Armageddon. Everyone was ecstatic as we had established ourselves as the giant of Icelandic banking. Kaupthing was almost the same size as the other banks combined.

As the worldwide liquidity bubble took off and the international appetite for debt became insatiable, expanding the balance sheet even further was an easy task.

Chapter Six

Where Does the Money Come From?!

'Armann, can you comment on the frequent rumours of Russian money being behind the Icelandic acquisitions?' I was in Barcelona, sitting on a panel at an annual seminar for Kaupthing employees. We did these management seminars, known as 'Kaupthinking', annually. Around 150 key people from across the group were invited to listen to both external and internal speakers for a couple of days.

As the acquisition spree had gone into overdrive, we were constantly asked the same question: 'Where does the money come from!?' The business pages were filled with headlines like 'The Iceman cometh' and 'The Viking Invasion'. People were scratching their heads. How was this tiny nation able to do so many transactions? Various creative theories were spun about the money behind the transactions. The most stupid, yet most widespread, was that Russians were laundering money through Iceland. We were repeatedly asked about our relationship with Russians, and when we informed people that it was non-existent, they often shook their heads in disbelief.

I looked over the audience at the seminar, as I contemplated the answer. The right thing to do was to cite the facts for the hundredth time and move on to the next question. But I was tired, sleepless and irritated. So I took the microphone, and said 'the truth is the only Russian I have ever met was at a London strip club and I can assure you that she was not giving me any money.' The stunned faces indicated I probably should have cited the facts.

But although it was inappropriate, my joke was close enough to the truth. There were no serious connections between Iceland and Russia, apart from the fact that Bjorgolfur Thor and his partners had built their brewery in St Petersburg. They sold the company to Heineken, so strictly speaking they had Dutch money! The rest of us really didn't know any Russians until the bank's final two or three years. Iceland would have been the worst place on earth to launder money. It is such a small place that any peculiar money transfer would be quick to attract attention. You really had to believe that the whole nation was in on the money laundering scheme to believe the Russian money stories.

The Danish tabloid *Ekstra Bladet* actually believed it had found evidence of a link between Russia and Iceland in 2006. The misunderstanding related to Luxembourg. Kaupthing dealt with the biggest law firm there in relation to holding companies for clients. Many holding companies are set up in Luxembourg every day, so law firms found a large number of holding companies and then sell them to clients, like Kaupthing Luxembourg, for a nominal price. Unbeknown to us, the law firm also worked for the Russian oligarch Mikhail Friedman. Because of that, some of the holding companies that were set up for high-profile clients of ours, like Baugur and Exista, had the same initial founding company as the holding companies set up for Friedman. When *Ekstra Bladet* got hold of this information in 2006, they were thrilled. Convinced that they had discovered proof of the link between Icelandic entrepreneurs and Russian oligarchs, they wrote a very damaging article. So convincing was it, I almost believed it myself. In the end we sued *Ekstra Bladet* in London, eventually settling out of court over a claim in their article that Kaupthing had been involved in tax evasion. Not surprisingly, that didn't exactly increase our popularity with the paper or the press in general.

The true source of the liquidity was a combination of real, pent-up wealth in Iceland, which had been waiting to be released internationally and, more importantly, the ever increasing use of debt financing.

When we began to take our first steps outside of Iceland in the late nineties, it was already one of the wealthiest countries in the world. The pension system in particular had financial assets exceeding the GDP of the country, and the young population of Iceland together with a high proportion of salaries going into pensions ensured the constant growth of the funds. Per capita, the pension funds of Iceland were bigger than the famous Norwegian oil fund. The funds had been locked up in Iceland, until we entered the European Economic Area and foreign investment restrictions were lifted in 1995. When the barriers were lifted and the new generation of entrepreneurs began identifying opportunities abroad, an avalanche started and the appetite for investments was almost limitless.

The second source of capital stemmed from the changes made to the Icelandic fishing system in the eighties. When the fish stocks in Iceland were overfished and began to shrink considerably in the early eighties, it became evident that there were too many fishermen and vessels chasing too few fish catches. That resulted in the establishment of a very controversial, but in most ways very successful, quota system that would revolutionise the fishing sector. Quotas – essentially rights to catch fish – were given to fishing vessels based on their recent historical catches. Each one would have the right to fish a percentage of the overall allowed catches in Icelandic waters. The total allowance was decided by the minister of fisheries, but he received his advice from marine biologists who tracked the sizes of the various fish stocks. Very importantly, the quotas were freely transferable and a very active market in quotas commenced. Gradually a big consolidation took place, where some fishing companies bought out the quotas from others, who would sell or scrap their vessels and close shop. The consolidators added the fishing quotas to their existing ship fleet, and gradually the number of vessels shrank dramatically, increasing the efficiency of the sector enormously. Iceland was practically the only country in the world who actually had a profitable fishing sector, while other nations were subsidising their respective fishing sectors.

There were two main controversies in regard to the system. One was that many small fishing villages depended heavily on the fishing companies in their town. When the owners of these companies sold the quotas, no more fish was brought to land there for processing, resulting in unemployment and people moving away. The other issue was the fact that the sellers of the fishing companies were of course cashing out big time. Many of these companies had never made proper money and in some cases had been badly run. Because the system created a sellable asset in the form of the future rights to fish catches, the owners of these companies suddenly had a valuable asset on their hands. People in towns and villages, who saw their livelihood being sold away while the person responsible for it was cashing out, were not happy.

Quotas became an asset that banks were happy to lend against, which further sped up the process of unprofitable fishing companies being bought out. The result was that in a short period of time a sizeable group of so-called 'Quota Kings' sold out of the sector with a substantial amount of capital to invest elsewhere.

In addition to the existing wealth and capital in Iceland that was waiting to get out after the mid-nineties, the success of the early steps created considerable capital. That in turn was immediately available to be invested again into new ventures and that's exactly what happened. The phrase, 'let the capital work for you', was very true in Iceland – the capital was working overtime and weekends! With the use of leverage, the purchasing power of the capital was multiplied many times over.

Baugur was a good example of this. When they acquired the 20 percent stake in Arcadia, the money was raised by issuing new shares in Iceland. This capital was obviously put to good use and when the shares were eventually sold to Philip Green, the total proceeds were close to £150 million. This considerable amount of money would then be put into new deals, mainly in the UK, but also in Scandinavia. The purchasing power for Baugur, however, was even greater than the £150 million, due to the use of co-investors and leverage. Typically they would acquire companies in leveraged buyouts, partnering up with other investors.

Early on, funding was more difficult to come by, and banks, including us, were quite conservative when extending debt into leveraged transactions. The first deals we did, which would be classified as leverage finance transactions, like Bakkavor's acquisition of Katsouris, had senior debt that equalled around two times the EBITDA of the underlying company. At the peak of the liquidity bubble in 2007 it wasn't unusual to see deals in the international markets structured in such a way that senior debt was six or seven times EBITDA. When debt came to be so easily available, and in large quantities, the growth in acquisitions further accelerated and they became bigger.

***

There is a Scandinavian folk tale called 'The Nail Soup.' A tramp is looking for shelter and food. When he comes across a woman, she is able but unwilling to provide him with both, until he claims he can make soup out of a nail. Curious, the woman invites him to her home to learn more about this exotic (and potentially frugal!) dish. The tramp puts a nail into a pot full of water, but then tricks the woman into adding real food to the pot, on the basis that it adds to the thickness and flavour of the nail soup. At the end he removes the nail, and the woman is ecstatic at the amazing soup, proclaiming it is the best she has had – 'and just imagine, all from a nail!' Although the structure of the Icelandic investment vehicles varied, most of the big ones developed in a way similar to a nail soup. Acquisitions were made on the back of an original base operating business, which then subsequently was sold out of the investment pot.

Pharmaco was an example of this. It was a boring wholesaler of pharmaceuticals in Iceland, which after listing on the Stock Exchange essentially became an acquisition vehicle of various generic drug producers in Bulgaria, Iceland, and other countries. After a while the original wholesale business was sold in a private transaction in 2002, and the remaining business became the third largest generic pharmaceutical company in the world after a series of takeovers.

Bakkavor followed a similar path. The original business that the two brothers had successfully built up was a specialised seafood business, but they used that as a platform to enter into the UK ready meal market on a grand scale. Later, they split the seafood business into a separate company and sold it to the management in 2003. Baugur was yet another example. They, of course, started out as Iceland's largest retailer, but gradually became an investment company with interest in various ventures in numerous countries. Eventually the Icelandic retail business was converted into a separate company called Hagar and spun out of Baugur, although the majority ownership continued to be in the hands of Jon Asgeir's family.

The most famous example of the 'nail soup syndrome' was Icelandair, the Icelandic national carrier, which was turned into the infamous investment company FL Group. The man behind the transition of Icelandair was Hannes Smarason, who had been the deputy CEO of deCODE. We had briefly played handball together when we were teenagers and our paths crossed again when I was studying in Boston. Hannes was then finishing his MBA from MIT, after having concluded his BSc in engineering from the same school. He worked for the famous consultancy firm McKinsey for a few years, until Kari Stefansson convinced Hannes to join him in establishing deCODE in 1996. After five years at the biotech company, Hannes left and began to focus on various investment activities. He had amassed a small fortune during his time at deCODE and his partnership with his father in law – who was considerably wealthy – established him as a serious investor. Athletic (he represented Iceland at a junior level in soccer) and energetic, Hannes spoke English and Danish fluently. A great presenter and a very good salesman, there was little doubt that he was highly intelligent, but also an aggressive and very bullish investor. Many saw him as the posterboy of the Icelandic expansion with all its excesses. In a country where many could be described as deal junkies, he still stood out.

In 2004 he and his father-in-law replaced Eimskip as the control-ling stakeholders in Icelandair. When the two had secured the stake, *Morgunbladid* wrote an editorial about the importance of Icelandair, and the responsibility its owners carried. The editorial ended by say-ing: 'With the ownership of such a big stake in Icelandair comes great responsibility. Jon Helgi Gudmundsson [the father in law] and Hannes Smarason, and their families have shown that they are worthy of being entrusted with such responsibility.'

The paper might have wanted to rewrite its editorial, as Hannes, who became chairman of Icelandair, began to take the company into new territory. A year after Hannes became chairman, the 'new' Icelandair began various investment activities and changed its name into FL Group. The airline activities were put into a separate subsidiary and in 2006 that 'nail' was removed from the pot and sold to an investor group that listed the carrier on the Iceland Stock Exchange again.

FL Group had various successes in the beginning, and by 2006 Han-nes was a star in Iceland as the stock price of FL Group multiplied in value during his reign. Apart from the fact that its investments were performing very well in the bull market at the time, there were other factors that pushed up the share price of FL Group. The company had large amounts of debt and when the value of the assets grew, the value of the debt was of course the same, save for the interest it accumulated. This meant that the value of the equity increased much more rapidly than the assets. When the market also began to value FL Group (and other investment companies) at a multiplier of 1.5–1.7 times to its net asset value, the value of the shares skyrocketed. Why did investors value the company higher than the net value of its assets? The only explanation was the belief that the company and its management were so clever in identifying profitable opportunities that its future value would be greater than the underlying assets. There are many similari-ties between what happened in Iceland and what happened in the US 80 years earlier, when the stock market crashed in 1929 and preceded the great depression. One of those similarities is between the Icelandic investment companies like FL Group, and the investment trusts in the US in the late twenties. Both were heavily leveraged, showed great performance for a period of time, and were valued at a multiplier to their net asset values.

***

Gradually, three main power blocs had developed in Iceland. Each one had a controlling stake in one of the three big banks. The old power bloc, 'The Octopus', had all but disappeared, its various tentacles having been ripped off by the new generation.

The Bakkavor brothers formed one of these groups. On the back of their fantastically successful investments in the UK, they had become the key shareholders in Kaupthing. This they had achieved in the beginning of 2003 by placing all of their shareholdings in Bakkavor into a holding company later known as Exista, which was the largest shareholder in Kaupthing. Exista held a stake in Kaupthing of over 20 percent, and was owned by those savings banks that still had connections to Kaupthing after our flotation. The brothers became 55 percent shareholders, and their timing couldn't have been better. The shares in Kaupthing took off and the value of their holding skyrocketed. Enormous capital gains from Kaupthing and Bakkavor's success, combined with easy access to debt, enabled Exista first to acquire VIS – one of the largest insurance companies in Iceland – and later Iceland Telecom, when it was privatised. They controlled a variety of different businesses, and I once asked the brothers whether they were trying to establish a one-stop shop for people who were looking for loans, life insurance, mashed potatoes and cheap calls to Kazakhstan. The thread that ran throughout all these investments was simply that they were all very strong companies and their portfolio of assets was undoubtedly of high quality. In 2006 they listed on the Iceland Stock Exchange with total assets of over £2 billion, and a market capitalisation of more than £1 billion.

Bjorgolfur Thor and his father Bjorgolfur made up the second bloc. Initially Magnus Thorsteinsson was part of their main investment company Samson, but after a while he went his own separate way. The father and son obviously worked closely together, but they still followed their own individual paths, and the structure of their holdings was sometimes a bit difficult to follow. The main assets were Landsbanki, which had grown rapidly after the privatisation, and Actavis (formerly Pharmaco), the generic drug company that also followed a path of expansive growth. Actavis was one of the companies that had the easiest access to international funding, and seemed to have endless ability to finance various acquisitions. The generic pharmaceutical sector was very much 'in' with banks, and finance ran freely to the sector. Bjorgolfur Thor also had telecom investments, which he made through his investment vehicle Novator. In co-operation with various other investors, Novator invested heavily in the telecom sector in Bulgaria, the Czech Republic, Finland and other countries, with great success. The Icelandic entrepreneurs were sometimes criticised for never exiting their investments, but that couldn't be said of Bjorgolfur Thor, who successfully exited most of his telecom investments.

Jon Asgeir, with Baugur as the anchor, controlled the third main group. Jon Asgeir gradually developed strong ties with Hannes's FL Group, and became the second largest shareholder behind Hannes. FL Group co-operated with Baugur in various investments. So did a number of Icelandic and UK investors, like Sir Tom Hunter, dubbed Scotland's richest man, Kevin Stanford and Don McCarthy, retail entrepreneur and chairman of House of Fraser. Typically, Baugur would own the largest stake in the various investments, but usually not a majority, with an investment consortium made up of several of these co-operatives holding the remainder. Jon Asgeir took Baugur private, not long after he sold the stake in Arcadia. He thus had more limited access to capital than before, so if he wanted to grow it would have to be through profits and leverage. He did both. With backup from us,

Morgan Stanley and others, Baugur and FL Group eventually managed to gain a controlling share in Glitnir.

All the three banks were then controlled by privately controlled investment companies. There was considerable rivalry between the leaders of the three groups, although all knew each other socially. As with the grand masters of chess, everyone wanted to be number one. But success wasn't measured in ELO points, but rather wealth and power. The rivalry undoubtedly pushed them to grow and expand, and that's exactly what everyone did. There were, of course, various other Icelandic investors, investor groups, companies and entrepreneurs that were following the lead of this group, many of these seriously wealthy.

For the new Arctic capitalists, the funding was almost endless. They ploughed all profits from the successful early investments back into new ones. Capital was raised from public sources, in the companies that were listed, and in private. Teaming up with other investors in particular deals further increased the ability to do deals. And debt funding wasn't limited either. The worldwide liquidity bubble had ensured that banks had endless amounts of funds to lend out.

In the summer of 2003 I was about to make a decision that enabled me to be at the centre of activities, as Iceland's acquisition spree was shifting into fifth gear. The real question wasn't where the money had come from, but where it was going.

Chapter Seven

London Calling

I felt like a poor immigrant on Ellis Island when I landed at Heathrow Airport in London on 18 June 2003. My wife, Thordis, my two children, Bjarki and Margret, and I had nothing but a few suitcases with us as we started our new life in the UK. As we walked down the tunnel, I felt slightly uneasy. We'd done quite a few deals in London, and I had some contacts, but building up a business in the world's financial capital was going to be no mean task.

I switched my phone on and found a message on my voicemail. It was from Kevin Stanford. He wanted me to join him in a meeting the next day to discuss the £620 million acquisition of Selfridges, one of UK's biggest and most famous department stores. My heart skipped a beat. I could hardly believe it, but it felt like we were off to a flying start.

***

A few months earlier, I had resigned from Kaupthing. The bank's success, and the fact that the key management team was very close, didn't mean that we never argued. We did. Most of us were headstrong, with sizeable egos, and we all had our opinions on how best to grow Kaupthing. Hreidar and Sigurdur set the course, but there were some aspects of it that I didn't agree with. The main difference came down to the fact that I felt we were too skewed towards acquisitive growth. I was particularly annoyed by the fact that the growth in Scandinavia, prior to the FIH acquisition, had diluted our shares substantially. We had issued more and more equity to enable us to acquire businesses, which often weren't really performing. The units we had built up organically, namely in Iceland and Luxembourg, were performing fantastically but now had to produce returns for a much bigger capital base because of these equity issues.

We argued about this, and we also debated other things, and eventually I came to the conclusion that I wanted to leave. This was no easy decision to take. I loved the place. For nearly a decade it had been the focus of my life. I turned it over for weeks and weeks, and eventually went to Sigurdur and Hreidar to give them my resignation. They were quite shocked, despite the quarrels we had had, and Sigurdur asked me not to announce anything until they had a chance to deliberate and speak to me again.

But as soon as I told them I quit, I realised I couldn't. Despite having thought long and hard about the decision, somehow it was only when I told them, that I realised I couldn't go through with it. The wrench felt like I was leaving my family. Before they called me back and invited me to lunch, I knew I was going to stay. Over lunch, we tried to clear the air. Hreidar told me that if I wanted to change environment they would be supportive of me moving to the UK. We were already doing a great deal of business there, and we could expand that even further if we were there on the ground. I went home with my head in turmoil again. I discussed it with Thordis, who was always open to new opportunities, and I gradually came to the conclusion that the change of scene might be just what I needed.

As luck would have it, the perfect opportunity came a few months later, in the form of a Dane called Lars Christian Brask. He had been a successful M&A banker at Merrill Lynch and Robertson Stephens in the tech boom of the late nineties and had set up his own firm, Brask and Company, with the backing of Kuwaiti investors, in 2000, specialising in M&A advisory in the tech sector. The timing was disastrous. Almost as soon as he had set up the business, the dot com bubble burst and they were unable to generate any income. So, in October 2002, Lars Christian approached us in Reykjavik to see if we were interested in taking over the business. For obvious reasons, we weren't particularly interested in doing advisory in the tech sector. However, the firm had a few things we were interested in, mainly a licence to conduct M&A business, an office and some infrastructure in London, and also close to a £3 million tax loss. We spent less than a couple of hundred thousand pounds, and we were up and running.

We concluded the deal formally in February 2003 although we had started to work from the office from November 2002. The day before we announced the deal to the Iceland Stock Exchange we required the former owners to change the name of the company from Brask and Company to BMY Advisory Ltd. The reason for this was the fact that 'Brask' in Icelandic means wheeling and dealing. Given our reputation for aggressive deals, we could foresee that we would be bombarded with cheap jokes if we had announced that we had acquired 'Wheeling and Dealing Ltd'!

Helgi Bergs and I decided that we would both move to London and build up the business, focusing solely on investment banking. I was already the group head of Investment Banking while Helgi's formal role was to run the UK part. We started to hire people who knew the London market. We focused on getting people who could project manage the M&A side, and debt people who could manage the financing of transactions for the bank in Iceland, as we had no balance sheet in the UK. At first we felt we could rely on our Icelandic clientele to generate the deals. I was pretty confident that we'd be successful in building UK contacts too. I was proved right, and even faster than I thought.

***

The Selfridges meeting was with Robert Tchenguiz. At that time, I had never heard of him, but Kevin Stanford told me he was a well-known investor in the UK business community, usually mentioned in tandem with his brother Vincent, although they had mostly separated their businesses at this stage. Later, I got to know Vincent and worked with him too.

When I entered Robert's offices in Curzon Street, it was obvious which of the seven people was the main man. Robert was 43 years old at the time and getting a bit out of shape with greying hair, but he was absolutely full of energy. The distinctive pink glasses he wore were a testament to his vanished playboy days. During those days, he had dated supermodel Caprice, and was rumoured to have introduced Dodi Al Fayed and Princess Diana. Robert's parents were originally from Iraq but had emigrated to Iran and Victor, his father, had been in charge of the mint for the Shah before the Islamic revolution. After the revolution, the family came to London, and the brothers started to make a name for themselves in the property world. They were not developers or really managers of property, but rather they were financial engineers, and fantastically clever at it. Their claim to fame was to buy property and property-related assets, managing through clever manoeuvrings to get debt funding exceeding the amount they had paid. I found Robert incredibly intelligent and creative, and over time we built an excellent relationship. At that time, he had become wealthy, but was struggling to get to the next level of seriously big deals. We enabled him to do just that.

He needed to raise finance for Selfridges in competition with the Weston family from Canada, the founding family of British Associated Foods, which Primark is a part of, but his hopes were fading. He'd been put in touch with Kevin by a mutual friend, but had no idea who I was, and had never heard of Kaupthing. Selfridges would clearly be a fabulous acquisition and I could see that we could probably close Robert's financing gap. He had a credit approved term sheet from RBS for the financing of Selfridges' property of some £500 million, but needed to fund the operating company with debt and equity to the tune of £120 million. At the end of the presentation, I told him we could probably put together the rest of the financing for him. Having hoped at most to get £10–20 million from Kevin, they were astounded. Were these strange Icelanders for real?

We were. After the meeting Helgi and I began to work on the deal. We couldn't provide the whole financing ourselves, but our contacts from other UK deals came in handy. We got HBOS in Birmingham involved, who had financed the Katsouris takeover. The deal was structured so that they debt-financed the operating company, and Kaupthing, R20 (Robert's investment vehicle) and Kevin provided the equity. In a couple of weeks we were ready to go. Robert was ecstatic.

Unfortunately, however, the part of the financing that was supposed to be secure, the property financing from RBS, suddenly started to look shaky. The bank was having problems with a similar kind of financing structure on the Le Meridien hotel chain and began to feel uncomfortable with this transaction. First, they refused to have any debt on the operating company. When we restructured the deal to accommodate that, they found a technical way of getting out of their commitment. After that the bid was history. Despite the failure, the deal enabled us to build a relationship with R20, and it was clear that other deals would shortly follow.

The timing of the London office couldn't have been better. The connection with Robert and R20 enabled us to build relationships with local entrepreneurs. The big Icelandic clients, like Baugur and Bakkavor, were now keen to explore other opportunities in the UK too, and having witnessed their success, other Icelandic companies were keen to do more business. The market was ideal for us. We spoke the language, international investors – even from Iceland – were welcomed, opportunities were plenty and valuations were low compared with the Scandinavian market. With each transaction, we built up a network of advisors, lawyers, accountants and bankers for further ventures. Our little office in London couldn't hire people fast enough to deal with the transactions coming our way. By the end of 2003 we had 10 people in the office, by Christmas 2004 the number had grown to 18, and a year later we had a staff of 40.

A couple of months after the failed takeover of Selfridges Jon Asgeir came to me with a new transaction, the acquisition of Oasis, a mid-size UK women's fashion retailer. It had been taken over by the private equity fund PPM Ventures a few years earlier, and they were now looking to exit what had been a profitable investment. Baugur was now focusing almost entirely on the UK. A few months earlier they had bought the famous Hamleys toy retailer. Oasis was, however, a much larger bite. We advised Baugur on the takeover, co-invested with them in the equity, and co-underwrote the debt financing with HBOS. These were the kind of deals that we particularly liked to do, where we could utilise all the different parts of the organisation. Prior to the merger with Bunadarbanki we always got another bank to do the senior lending, but now we were able to participate in that part as well.

The purchase price of Oasis was around £150 million, so if Baugur had bought the business straight out, without any partners or banks, it would have used all the proceeds from Arcadia. For Jon Asgeir that would have been too small a bang for his buck. Instead, they bought it in the form of a leveraged buyout and we partnered them as equity holders. Of the £150 million that was paid for Oasis, around half of that amount came in the form of senior debt from HBOS and Kaupthing. We then also underwrote around £20 million in so-called mezzanine financing (debt that ranks ahead of equity, but behind the senior debt and thus carries much higher interest rate). The mezzanine debt we subsequently sold down to our high net worth clients in Iceland and Luxembourg. The equity part of the transaction was less than £50 million. We took a small part of it so in the end Baugur invested a total of around £35 million in Oasis. They didn't own it alone, but that went largely unnoticed. To the outside world they had swallowed up another chunk of the British high street.

FL Group was also eager to make its mark in the UK. In the autumn of 2004 Hannes came to my office in New Bond Street, asking for our assistance in building a sizeable stake in the low-cost carrier Easyjet. He believed the company to be undervalued and that was mainly based on his, and his Icelandair colleagues' insight into the value of aircraft options. Easyjet had options to buy a large number of aircraft from Boeing at prices much lower than their market price, and Hannes felt the market was not valuing that correctly. We began to accumulate shares for him through a broker in the UK and, over the next year and a half, FL Group reached a 16.9 percent stake holding and became the company's second largest shareholder after the founder Stelios Haji-Ioannou. Hannes was interested in looking into the possibility of bidding for the whole company but eventually aborted that plan. When Stelios, following rumours of a possible bid for the company from FL Group, told journalists that he had no intention of selling his stake, Hannes famously quipped, 'everything can be bought!' Eventually, though, FL Group sold its stake in a block trade in April 2006 for a handsome profit of over £100 million, making it one of their most successful investments.

Shortly after the Oasis acquisition we initiated another transaction to create one of the largest fashion retailers in the UK. I had introduced Jon Asgeir and Kevin Stanford earlier, and the idea of putting the two companies, Oasis and Karen Millen, together was born soon after. Kaupthing was a shareholder in both companies and we could see the logic and synergies in merging the two. After some negotiations a deal was reached. As lenders and shareholders to both businesses, we were so conflicted that I couldn't advise either company. I still spent a massive amount of time in getting the deal together and agreed with both parties that they would pay a sizeable 'mediation fee' – an unknown phenomenon until then.

It was sentimentally difficult for Kevin and Karen to sell off the company they'd built together. Accepting co-investors was one thing, but after merging with Oasis they would become minority investors and would cease to work for the company. The deal almost fell apart a couple of times. There was one clause in the agreement on the sale that stipulated earn-out payments for Kevin and Karen (additional payments if the company performed exceptionally well). But the amount payable could be subject to interpretation and possible dispute. After lengthy debate, both parties agreed to put in a very unusual clause that stipulated that if there was any disagreement, Armann Thorvaldsson would decide what was fair. I was proud that both parties had entrusted me with the role of Solomon, but I silently prayed that it would not come to a dispute.

This merger created a £500 million turnover retail giant that was named Mosaic Fashions. Shortly after that, the company doubled in size when it acquired another Icelandic-owned retailer called Rubicon. We had also played a big role in creating Rubicon soon after I came to London. The investors we had helped buy into Karen Millen had approached us with another opportunity, Shoe Studio, the largest shoe retailer in the UK. We assisted them in acquiring a large minority stake together with Baugur, while the CEO, Don McCarthy, and his management team held the majority. Things happened fast and, shortly after that deal was done, another opportunity came in the form of Rubicon, a retail business that had been spun out of Arcadia around the time when Baugur was building its 20 percent stake there. We advised and funded the takeover of Rubicon by Shoe Studio, the combined company keeping the Rubicon name. The final piece of the puzzle was then the merger of Rubicon and Mosaic under the latter's name in late 2006. Shortly before that, Mosaic had been listed on the Iceland Stock Exchange, in an attempt to bring a greater variety of investment opportunities to the Icelandic market, but with limited success. Baugur, with various other investors, later took the company private, after it started to experience problems. For better or worse, we were party to all the various transactions, and there were so many advisory, funding and co-investing roles that it was difficult to keep track. Although the initial merger between Oasis and Karen Millen was a sensible transaction, the following acquisitions proved too much. With too many brands, the profits of the consolidated entity started to deteriorate.

Bakkavor also wanted to expand their successful UK business. The ideal target for the brothers was Geest, the leading UK producer of fresh food. With a turnover many times that of Bakkavor, it was also highly ambitious. But that was nothing new for them or us. We approached the board of Geest in 2004. The response left nothing to the imagination – we were swiftly dismissed and the board even declined to have their advisors meet with Bakkavor. It is not unlikely that they simply didn't see the approach from such a small company as realistic, and didn't take it seriously. Also, as we would find out through various other transactions, the boards and management of many UK publicly listed companies rarely had much interest in entertaining bids if they could avoid it. It simply wasn't in their interest. The members of the board or even management rarely had such a vested interest in their business that a takeover would reap big gains for them. A takeover usually meant that their board seats and jobs were at risk. Understandably, perhaps, their interest was muted.

Whatever the reason, the brothers were brushed away. That, of course, only made them keener. Getting rid of them was like trying to throw away a boomerang. They soon came back, and this time they invited themselves to the party. By selling the seafood business and raising a considerable amount of funding through a bond offering in Iceland, they had accumulated a sizeable war chest. They now deployed these funds into accumulating a sizeable stake in Geest from the market. By the end of 2004, they had reached a 20 percent shareholding, and this time the board of Geest did engage with them. In March 2005 the board approved the takeover bid. For Bakkavor it was a big bite, but in addition to the war chest, the company had paid up all its debt from the acquisition of Katsouris. The UK banks were lining up to fund further acquisitions for them. This was the first public takeover Kaupthing worked on outside Iceland, and not a small one – the enterprise value was close to £600 million. We were also interested in underwriting a big part of the debt that the company was looking for to fund the acquisition, but in the end Barclays offered such good terms, that they solely underwrote the £500 million debt package. Only four years earlier, I had been throwing up caviar, trying to convince Commerzbank to lend

Bakkavor one-tenth of that amount without success. It also dawned on me that the presentation Agust had given the first time I met the brothers, and which I had concluded bordered on insanity, had drastically underestimated the real growth of the company. They had now surpassed their goals by a wide margin.

By this time, Baugur was also acquiring businesses as if a worldwide ban on takeovers was looming. Their acquisition spree prompted Sir Tom Hunter to ask Jon Asgeir if he was dying. It seemed like he was trying to achieve his lifetime goals in a matter of months. Many of the acquisitions were in Scandinavia. The most noteworthy one was in Denmark, where they acquired Magasin de Nord, the Danish equivalent to Harrods. Most of the deals were still in the UK, but we had gradually become less involved. In the beginning we were the only bank that could help them close transactions, and they were one of the few clients that came to us with interesting international deals, but now that had dramatically changed. Kaupthing had substantially expanded its client base, and Baugur had built up relationships with various other banks. We also had limits on what we could and wanted to lend to them and their ventures.

Baugur was still constantly looking for new sources of debt financing. Jon Asgeir wouldn't buy a toothbrush unless he could borrow against it. After the initial success of transactions like Arcadia, Oasis, and others, there was no shortage of willing lenders. Following the privatisation of Landsbanki, they became very eager lenders to Baugur, and in the latter part of the noughties they were their main Icelandic lenders. Various UK banks were involved as well, RBS financed the takeover of Hamleys, Barclays supported them in the takeover of MK One and HBOS partnered up with them in various transactions.

Baugur's most successful takeover ranks among UK's most successful leveraged buyouts in the first decade of the millennium. It perfectly showcased Jon Asgeir's talent in identifying and putting together deals, and also in getting the best people to work with him. Big Food Group owned the wholesaler Booker and the frozen food retailer Iceland. Jon Asgeir had been watching the business since 2002, and I had been to a couple of meetings with him and Deutsche Bank to discuss the possibility of a bid. Financing the deal, however, was proving tricky, mainly because of the lacklustre performance of the Iceland chain.

Baugur still began to build a small stake in the ailing company, and continued to find ways to finance a bid. There was bid speculation, but people found it difficult to see that an entity the size of Baugur could close a transaction of this size. One unflattering analyst told a journalist, 'The Iceland business has effectively been up for sale for the last 10 years. But it's been waiting for the 7th Cavalry, and then a bloke on a donkey turns up.' He was underestimating the bloke on the donkey.

After more than two years of huffing and puffing, Baugur was able to put together a consortium large enough to make a public bid for the food group, at year-end 2004. They teamed up with various people, including Sir Tom Hunter and the property tycoon Nick Leslau, with HBOS, Kaupthing and Landsbanki debt-funding the transaction. The plan was to acquire the whole company, but immediately split it into three separate companies, Iceland, Booker, and a special property company formed around the real estate of the two operating companies. It was a big deal – the enterprise value was close to £600 million – and a risky one. Booker was deemed to be the stable performer, while Iceland was the one that no one wanted to finance. We had declined to put debt on the business and so had other banks, but Baugur had been able to convince Landsbanki to fund Iceland, which made the whole deal come together. Kaupthing and HBOS financed Booker, and HBOS provided the debt to the property company. In December the board of Big Food Group approved the bid, and the company was split into the three parts.

The ugly duckling, Iceland, turned out to be a beautiful swan, thanks to the management team led by Malcolm Walker. Walker had founded Iceland in the seventies and built it into a very successful chain of 84 stores when he floated the company on the London Stock Exchange in 1984. He continued to grow the company into the new millennium, until Iceland acquired Booker in 2000. Stuart Rose was the CEO of Booker, and the plan was for him to take over as CEO of the combined business while Walker would step down. Rose, however, left for Arcadia immediately after the takeover, and instead Bill Grimsey took over as CEO. A few months after he took the helm, Grimsey announced that big problems had been identified in the business and made a whopping £145 million write downs of exceptional items.

When it turned out that Walker had sold more than £13.5 million worth of shares a month earlier, the FSA and the Serious Fraud Office placed him under investigation for insider trading. He endured more than a three-year investigation before he was cleared. Iceland's website describes the 2004–2005 period in which Grimsey was in charge as 'the dark ages.' When Jon began to look at Big Food Group, he came into contact with Walker and convinced him to team up with the consortium. I suspect that part of Walker's decision to take over Iceland again was at least partly to prove a point. He certainly did that, as he and his team completely turned around the fortunes of Iceland, via a back-to-basics strategy. Profits exploded, and within four years, two refinancings had enabled the shareholders to pay themselves over £330 million in dividends. By the middle of 2009 the company had repaid all its debts and was producing an annual EBITDA of £150 million. When Big Food Group was taken over, Iceland was valued at close to £150 million. A realistic valuation of the company now would imply that the total value created since the takeover is in the region of £1.5 billion.

The property realised quick profits as rental yields dropped rapidly following the takeover. Booker, however, struggled immensely after the takeover, and was not the stable business we expected. Credit from suppliers quickly became a problem, and only a few months after the takeover the business was in serious danger of going into bankruptcy. The saviour came in the form of Charles Wilson. He had been Stuart Rose's right-hand man at Booker, Arcadia and Marks & Spencer, and highly respected as an operations manager. Jon Asgeir, very much to his credit, managed to convince Wilson to take over Booker. The company was practically bankrupt so a major restructuring needed to take place where the banks converted a part of their debt into equity. Wilson did a superb job, turned the business around, and when it was listed on the AIM market in London, through a reverse takeover of a smaller competitor, Blueheath, the banks had recouped their initial funding.

Although Icelandic clients were still crucial, UK clients became more and more important for us. Eventually, we closed our first deal with Robert Tchenguiz. That was the acquisition of the pub chain Laurel, which we funded together with Dresdner Bank, in addition to taking a small stake in the business. A couple of add-on acquisitions of other pub chains followed shortly after. A more sizeable transaction reared its head shortly after the initial Laurel deal.

In early 2005, Robert called me and informed me that he was in discussions with Barclays Capital and Apax, the private equity fund, to make a bid for Somerfield. Even though we had been involved in very sizeable deals previously, like Big Food Group and Geest, this was still in another league. The total enterprise value of Somerfield was in the region of £1.8 billion. He enquired whether we were interested in being part of the consortium and providing part of the financing. We would have seized the opportunity, as we would have been very interested in working with Apax and Barclays on the equity side. The problem was that we were already involved with another interested buyer, none other than Baugur.

Jon Asgeir had identified Somerfield as a great opportunity some time earlier. To him it was the chance to create the value he had missed out on in the Arcadia deal. He had assembled a small percentage of the shares, as he tended to do when he was considering bids, and then began to approach us and others for financing. The size was enormous and we needed to get other banks and equity investors involved. Jon Asgeir approached Sir Tom Hunter, and shortly after that I flew with him to Scotland for a meeting at Hunter's home. There we met Peter Cummings, Head of Corporate Banking at HBOS, and in Hunter's living room the four of us informally agreed on the bid and financing structure. Kaupthing and HBOS were going to provide the debt, with HBOS taking the bulk, and all four parties were going to participate in the equity.

By the time Robert called me in April, the Baugur consortium had already approached the board of Somerfield with a bid of 190 pence per share. The board had rejected it. That sparked interest in Somerfield, and a couple of other property moguls, the Livingstone brothers and the Zakay brothers, began to sniff around. It wasn't a coincidence that it was property people that showed the most interest. Somerfield had a large property portfolio of stores which, at the time, was very easy to get financing against. So I had a problem on my hands, with both groups clamouring for finance. The logic in joining forces soon became obvious. I set up a meeting at Robert's house with Jon Asgeir and people from Robert's consortium. After that meeting and a couple of others, Baugur and ourselves joined R20, Barclays and Apax and we began to prepare a new bid for Somerfield. HBOS and Tom decided not to continue, and Citigroup now led the debt financing.

Everything was progressing as planned, and the other two bidders didn't seem likely to conclude the financing for their bid. Jon Asgeir's dream of getting a second chance at the deal of a lifetime was getting closer and closer. He even had slides in his presentation on Somerfield with the headline 'Better than Arcadia.' It should have read 'Exactly the same as Arcadia.' In the beginning of July, at the end of the three-year investigation that began with the house raid at Baugur, leading it to being forced to sell its shares in Arcadia, the Icelandic prosecutor charged Jon Asgeir, his father and sister and three other individuals on a total of 40 different counts. Many of the charges were serious and included charges of embezzlement, breaking company law and avoiding import duties. Some of the charges were minor in relation to amounts, and even related to purchases of hot dogs. Eventually, after going through the various stages of the Icelandic judicial system, Jon Asgeir was in 2007 convicted for false accounting and sentenced to three months deferred time in jail. The invoices that had sparked the investigation had not been proof of embezzlement, but according to the court ruling had been used to show Baugur's accounts in a favourable light. Ironically the disgruntled business partner, Sullenberger, received the same sentence as Jon Asgeir for his part in issuing the invoices. The former deputy CEO of Baugur was convicted on charges of embezzlement, although the amounts were quite small. He had used the company credit card and according to the court charged Baugur for a total of £3500, mainly for the purchase of a lawnmower.

Just like the Arcadia deal, the actions of the Icelandic police resulted in Baugur being thrown out of the Somerfield syndication. Barclays Capital made it immediately very clear that they would not accept that someone charged with embezzlement would be part of the bidding consortium. After some desperate attempts by Baugur to have them change their mind they gave up – this was a battle they couldn't win. I met Jon Asgeir on the day it became clear they couldn't continue. He was a broken man. He still managed to negotiate with R20 to buy the shares he had in Somerfield, on which he made some profits. I was mostly disappointed that we'd miss out on the considerable 'mediation fee' I had successfully reintroduced for putting the two consortia together.

After Baugur left, the path was clear for the consortium to close the bid, and although there were some rocks on the road, in October we closed the £1.8 billion transaction. Kaupthing was the second-largest provider of equity after Apax, although we subsequently sold a large part of it to our high net worth client base. The acquisition was a success. After selling off the money-losing Kwik Save chain and some of the property, the management team rationalised the core operations. Despite the fact that sales were falling, they were able to grow profits by cutting costs. The business was put up for sale in 2008 and in February 2009 the sale of the business to the Co-operative Group was closed, returning slightly less than two times the initial investment. That was a great result in light of the fact that the business was being sold at the height of the credit crunch.

***

I had not been able to focus much on the Somerfield deal in the last stages of the acquisition. We were simultaneously working on our own acquisition of Singer & Friedlander, which would revolutionise our operations in the UK. It was a long-standing merchant bank, and one of the very few small independent banks left in the market. We initially learned of them as they were the largest shareholder in Carnegie, one of our competitors in Scandinavia and the largest investment bank in the region. We began to accumulate a stakeholding in 2003 and built up to 9.5 percent by the end of the year, and by February 2004 we owned over 20 percent of the bank. Hreidar had initiated it, after concluding that the market was undervaluing the stock. But he was also beginning to consider a full takeover. In 2004 we were preoccupied with the acquisition of FIH, but a year later, when we had absorbed FIH properly, Singer came back on the agenda.

I wasn't interested in Singer and argued against the takeover. My experience from building the office in the UK had only strengthened my view that our emphasis should be on organic growth. We had done it very successfully in Iceland, Luxembourg and now in London. The London office was extremely successful. Hiring in all the people, save for one that came from Brask & Company, meant that we had created a Kaupthing culture. What I really wanted to do was expand into brokerage, which would fit well with the investment banking operation.

But Sigurdur and Hreidar had made up their minds. I then agreed with them to take over the business to ensure it would become an integrated part of the bank. You would have struggled to find two more different cultures than Singer and Kaupthing, and just putting a Kaupthing sign in the window would do nothing to change that. I took over as the CEO of Singer following the acquisition, with the aim of merging it quickly with the existing Kaupthing investment banking business in the UK. The agreed purchase price was over £500 million, but relative to FIH Singer would be much easier to swallow. At the time it was only equivalent to one year's profit for us. Singer had a balance sheet of almost £3 billion, which was slightly more than 20 percent of the overall balance sheet of the group.

The negotiations were conducted with the CEO, Tony Presley Shearer, Paul Selway-Swift, the Chairman and their advisors. Tony Presley, tall and dark haired, was a real character. He had changed his middle name to Presley, to show his devotion to the King, and went to Memphis annually to pay tribute. Tony Presley had taken over as CEO only a few months before our approach, and I believe he was not particularly happy with the takeover. After I got to know the people at Singer, a few told me that the CEO job had been his dream position. He seemed keen to continue as CEO, but unfortunately we didn't plan to keep him on. His attitude towards us changed very much when we informed him of our plan that I would replace him. We offered him a role as executive chairman for a limited time of 18–24 months to help with the transition after the takeover, but he declined.

After extensive due diligence and negotiations on the price, we reached an agreement with the board of Singer on 22 April 2005. It's not difficult for me to remember the date, as our son Atli was born in London that day. I was at the hospital negotiating the last points over the phone, although I took a break while Thordis gave birth. The common date was appropriate: dealing with our extremely lively son would be as hectic for Thordis as the coming reorganisation of Singer was for me.

The takeover was complete in the summer, but I only took over as CEO at the beginning of December. At the end of the year I was slightly nervous at the task at hand, but I was also looking forward to it. Fortunately I wasn't going to do it alone. Kristin Petursdottir agreed to join me as Deputy CEO. She had joined the bank in 1997, after having worked for Statoil in Norway and Shell in Iceland. When I was in charge of the funding of the bank, Kristin worked with me, and took over when I began to focus solely on investment banking. Athletic, blonde and very good looking, she was probably the toughest manager of the lot of us, and didn't shy away from difficult decisions. That would come in handy for the tasks ahead.

It was a time to be optimistic. Kaupthing was doing better than ever before, the achievements in London were fantastic, with faster and more profitable growth than anyone could have expected. When I left as group head of Investment Banking at the end of the year to take over at Singer, I was proud. The division was the most profitable in the bank and made over £200 million of gross profits. Other parts of the business were also doing well. Our Nordic operation, in particular FIH, was performing very well, and the same was true of Luxembourg and Iceland. The bank's assets now exceeded £20 billion. With record profits of over £500 million it was easy to understand why the market capitalisation of Kaupthing exceeded £4.5 billion.

We were not the only Icelanders who were prospering. The other banks had grown too and were reporting record earnings. The same was true for most of the big international companies, like Ossur, Bakkavor, Actavis and Alfesca. The wealth poured into our tiny country. But Icelandic society also changed dramatically, and not to everyone's liking.

Chapter Eight

The Champagne Island

The sun was setting as I looked over the Mediterranean from the upper deck of the 120-ft yacht. It was the end of May, the Friday of the Grand Prix weekend in Monaco, probably the most glamorous event anywhere in the world. I faced a crowd of 80 people, including some of the wealthiest people in the UK, gazing up at me in anticipation. They were waiting for me to sing 'Delilah', the Tom Jones song. It had become my signature song, and the only one I knew– I'd sung it to five people and to a crowd of 1500, in fishing cabins, private jets, a zodiac and a scheduled airline flight. This time though, I didn't know most of the audience, they were all pretty sober and worst of all, so was the singer. I was acutely aware that I normally sang with more emphasis on volume than quality. But eventually, to avoid further embarrassment and the tuneless chanting of my colleagues who were keen to do the backing vocals, I gave in. Probably because I was unusually sober, for the first time ever I sang surprisingly well. My colleagues and clients loved it. But how the hell did I end up singing 'Delilah' on a yacht in the south of France to assembled millionaires and billionaires? Only ten years earlier I thought I'd be a history teacher, working in one of the fishing villages in Iceland.

But then, there was a party atmosphere everywhere, and nowhere more so than back in Iceland. Singing on a yacht in Monaco seemed completely fitting. By 2006 the economy was going like a steam train. We were witnessing wealth creation on a scale rarely seen before in human history. The Icelandic banks were obviously at the heart of this. Kaupthing was the largest, but we weren't the only ones. Internationally, Kaupthing went first, but the others soon followed.

***

Landsbanki and Glitnir had taken small steps outside Iceland in 2000. Landsbanki bought the small UK property lender Heritable, and Glitnir bought Raphael & Sons in the UK and the Danish internet bank Basisbank. But these hadn't been particularly successful. Heritable did well, but attempts to add private banking to its services failed and was closed down. Both of Glitnir's acquisitions turned sour. After this, both banks retracted and focused mainly on the domestic market for the years in which our international expansion was at its most aggressive. Soon, though, it became difficult for the others not to follow suit. Undoubtedly, it was annoying for them to watch us get all the glory attached to 'making it' abroad. We were attracting more and more clients, and the best staff too.

Under the leadership of Sigurjon Arnason and Halldor Kristjansson, Landsbanki focused primarily on organic growth. They made a number of relatively small acquisitions in the broking sector in Europe, the noteworthy ones being Teather & Greenwood in the UK, and Kepler Securities in France. These were consolidated into one platform called Landsbanki securities, with modest success. Landsbanki's assets tripled between 2003 and 2005 as they aggressively grew their loan books. The attempt to acquire FIH had been an aberration, rather than a normal part of their growth strategy. But it seemed clear that they aspired to Kaupthing's international profile. A Landsbanki employee told me that at one Christmas Party Sigurjon referred five times to Kaupthing in his welcome speech. After they were privatised they aggressively went after our clients and began to lend in the UK and other countries. Their heads of Broking and Investment Banking were both former employees of Kaupthing, so naturally there were similarities. Their market value grew in line with profits, and at the end of 2006 the bank was worth £2 billion.

Glitnir was a slightly different animal. It had been formed with the merger of FBA and Islandsbanki in 1999, at which time it was the largest bank. Until 2006 they had a more diversified shareholder base than Kaupthing or Landsbanki. Bjarni Armannsson, their CEO, was a former Kaupthing colleague. Bjarni was very intelligent, a fantastic orator and presenter. Raised on a farm, he revelled in his quirky image – he had appeared on TV exhibiting his embroidery and digging his potato garden in his wellingtons. Following this, he was sometimes called Puss'n Boots, as much a reflection of his reputation for being cunning as anything else. I worked with him at Kaupthing; both there and at Glitnir he was very popular with the staff. Massively extroverted, Bjarni got to know people quickly, and was famed for his love of singing, which he did at every opportunity.

Despite all this, there was no hiding his determination. He seemed to struggle to build a cohesive management team at Glitnir and there were regularly people changes at the top. Still, Glitnir was a very well-run bank under his leadership, and focused clearly on retail and corporate banking, with little emphasis on investment banking. The bank wanted to build its expansion outside of Iceland on the country's two major industries, fishing and energy. To that end (at least I could see no other plausible reason), it concentrated its international growth almost solely in Norway, a leader in both sectors, where it acquired two regional banks, Kreditbanken and BN Bank. Bjarni was very well liked by international creditors and bondholders, who perceived Glitnir to be the most conservative of the Icelandic banks.

When FL Group and Baugur established themselves as the controlling shareholders of Glitnir in 2006 and 2007 it was clear to everyone that Bjarni's departure was a case of when, not if. The shareholders were keen to take the bank in the direction of investment banking and there were rumours of personal tensions with Bjarni. He still stayed on until the middle of 2007, and seemed to be implementing a strategy in line with the wishes of the owners – as Glitnir became more involved in investment banking deals, and began to expand through acquisitions of FIM, a Finnish asset manager, and the Swedish broker Fischer Partners.

After a compromise agreement with his board, Bjarni finally left in 2007 and moved to Norway. He was replaced by the 30-year-old Larus Welding, who had previously been the head of Landsbanki's UK branch and the main relationship manager for Baugur. Larus was very likeable and sensible but this was an unfortunate shift – not least because he lacked Bjarni's experience. His appointment was also viewed by many, including international creditors and analysts, as a sign that Baugur was heavily influencing the direction of the bank.

Apart from the big three, other still sizeable players also did relatively well in the market. The investment bank Straumur, like Landsbanki, had Bjorgolfur Thor as its main shareholder. The savings bank system had mushroomed too. Collectively the banks had a market capitalisation of £13 billion in 2006, which was over 75 percent of the total market capitalisation of the Iceland Stock Exchange. This was remarkable, not least because several fairly large multinational companies were listed on the exchange.

The growth of the banks was first and foremost on the back of what seemed like an endless appetite in the European bond market for bonds issued by the Icelandic banks (and others). Liquidity was ample and the banks had strong single A credit ratings from the rating agencies of Moody's and Fitch. In 2005 alone the banks issued over €15 billion worth of bonds, 150 percent of the GDP of Iceland.

The engorged banking sector changed every aspect of the economy in Iceland. Obviously, accountants and lawyers were constantly busy with advisory work on loan agreements and takeovers. But every business in the country felt it – florists, taxi drivers, advertising agencies, restaurants and hotels. Corporate entertainment reached ludicrous proportions. Each of the banks had numerous fishing trips every summer, causing the cost of fishing licences in the salmon rivers to skyrocket. That was despite the fact that fishing tours, which five years earlier had been looked upon as extravagant, were now almost considered lame. Banks, and to some extent the other international businesses, were now organising trips to the opera in Milan, skiing in the Alps and watching the final of the football World Cup in Berlin.

The banking sector had become so big that finding enough talented and experienced people in our tiny country became a big problem. Other businesses became frustrated as all their best people were headhunted by the financial institutions. The situation climaxed in 2007 when a GP enquired about a job with us in the communications division! When interviewed, he claimed that the job would be ideal for him – as a doctor he was communicating with people every day. Apparently, everyone wanted to work in a bank.

The banks in general, and Kaupthing in particular, sucked the talent out of the Icelandic universities like a big black hole. In 2005 a survey carried out at the University of Iceland showed that Kaupthing was by far the most sought after place to work. And it wasn't only the business graduates that we attracted. The top students from engineering, law, and even the best history and psychology students were hired into the bank. They were often being hired many months before they finished their studies for salaries that were beginning to look ridiculously high. An apocryphal story went that the car park at the university was so full of student cars that the professors had difficulties finding places to park their bicycles.

The trend of hiring in talent, even if people knew little about business, started shortly after I joined Kaupthing, with Stein Karason, who later became our Head of Risk. I knew Stein originally through my brother, who had studied engineering with him at the University of Iceland. When I moved to Boston, Stein was doing his PhD at MIT and we became good friends. Stein was a brilliant engineer, and when he graduated from the University of Iceland, one of his professors said he was the most promising engineer to come out of the country in a decade. But at over 6ft 6 inches tall, weighing more than 250 pounds and with an enormous beard, he looked slightly incongruous, more like a bitter Santa Claus than a top engineer. Shortly after I joined Kaupthing, I mentioned Stein to Sigurdur, who was always on the lookout for talented and intelligent people whatever their academic background. In the spring of 1996 I went back to visit Boston. At a party at Stein's house I convinced him to join Kaupthing and we signed a letter of intent to that effect on a napkin. Instead of signing it in blood, we settled for pouring beer over it. A few months later, Stein showed up at Kaupthing to meet with Sigurdur, clutching a battered and incomprehensible napkin. He was hired.

If it wasn't in a bank, most people would surely have tried to work for some of the international giants that had been built up through the various acquisitions and were headquartered in Iceland. And these were great companies. On the Iceland Stock Exchange you could now find the second largest prosthetic company in the world, Ossur, the fourth largest generic pharmaceutical business in the world, Actavis, the UK's largest producer of fresh food, Bakkavor, and France's leading producer of foie gras and smoked salmon, Alfesca. Although not as big as the banks, these were all very sizeable businesses on an international scale. Their market capitalisation was in the hundreds of millions of pounds, and Actavis exceeded a billion. You weren't really investing in Iceland if you bought shares on the Iceland Stock Exchange. More than 70 percent of the income of listed companies came from abroad. The ownership was still very Icelandic, as very few international investors were interested in going through the hassle of having investments in Icelandic kronur in their portfolio. The valuations were also becoming a bit scary. In just three years – from the end of 2003 until the end of 2006 – the ICEX index rose by 203 percent and the market capitalisation grew from £4 billion to £16 billion. Ten years earlier the total market capitalisation of the stock market was barely half a billion pounds. This growth in value was a combination of a number of things, namely pros-perous operations, relatively high valuations and the fact that most of the companies were leveraged. That meant that the value of the shares increased very rapidly when the companies performed well.

With almost all of the companies in the hands of Icelanders, the wealth effect that the stock market created was nothing short of enor-mous. In three years a wealth equal to more than the total GDP of the country had been created in the stock market. Some of this wealth was cashed out; the largest example of that was when Bjorgolfur Thor's Novator bid for all the shares in Actavis in early 2007 for a total of €2.0 billion. That takeover was financed by Deutsche Bank, but most other takeovers of companies on the stock exchange were funded at least in part by the Icelandic banks. Because the banks were so big, doing a leveraged buyout of practically every domestic company was easy. And there was ample interest from wealthy investors to provide equity for those transactions. Transaction after transaction saw all three oil com-panies in Iceland being taken over, plus many of the fishing companies, the shipping companies and the national airline. Debt was placed on the operating companies to finance the takeover. At the end of 2007, corporate Iceland was leveraged to the hilt.

For some reason Icelanders have big appetite for debt. The word for loan in Icelandic, 'lan' actually also means luck. Telling someone that you had been granted a loan you literally say 'I got lucky'. This is probably telling. Until the nineties, loans were incredibly difficult to get. People would queue up outside the office of the branch manager of their bank to ask for a loan to buy a car or a house, and he would arbitrarily make loan decisions in a godlike fashion. Knowing a well-connected politician was often the only way to get a sizeable loan. Throughout much of the seventies and eighties there was incredibly high inflation, which ate up the real value of mortgages in a decade's time. Likewise that meant that sensible savers were punished as the inflation reduced the real value of their savings. Eventually this led to the extensive use of inflation-linked loans in Iceland, but prior to that receiving a loan was actually truly getting lucky. Another possible reason for how lightly we treat indebtedness is the fact that Icelanders have a very determined belief that they can always work themselves out of difficult situations. We have a special word that means things will sort themselves out – 'reddast'.Whatever the reason, the debt flowed and fuelled the boom.

Given the economic boom, one would have been forgiven for thinking that this would have been the time for the government to retract, maybe increase taxes, and keep investment programmes to a minimum. In fact, the opposite happened. In 2003 the national power company Landsvirkjun commenced the building of one of the largest hydro power plants in Europe to provide electricity for two aluminium smelters built on the east and west coasts of Iceland. The total cost of these projects was close to $4 billion, around 35 percent of Iceland's GDP. Corporate and individual tax, as well as VAT, all came down; after all, the increase in revenues was so big that the Treasury could easily pay down debt – by the end of 2005, the government claimed it had practically no foreign debt. That was only true if you excluded the guarantees that had been entered into for the loans of Landsvirkjun and the Housing Financing Fund, which collectively were taking on billions of pounds of liabilities.

The Housing Financing Fund (a government agency similar to Freddie Mac and Fannie May in the US, and the primary mortgage lender in Iceland) eased its lending restrictions and lowered the interest rates on mortgages. Because of the government guarantee it had always offered lower rates than the banks were able to do and practically all households in Iceland had mortgages with the fund. The banks would not compete with the fund, instead providing second mortgages, ranking behind the fund's.

In the summer of 2004, all this changed and Kaupthing began to offer up to 80 percent financing on first priority mortgages at the same rates as the Housing Financing Fund. This was Hreidar's initiative. He and others had complained regularly about the existence of the fund, which they saw as unfair competition with the banks. Hreidar even referred to the fund as the Housing Financing Bank, to drive home the notion that it was competing with the banks. His complaints were in vain so eventually he lost patience and began competing head-on with the fund. The Housing Financing Fund rose to the challenge and began to lower the interest rate on its mortgages and lending at higher loan to value ratios. This sparked a big property boom, which until then had lagged behind the property boom happening elsewhere in the world. Two years later prices of property in Reykjavik had almost doubled.

Perhaps most tragic were the actions of the Central Bank of Iceland. Make no mistake about how difficult their role was. Not only was the economy booming on a scale seldom seen in developed countries, but the traditional weapons of a central bank, interest rates, just weren't working. By the end of 2005, the Central Bank Policy rates were 10.5 percent, and a year later they exceeded 14 percent. The problem was that increasing short-term interest rates had practically no effect on private households. Almost no borrowing, save for overdrafts and credit card debt, was based on short-term nominal interest rates. Around ninety percent of mortgages in Iceland had fixed interest rates and were inflation linked. Those who didn't borrow inflation linked, borrowed in foreign currency and, in particular, cars tended to be financed in foreign currency because of the lower interest rate. An increase in the Icelandic krona interest rate had no effect on the rates paid on the foreign borrowings. While a one percent interest rate hike in the UK would result in house owners appearing on television explaining how much their monthly mortgage cost had gone up by, a five percent interest hike in Iceland only resulted in people shrugging their shoulders. They didn't care.

The interest rate hikes did have an effect – but it was the opposite of what it was supposed to be. The very high interest rates made it very attractive to investors to invest in Icelandic kronur. While you would be paid 3 or 4 percent interest in currencies like euros and pounds, an investor would be paid almost 10 percent higher rates if he placed his money in kronur. That created a demand for kronur and severely strengthened the Icelandic krona. Between the end of 2001 and 2005, the krona strengthened by an amazing 34 percent, measured against other major currencies. A stronger krona in fact meant reduced inflation, as imports such as cars, TVs, electronics, etc., became cheaper. For those with inflation-linked mortgages this meant that the total interest they paid was lower as the inflation part was kept low. The same was true of those that had borrowed foreign currency: when the krona strengthened the krona value of their loan decreased. Thus, the Central Bank's interest rate hike resulted in lower financing cost for households, the opposite of what you would see in other countries.

During this massive economic boom the Icelandic government had two entities that seemed to have two different agendas. The Housing Financing Fund was lowering its interest rates and expanding its balance sheet, while the Central Bank was raising rates to no avail. Both had the effect of further fuelling the boom.

Importantly, the high interest rates pushed more and more people into borrowing in foreign currency. When the krona eventually tanked, this led to catastrophe. So-called carry traders loved the high interest rates. Carry trading is a term used for investors that borrow in a low-interest currency (often Japanese yen and Swiss francs) and invest the borrowed funds in a high interest currency like the Icelandic krona. While the krona is stable they pocket the interest rate differential, their risk being that the krona weakens. The carry trading in the krona was well publicised, but there were two common misconceptions. For one, the strengthening of the krona was only to a small extent driven by true carry traders. Most of the demand for kronur came from private investors in Europe, often summarised as 'Belgian dentists', investing part of their portfolio in the high-yielding Icelandic krona. Since they were not borrowing in lower yielding currencies they were not, strictly speaking, carry traders. The other misconception was that the funds being invested in the krona had flooded the Icelandic banks, and these funds were funding the growth of the banks and the Icelandic expansion. The Belgian dentists didn't actually buy bonds or other krona securities from the Icelandic banks, but rather from various international banks that began in 2005 to issue so-called Glacier Bonds, which were bonds denominated in Icelandic kronur. The truth is that these investments never provided funding for the Icelandic banks.

The Glacier Bond issues were actually driven by other financial institutions than those issuing the bonds, the most famous being the Canadian bank, Toronto Dominion. They would approach banks with AAA credit ratings, the highest possible, like Rabobank and the European Investment Bank, with a proposition to secure them funds at lower rates than they were getting through normal funding routes. Toronto Dominion (quite legitimately) would sell kronur denominated bonds with a high interest rate, issued by the AAA banks, that were snapped up by the yield-hungry dentists. The issuing banks had of course no interest in having debt outstanding in kronur as they had no assets in Iceland. The Canadians thus also entered into so-called swap agreements with the banks, effectively converting their liability from kronur to other currencies, typically euros. Toronto Dominion then entered into the opposite swap with one of the Icelandic banks to hedge their own position. Because the bonds were sold to the private investors at interest rates slightly lower than those prevailing in Iceland (but still high compared to what they would get in other currencies), the likes of Rabobank ended up paying lower interest in euros than they would have, if they sold euro bonds directly. The Canadian bank took fees for arranging the bond issue and some margin on the swap agreements, and made a fortune.

Over the period of a few years the amount of Glacier Bonds outstanding in kronur reached an enormous amount, estimated at £2.5 billion at its peak, equal to about 25 percent of Iceland's GDP. This created a ticking time bomb. The people taking the risk on the krona were by definition speculators. Their demand for kronur, spurred on by the enormously high interest rates, pushed up the value of the currency. But they weren't long-term investors in Iceland. The question was: when would their interest in maintaining the risk on the krona cease?

Everyone knew that if something went wrong in Iceland, they would run from the krona like it was a burning building. If that happened, the currency would completely collapse.

***

Managing an open economy with a huge banking sector and a very international corporate sector had become all but impossible. The inflation linkage that ran through society made the task even more difficult. The changes that had happened over the last ten years, in my opinion, meant that we couldn't maintain an independent currency. Many people shared this view, even the chief economist of the Central Bank was quoted in a German newspaper saying the euro would bring stability to the Icelandic economy. There was an active discussion about the logic of applying for membership to the European Union. Most business leaders, frustrated by the problems associated with the small currency, were supportive. Sigurdur Einarsson was one of the biggest promoters of going down the EU route and voiced his opinion regularly in public.

The most influential opponent of the entrance into the EU, however, was David Oddsson. He was no longer Prime Minister but, in what would turn out to be an amazing twist of fate, had taken over as Governor of the Central Bank. Oddsson had not left politics a content man. And while Jon Asgeir blamed Oddsson for wrecking his dream deals, Arcadia and Somerfield, Oddsson blamed Jon Asgeir for his political demise. In 2002 Jon Asgeir had gained control over the struggling *Frettabladid*, the only free newspaper in Iceland, and in a short period of time, turned it into the most read publication in the country. A year later *Frettabladid* opposed Oddsson's Independence Party in the bitterly fought 2003 parliamentary election when there was talk of corruption, bribery and abuse of the police. Despite the prosperity in Iceland under Oddsson's leadership, he suffered a humiliating defeat. Icelanders saw Oddsson as having become over-powerful. Although his party continued in government, the results of the election caused him to relinquish his position as Prime Minister and take over as Foreign Minister for a short period of time.

Oddsson was furious and he blamed Jon Asgeir and *Frettabladid* for his defeat. Shortly before he stepped down as Prime Minister he introduced a hugely controversial bill which would have made it impossible for large private companies to own more than 15 percent in any one media, and under which newspapers and television stations could not be owned by the same companies. This legislation was seen to be directly aimed at Baugur, which by then had bought the largest private television station. Oddsson still had amazing influence in the parliament and was able to push through the bill, but in another controversial move, the president of Iceland, Olafur Ragnar Grimsson, refused to ratify it. For the first time in the history of the republic a president had used his power not to ratify a bill. Oddsson withdrew the bill, and not long after that he withdrew from politics, at least publicly, and was appointed the Governor of the Central Bank.

One of our managing directors learned about the changes, shortly prior to the formal announcement. He went to the CEO's office and first told Hreidar and Sigurdur that Oddsson had decided to withdraw from politics. Hreidar, tired from his battles with the former Prime Minister, leaped up and said 'this is a cause for celebration. Let's call for champagne!' When he heard the rest of the story, he sank back into his chair and said 'Let's hold off on the champagne. This is bad news – very bad news.'

Amazingly, the Governorship was historically seen as a retirement job for politicians even when, like Oddsson, they lacked the necessary background in economics. His appointment was criticised, but so were many other similar ones in the past. In any case the mighty Oddsson had now become the lender of last resort to Kaupthing and the other banks. Although at the time the possibility of having to go to the Central Bank for assistance was not in anyone's mind, this augured badly.

Oddsson disliked the European Union intensely and was intent on keeping the krona. In any case, landslide support for the EU was highly unlikely whilst the economy was booming. If it ain't broken, why fix it? And for most Icelanders things certainly didn't seem to be broken. The economy of Iceland grew an astronomical 30 percent in three years, between 2003 and 2006. Unemployment figures were similar to many European countries, except there was a dot before the Icelandic number – it didn't even reach one percent. This was despite the fact that the boom years had seen an unprecedented inflow of foreign labour. By the end of 2006 almost 10 percent of the labour force had come from abroad, mainly from countries like Poland and Lithuania. In some fish processing companies the number of Poles exceeded Icelanders. Waiters and the people at the checkout counters of the supermarkets rarely spoke Icelandic.

The strong currency had artificially inflated people's purchasing power and a consumption boom followed. People couldn't get enough flatscreen TVs and cars. The older generation shook their heads as their children purchased jacuzzis, trampolines, and chocolate fountains. The sale of champagne increased by 82 percent. The luxury electronics maker Bang & Olufsen sold more in its store in Reykjavik than any other store worldwide except for Moscow. And amazingly, more Range Rovers were sold in Iceland in 2006 than collectively in the other Nordic countries combined! By the age of 15, I had been on a holiday abroad just once. Now the typical family was going abroad once or even twice a year.

I should have picked up that something was wrong when I went for dinner at my parents' house and my father greeted me in a custom-made Armani suit. Armani was doing such business in Iceland that they sent a tailor from Italy to make suits to measure. My brother had taken our father to the store and bought him a suit. For a man who tucked his tie into his trousers religiously, and bought shoes only when they were on sale (and usually when they didn't fit) this was a sea change indeed.

The life of the average Icelander had never been better, at least if measured in terms of material possessions. Although practically everyone benefited, some people really stood out. The young entrepreneurs that had started it all had become enormously wealthy, even by international standards. Jon Asgeir, the Bakkavor brothers and Bjorgolfur Thor regularly featured on lists of the wealthiest people in the UK, and Bjorgolfur Thor became the first Icelander to be featured in Forbes list of the world's richest people. More impressively, Bjorgolfur Thor was elected the sexiest billionaire in the world by *Financial Times*! Their estimated individual wealth, at the peak, ranged from £500 million to £2 billion. But various other Icelanders could count their net worth in millions of pounds, and there was an amazingly large number whose value exceeded £10 million. Little more than ten years earlier a book entitled *Icelandic Millionaires* revealed that the wealthiest person in Iceland was worth less than £15 million. The change was dramatic. Many people had become super wealthy by simply investing in the stock market, which had created dramatic returns. Many of Kaupthing's shareholders had become Icelandic krona billionaires, without ever dreaming that would be possible, simply by holding on to their shares as the price rose continuously.

When I began my career at Kaupthing, the salary range in Iceland was incredibly narrow compared to most other countries. The CEOs of the biggest corporations were the highest earners with annual salaries of around £100,000 whilst the lowest salaries were close to £10,000. With tax taken into account, the difference was approximately five fold. By 2006 banks were paying more than £100,000 to new graduates. The rain makers were receiving many times that amount, and the executives of the banks even more.

The most famous outbreak of anger at the super remuneration had happened as early as at the end of 2003. Maybe not surprisingly the bank in question was Kaupthing and the wrath came from a familiar direction, the Prime Minister Oddsson. The bank had announced to the stock exchange the awarding of share options to its key employees and the amounts caused jitters. In particular the board had awarded Sigurdur and Hreidar individually almost ten times as many shares as the second tier management. Although the shares could not be sold for five years, people could calculate that on day one the two were in the money by over two million pounds. That did not go down well. The reaction to the announcement was extremely negative and amazingly resulted in Oddsson announcing that he had withdrawn his deposits from the bank. He told a journalist that the share options should be condemned saying that 'all clients of the banks must consider whether they want to be clients of an institution that behaves like this. I don't have a lot of money there, but I still have 400 thousand kronur (around £3000) on a savings account. I will withdraw it.'

The lifestyle of the 'rich and famous' covered the pages of Iceland's glossy magazines. Some time earlier, flying business class was seen as a sign of excess. Executives at the banks and the international companies filled the business class section of Icelandair. Because successful Icelanders were often so young, I once told an English journalist that Icelandair was the only airline that provided its business passengers with crayons and colouring books. By 2007, however, the transportation of choice for many had become the private jet. Seeing five or six jets parked in Reykjavik airport, which is located practically in the centre of town, became a common sight. Most of the wealthiest entrepreneurs owned their plane – Bjorgolfur Thor's had the logo of his investment company Novator painted on the tail. Jon Asgeir's private aircraft and his yacht were both painted in his signature black. Elton John played when Olafur Olafsson celebrated his fiftieth birthday in Reykjavik and 50 Cent and Jamiroquai provided the music at Bjorgolfur Thor's birthday party in Jamaica.

For the Icelandic nouveau riche the wealth created new and previously unknown problems. Staff issues became the centre of discussions between housewives. The driver was lazy, and the cleaning ladies were doing a lousy job. Children complained about the constant travelling to places like Courchevel, St. Tropez and Dubai, preferring to stay at home and go cycling. Wine selection became an issue. A few years earlier everyone drank gin and tonic, but now you were lame if your red wine was younger than you were.

Some of the behaviour got out of hand and money was flashed more and more obviously. At an international charity dinner I witnessed an Icelandic husband and wife, sitting on the same table, bid against each other for hundreds of thousands of pounds. In a famous UNICEF charity auction in Iceland in 2005 a yet-to-be-painted picture by one of the country's contemporary painters was sold for almost £200,000. The painter would normally have fetched around £5000 for his pictures. Although money was going to charity people frowned upon what they saw as a total lack of respect for money.

Icelanders are not by nature envious people, and I think to some extent people accepted the high life of people that had built their businesses from scratch and were reaping the benefit of their success. But in a small country, feathers were undoubtedly ruffled. Iceland was usually referred to as a classless society, but to many that had now changed. A special class of people, whose wealth far exceeded that of the normal Icelander, had been created.

And what about me? Over in London, I played my part in the extravagant living, maybe even more than most. Although far from wealthy compared to most of our high-profile clients, I was very well paid by any standards. Money is like good looks, though. People want to have them, but if you have no other qualities, they won't bring you happiness. While at Kaupthing I was offered millions of pounds to join other banks, and that included offers to become group CEO of both Landsbanki and Glitnir. I entertained neither offer. That doesn't mean I was the Mother Theresa of high finance, but I was wedded to Kaupthing, I was very well paid, and for me working with people who were almost like family was very important. I had tried to leave once without success and I wasn't going to try again.

My claim to fame in Iceland was the New Year parties that I threw in London from 2004 until 2007, seen as an example of the extravagance of the nouveau riche. I first threw a party for around 60 people, mainly childhood friends and family, but also colleagues and some high-profile clients, at my house in Iceland in January 2003. Everyone loved it, and pestered me to do it again in London the next year. It was low key, around 80 people at a restaurant, but it was fantastic, and I began excitedly preparing for the next year. In January 2005 I took it up a notch, and we invited over a hundred people for a party in the Oxo Tower, where the highlight was a fireworks display on the Thames at midnight.

Only weeks after I moved to the UK in 2003, I had been invited to a charity event in the Natural History Museum. I thought it was the most fantastic venue I had ever seen. I promised myself that if I could, I would throw a party there one day. In 2006, that was exactly what I did. By then, I'd been in London for almost three years, so I invited more than 200 people, and for the first time there were not only Icelanders there, but many of the high-profile UK clients.

My predilection for 'Delilah' was well-known by this time. People thought I had gone all-out when they saw the big band take the stage. I went up to join them, but taking the microphone I announced, 'instead of the cheap Icelandic version, why not get the real thing and the best singer in the world!' Sir Tom Jones strutted on stage. Many of the guests thought it was an imitator, one English friend told me he had listened to five songs before realising it was the real thing. Backstage, when I met the man himself, I had joked that I would introduce him with the line 'instead of the cheap Icelandic version, here's the cheap Welsh version!' The stony faces of his entourage told me I had gone too far.

Although it was my party, by now it had become a collective effort and various guests funded parts of it like the wine or the entertainment. I still spent a ridiculous amount of money on it, and Thordis was furious with me. My logic was that memories like these were worth more than most things, and I still stand by that. I grew up in the shadiest neighbourhood in Reykjavik and my closest friends today are the ones I made there. To be able to invite them and my family to events like the one at the Natural History Museum was what really made the money worth having.

Almost without trying, Kaupthing quickly became known in London as the bank of the wealthy and well-known. Singer had a Private Banking division whose clients included TV actors, film stars, and supermodels. To this Kaupthing added the entrepreneurs. When we merged the two and added a brokerage division, we could service wealthy individuals in many areas. New clients came to us through word of mouth, as well as through social occasions and holidays.

In the summer we decamped to the South of France, where most of the ultra high net worth Londoners spent their holidays. Hreidar, Magnus and I would go there together with our families, who would complain about the fact that we were spending almost all the time meeting with clients at restaurants or on their boats. Eventually, I actually stopped going on these trips, as it had simply ceased to be holiday. I also met new clients at various events in London, mainly charity dinners. We socialised and networked at high-profile events at venues like Elton John's home, the Winter Palace in St Petersburg and Hampton Court Palace. For a small town boy it was an adventure suddenly to be at parties conversing with celebrities as diverse as Michael Caine, Ivanka Trump, Alan Shearer and Shirley Bassey. I sat at tables with Elle McPherson and Sting, and stood at urinals with Rod Stewart and Hugh Grant on either side of me.

The Formula 1 Grand Prix weekend in Monte Carlo was the highlight of our networking calendar. We first went there in 2002 on a corporate entertainment trip with some of our best clients. Hotel rooms in the city were so expensive that we could only invite a select handful. Those of us from Kaupthing shared a room and bed together. When I woke up one night spooning with Hreidar I swore that would be the last time. After seven years, in the end we knew so many people that we hopped from one yacht to another. We also chartered a boat and hosted parties on board, which was a great way to meet clients. It was in Monaco that I met Mike Ashley, the owner of Sports Direct and Newcastle Football Club, Sir Tom Hunter, and the Candy brothers, who all became clients of ours. By 2007 I personally knew around a third of the *Sunday Times* top 100 Rich List. Most did business with us.

In less than five years, my life had changed from being preoccupied with listing fishing companies in Iceland to being an international banker to the billionaires. Yet it all seemed very effortless. As humans, I've learned that we are hugely adaptable; we can get used to anything very quickly, no matter how bizarre things seem.

Building the bank was still a round-the-clock job, despite the high life. The year after the Singer acquisition was the most difficult one I experienced in all my Kaupthing years. Until the end of 2006, I worked on average 13 hours a day, essentially creating a new bank out of the two legacy businesses. I only saw my newborn son at weekends as he hadn't woken up when I left in the mornings, and was in bed when I arrived home in the evening. It wasn't just that it was a lot of work, it was also incredibly difficult work. Enforcing unpopular changes, making people redundant and dealing with the FSA lacks the adrenaline rush of working hard on a deal you can close and celebrate. By the end of 2006 Thordis commented that it was like happiness had been surgically removed from my soul.

Singer & Friedlander had been set up like a group of independent companies, and had a large number of subsidiaries, many of which were dormant. My plan was to create one bank with various divisions, rather than independent subsidiaries. We embarked on a programme to simplify the legal structure and eventually we reduced the number of subsidiaries from almost 100 to less than 30. The organisational structure was also changed. We centralised the support functions, such as IT, finance and human resources, and created six business units. I managed to persuade the CEO of KBC Peel Hunt, one of the most successful mid cap brokers, to join us to build a new Capital Markets business. He managed to attract a lot of talent from the UK market and the division became very profitable. In the summer of 2006 we moved the headquarters of the bank from the City to Hanover Street in the West End.

I desperately wanted to make all the changes I felt were needed before the end of 2006, so we could have a fresh start to the new year. The most difficult part was the staff changes that I felt were needed. In 12 months we hired over 40 people into the new Capital Markets unit, but a large number of people left from the Investment Management side. I met so many people, I sometimes wasn't sure whether the person coming into the office was resigning or whether it was someone I was convincing to join us. Eventually things settled down, and as 2007 approached we had built a strong organisation with fantastic people. We could now service our core clientele in almost all areas of financial services, whether it was investment banking, brokerage, financing or private banking. We emphasised cross-selling between divisions – and clients in one area were quickly introduced to other parts of the business.

As the new year began in 2007, we quickly started to reap the benefits. All the businesses were contributing, and for the first six months of 2007 we were very profitable with return on equity in excess of 16 percent. When we took over Singer it had been operating on a return on equity of around 6 percent. Our success was one of the main reasons why Citigroup gave Kaupthing a 'Strong Buy' recommendation in their flash report in July.

In July, I was full of optimism as I prepared to fly a group of clients from the UK to Iceland for salmon fishing. Henrik and I had been trying to organise a trip like this for some of our key clients in the UK for a few years but somehow it had never come off. But that year we managed to put together a trip with a good group of people for two days of fishing in Laxá in Kjós not far away from Reykjavik.

Although there were some relatively high-profile business people in the group it was the presence of Gordon Ramsay, the famous chef, that created most interest in Reykjavik. Gordon had been a client of Singer for a few years and had a strong relationship with Iain Stewart, my head of Private Banking, who had supported him in the early stages of his career. I had only come across him once before the salmon fishing trip, when Iain and I met him and his business partner and father-in-law, Chris Hutcheson, for lunch earlier in 2007 to discuss how we could expand the relationship.

If anything, Gordon was more charismatic off-screen, with a great sense of humour. His short attention span made him look a bit like he wasn't very interested in the conversation but after a while you could see that wasn't the case, at least not always. Before the trip guests were requested to send information about their height and shoe size so we could get the correct waders and wading shoes. When the information came from Gordon I first thought it was a mistake – he had written that he wears size 15 shoes. We are about the same height but I'm a pretty normal size 9 so this looked fairly strange, I started to wonder how I avoided tipping over, with such tiny feet! After some searching we managed to find wading shoes that fit Gordon, although they looked more like clown shoes than fishing boots.

As part of the trip we planned a night out in Reykjavik on the Friday before we were scheduled to start fishing. We flew to Iceland on the Friday afternoon and met at the bar of Hotel 101 in Reykjavik early evening for a drink before going out. I had reserved a table at one of my favourite restaurants in Reykjavik, the Seafood Cellar. I had spoken to the manager of the restaurant to let him know that Gordon would be there, thinking it only fair. The food was very good but the waiters were shaking with nerves around the great chef, the plates wobbled perilously on the end of his rough humour and sarcastic comments.

Later, we went to Reykjavik's hottest nightclub where we stayed until five in the morning, which is pretty standard in Iceland in the summer, where almost constant daylight leads to a carnival atmosphere. When we arrived at the club our table quickly became the centre of attention, mainly because of Gordon's presence. Although he wasn't actually well known in Iceland at the time – I never tired of explaining to him that everyone knew Jamie Oliver but that he was a nobody – enough people recognised him for it to spread quickly in the club that someone famous was at our table. Icelandic girls, in addition to being generally very attractive, are also quite happy to take the initiative. One of our guests commented: 'I haven't been hit on like this since I was last in a strip club!' Gordon obviously got the impression that throwing alcohol around was the done thing in Iceland. At the end of the night he high popped the cork out of a bottle of champagne and sprayed one of my friends until he almost drowned.

The fishing trip was great, apart from the fishing itself. The weather was uncharacteristically sunny, calm and 25 degrees, which is great if you are working on your tan, but pretty awful if you are fishing for salmon. The scenery by the river in Hvalfjordur when the weather is like that is absolutely breathtaking so our guests had to accept that as consolation for the fairly low number of salmon caught. One person, however, was thrilled with the fishing, despite the low catch. That was the most experienced fisherman in the group, Ray Kelvin, the founder and majority owner of fashion retailer Ted Baker. Ray, despite being a very keen fisherman, had never caught a sea trout so he was absolutely thrilled when he managed to land one on the second day. To make the trip even more memorable for him Gordon offered to cook it, baking it in a wet newspaper – a method Ray swore by. As he watched Gordon Ramsay cook the first sea trout he had ever caught and looked outside our cabin where the sun was setting over the beautiful fjord, Ray looked at me and said, 'If Carlsberg did fishing trips, this is what they would be like!'

Later on that evening we had the traditional arm-wrestling contest. As always, I lost quickly. Despite some close matches with a couple of my Icelandic colleagues Gordon was victorious in the end – I assume carrying pots and pans around all day does wonders for your biceps. The shame of losing was only exacerbated a couple of weeks later when I received a letter from Gordon mockingly apologising for his win.

From the rivers of Iceland I went with Thordis to the French Riviera to meet our school friends for a yachting holiday in the Mediterranean. For childhood friends this was a dream come true. On the last day we went for a closing lunch party at La Voile Rouge, one of the most famous beach restaurants in St Tropez. It was nothing short of deca-dent. Perhaps it was the Russian billionaire sitting in an actual throne with a crown on his head drinking Chateau Lafite from the bottle. It could have been the waiter dressed up as Spider Man, holding a 20 litre Melchizedek champagne bottle, which he sprayed over the guests. Or it could have been the sight of my Icelandic friends, many in their youth known as the neighbourhood bullies, taking tequila shots with the former chairman of one of UK's largest banks.

Whatever the reason, the thought crossed my mind that this was like the last days of Rome.

Chapter Nine

The Beginning of the End

In early June of 2007 I was sitting on Joe Lewis's superyacht, which was moored outside St Tropez. We were discussing possibilities for working more together. I had met Lewis on a number of occasions and was keen to build a stronger relationship with him. Estimated to be one of the 20 richest people in the UK, Lewis was very comfortable in his own skin. Short and balding, in his early seventies, he was pleasant and calming to be around, although behind that exterior he was as sharp as a nail.

We were talking about the market, and possible opportunities. He told me that for a while he had practically been out of the market, preferring to place most of his funds in cash. In his opinion the good times would come to an end at some point. 'I don't know when or how, I just know from experience that the time will come that liquidity will dry up, it always does.' I didn't disagree. Despite being more than 30 years his junior, I had still been in business long enough to go through a couple of periods of liquidity shortage. But it was still difficult to imagine a major liquidity shortage at the time. The world was absolutely filled with cash, it seemed. Various funds had been raising billions and billions to invest in listed and unlisted shares. Banks were so liquid that takeovers needing tens of billions of bank debt were being seriously contemplated. I told him I thought it would probably be some time until we felt a proper liquidity crunch. Joe shook his head and said 'you'll see.'

Lewis was right, and probably sooner than even he could have imagined. Little more than a month after our meeting, the biggest liquidity squeeze in nearly a century would be upon the world. The notorious credit crunch was just around the corner. As we spoke in the French Riviera, the severe losses being incurred in the US subprime market were beginning to creep to the surface. Banks were about to realise that a significant part of their balance sheets, invested in various securities with subprime exposure, was lost. The losses undermined the faith in the banking system as a whole, and the large financial institutions were suddenly unable to access funding from investors – a scenario few had imagined. With losses eating into their equity, and a shortage of liquidity a fact, the banks gradually ceased to lend to their clients. They didn't even want to lend to each other. Because of the complexity of the various subprime securities, people weren't sure of the extent of the losses. Eventually the total losses were estimated to be in excess of $1.5 trillion. The trust in and between banks disappeared, and consequently the liquidity in the system disappeared too, just as Lewis had predicted. Liquidity is the bloodstream of the financial markets, when it goes away the system starts to sputter. Asset values are estimated to have crashed around 25 percent in the 18 months from the summer of 2007, most major stock markets almost halved in value and shares in financials lost almost all their value. In the autumn of 2007 RBS bought the Dutch bank ABN Amro for almost $100 billion. Twelve months later the value of banks had deteriorated such that for the same amount you could have bought Citibank ($22 billion) plus Goldman Sachs ($21 billion) plus Merrill Lynch ($12 billion) plus Morgan Stanley ($11 billion) plus Deutsche Bank ($13 billion) plus Barclays ($13 billion), and still have a few billion left. The value destruction was unbelievable.

The impact was so severe that even those who predicted the collapse still lost money, as they underestimated how bad things would get. Lewis himself lost close to $1 billion on his stake-building in Bear

Sterns, when the investment bank dramatically collapsed and was taken over by JP Morgan in March 2008. Hedge funds that made enormous amounts of money in 2007 on predicting the subprime crisis, went belly up in 2008 as they failed to foresee how far the deterioration in the markets would go.

***

Even though times were good in the early summer of 2007, we had had a taste of what was to come in the so-called Geyser crisis of early 2006. Until then the Icelandic banks had gone pretty much unnoticed by the international capital markets. None of the banks had any international shareholders to speak of and therefore there were no equity research departments that thought them worth paying any attention to. The rating agencies regularly issued reports on the Icelandic financial institutions, which had been very positive and the ratings had climbed steadily, both for Iceland and its banks. Of course, we were mentioned in relation to our role in supporting our clients in their high-profile acquisitions, but the focus was always on the clients and the company they were acquiring. Nobody seemed to be interested in Kaupthing itself, or the other two banks.

By the end of 2005, however, we had become a noteworthy player in the financial markets, as all the banks tapped the European bond markets aggressively for funds. This led to two very important developments. First of all the credit research departments of various banks began to focus their attention on us, and to issue reports on the banks. Not less important was the fact that, in the autumn of 2005, for the first time so-called credit default swaps (CDSs) were written on Kaupthing. Initially this event was a cause of celebration within our Treasury department. We thought it was prestigious; we were now a significant player in the capital markets. As we quickly found out, the CDSs were no cause for celebration. I don't think anything caused us as much damage in so many ways as the CDS market, and it eventually played a prime role in the collapse of the Icelandic banking system.

Credit default swaps were an invention of JP Morgan, which wrote the first ones in 1997. It is best described as an insurance that investors can buy to compensate from a loss if a particular firm or a bank defaults on its obligations. When the first CDS was written on Kaupthing, the price of this insurance was 20 basis points or 0.20 percent. If you held a million dollar bond, issued by Kaupthing, on which you wanted to insure yourself against a possible default, you needed to pay an annual fee of 0.20 percent of one million, or $2000. The pricing of a CDS was highly correlated to the prices of the bonds you were insuring, of course. If the Kaupthing CDS was trading at 0.20 percent, you would expect the bank to sell its bonds at 0.20 percent margin over LIBOR rates.

The legendary fund manager George Soros wants CDS trading to be banned, and the famous investor Warren Buffet calls them financial weapons of mass destruction. And to many aggressive hedge funds, they were a weapon. The most serious issue was the fact that you didn't need to own any underlying bonds issued to write a CDS on a bank. By paying a small amount of money, in our example $2000, a hedge fund could potentially make one million dollars on the downfall of Kaupthing. That kind of situation is unpleasant for any company but particularly unpleasant for credit institutions, who are dependent on confidence and trust. The word 'credit' derives from the Latin word *credere* and means 'to entrust'. Suddenly you could be faced with funds that had invested tens or hundred of millions of pounds betting on your downfall. By undermining people's confidence, they are promoting their own bet. If a mafia hit man and all his friends bought cheap life insurance on you, would you sleep well at night?

The CDS spreads also became an indicator of a bank's well-being. Media reports would measure a bank's riskiness on the basis of the spreads. In theory that sounds right; in practice there were so many factors influencing the spreads, including manipulation, that it was far from reliable. But it was a great quantifiable measure for the newspapers when they wanted to make the point about how risky the market perceived the Icelandic banks to be.

We quickly felt the effect of the CDS market. The first noteworthy fund to begin trading CDSs on Kaupthing was the massive Norwegian Oil Fund. One of the fund's traders had compared the cost of buying protection on Kaupthing to that of Barclays Bank, which was trading close to 0.20 percent, and came to the conclusion that it didn't make sense that the cost was identical. Apparently he wasn't particularly negative on Kaupthing, he just felt understandably that an Icelandic bank was more risky than the mighty Barclays bank. Thus he shorted a CDS on Kaupthing and went long on a CDS on Barclays. The demand from the fund to buy protection on Kaupthing and the other Icelandic banks began to affect the price in the illiquid CDS market and the spreads on the banks began to rise. In the market people started to take notice.

By mid-November 2005, the first negative credit report on Kaupthing appeared from RBS. It mentioned that the market was worrying about the bank, as could be seen from the CDS spreads. It then went on to list all the various rumours going around in the market about Kaupthing. What followed was a series of credit reports, the most famous from Merrill Lynch and Danske Bank, which were very negative. Some of the criticisms in the reports were fair. They mentioned the low portion of deposits in the total financing of the bank, its dependence on the wholesale markets for issuing bonds, cross ownership with Exista and the size of the bank compared to the size of Iceland. The other banks were also covered, but most of the attention went to Kaupthing as it was by far the largest bank in the country.

At the same time as more and more funds began to short the CDS on the Icelandic banks, some also began to short the Icelandic krona. They had watched the strengthening of the krona on the back of the high interest rate and the ever-growing carry trade. In their opinion, the krona was overvalued, and they began to bet on its correction. One of the noteworthy shorters of the krona was a hedge fund manager called Hugh Hendry, who claimed he heard voices in his head when he was picking investments. In an interview with *The Times* in the summer of 2006 he told the journalist he wanted to become known as 'the man who bankrupted Iceland.' Gradually the krona began to weaken, and by May it had dropped over 20 percent from the beginning of the year.

We had realised that we were under attack at the end of March, when Barclays Capital and UBS brought a group of investors to Reykjavik. During their visit at Kaupthing's headquarters, a presentation by Hreidar almost turned into a shouting match, as some of the fund managers interrupted with exclamations such as 'This is not a bank but a hedge fund!' With its big banking system and small Central Bank, Iceland had clearly been singled out by the hedge funds.

As more and more hedge fund sharks smelled blood in the Icelandic waters the situation turned into a feeding frenzy. Anything Icelandic was under attack. The funds shorted the currency, the bonds of the banks, and even shorted the Icelandic government's CDS.

Suddenly everyone was interested in the little island in the Atlantic. Newspapers from the UK and the Nordic countries began printing articles with headlines such as 'Red lights blinking in Iceland' and the ubiquitous 'Iceland melting.' Our communication people spoke to the journalists, trying to convince them of the soundness of the banks, and pointing to the high credit ratings the banks enjoyed from Fitch and Moody's. But every argument was met with the same question: 'If that's so, how come the CDS spreads are so high!?' Consequently, the articles had further negative effects on the currency and the CDS spreads, which in turn spurred new articles. As the CDSs reached almost 100 basis points, or 1.00 percent (at that time, an incredibly high number), people began to speculate that the banks would not be able to access any funding internationally. Forecasting that a bank cannot fund itself can very quickly turn into a self-fulfilling prophecy. If the market believes you are running out of money, it is not going to lend you any. We were in a vicious circle and the situation was becoming incredibly uncomfortable.

What eventually got us out of the situation was the fact that the world was still drowning in liquidity. Although the European bond market had had its fill of Icelandic bank exposures, money was available from other markets at a price. The circle was cut in the spring and summer as the Icelandic banks issued billions of dollars worth of bonds in the US. The pricing was very high compared to what other banks was paying, almost 1 percent over LIBOR rates, but it was necessary. Although there were other things that contributed to the end of the crisis as well, it was the access to liquidity that was of primary importance. When the market realised that the banks did have access to funds, although expensive, the hope for collapse faded away. The krona stabilised and the CDS spreads narrowed gradually over the summer, though it didn't go down to previous levels. The crisis was over – or so it seemed.

The Geyser crisis did have a big effect on us and the other Icelandic banks. We took various measures to answer the criticism, which strengthened the banks. Landsbanki launched its internet deposit product, Icesave, in the UK and it became an instant hit. They paid comparatively high interest rates and the product was cleverly marketed. In an editorial, *Morgunbladid* wrote that the fantastic success of Icesave would be studied by market researchers for years to come. Within a year they had raised billions of pounds and their reliance on the wholesale markets diminished drastically. We took various actions, including the diversification of our funding base by issuing bonds in markets as exotic as Japan, Australia and Mexico. We sold and distributed to our shareholders the shares we owned in Exista, thereby cutting the cross holding that we had been attacked for. Our private equity investments, which had been criticised, were now done from a fund with third-party investors. Finally we strengthened our liquidity policies, requiring the bank to hold enough liquidity to endure 360 days without any new funding – up from 180 days. The one criticism that we did nothing about read as follows in one of the credit reports: 'Kaupthing Bank with a balance sheet 2.5 times Iceland's GDP is too large to be rescued by the sovereign.'

It has been said many times that the Geyser crisis had been a blessing in disguise, because of the actions we took following it to strengthen the bank. Looking back, I'm not so sure. What the crisis, or rather the fact that we got out of it, also did was to boost our confidence. The same can be said of the other two banks and Icelanders in general.

As 2006 drew to a close, the memories of the Geyser crisis had rapidly faded. In a sign that the international markets seemed to have forgotten about their scepticism about Iceland, Citigroup, Morgan Stanley and Fox-Pitt Kelton successfully executed a €650 million international placing of Kaupthing shares. For the first time, we had a large number of foreign institutional investors on our share register. And despite the scare in the early months, 2006 turned out to be a record year for Kaupthing. Profits almost reached an amazing billion euros.

And until the summer of 2007 on Joe's yacht, it seemed like the good times would never end. The business was doing fantastically well, in the group as a whole and not least in the UK. KSF was blossoming. By word of mouth alone, clients poured in from every direction. Every division of the bank was making good profits, from Asset Finance to Investment Banking.

The newspapers started to pick up on the deals we were doing with many of the high-profile entrepreneurs in the UK. We worked with John Hargreaves on his £817 million successful takeover of Matalan, underwriting over £400 million of debt, which we sold immediately. Our Capital Markets team worked with Sir Tom Hunter on his stake-building in Wyevale garden centres, and Joe Lewis's Enic with the takeover of Tottenham Hotspur. The Banking team financed the Shard of Glass skyscraper project in London for Irvine Seller's consortium, which later sold it on to Qatari investors. We did deals for the Candy brothers in London and Beverly Hills.

We also forged a relationship with Mike Ashley about the time he was floating his company Sport Direct, the largest sports retailer in the UK. We put together his bid for Newcastle football club, and helped his stake-building in Adidas. Mike was normally friendly and cheerful, but frighteningly tough. He never wore a suit when I met with him, favouring jeans and a polo shirt – he completely lacked pretension. Once when we went for lunch I had forgotten to inform my PA that Mike wasn't the typical billionaire, and she booked a table at the Michelin-starred Sketch. When we asked for sparkling water and the waiter brought a cart with five different sparkling waters from equally many countries, I knew we were in the wrong place. Not a gourmet myself, I leaned over to Mike and said 'we should have gone to Burger King!'

Although we were constantly expanding our client base, we continued to do work for our Icelandic clients. In general we and our countrymen were very active in 2006 and early 2007. Bjorgolfur Thor was mainly focused on the delisting of Actavis, which was a big bite, even for him. Baugur's most noteworthy deal was the takeover of House of Fraser, the well-known department store. They teamed up with a number of co-investors, and this time it was Glitnir together with HBOS that provided the funding. Exista's biggest transaction was the building of a 20 percent stake in the Finnish insurance giant Sampo. Kaupthing, on the back of prior successes in building stakes in various financial companies, also made a big investment in the insurance sector. Our stake-building was in Norway's largest insurance company, Storebrand. When shares in financial companies began to drop, these investments in the insurance sector would create substantial losses for both Exista and Kaupthing.

Between 2006 and 2007 asset prices were booming – from companies to property, and even wine and art, but it was difficult to see value. Liquidity was plentiful, and more and more people had become rich as a result of the asset bubble. Nowhere was that truer than in Iceland, where it seemed every other person was a millionaire. Some of those that had come into riches in Iceland focused their attention locally, but most wanted to go abroad and invest. Investing in Iceland, despite the name, was not considered cool. As more people went abroad to invest the quality of the investments started to waver. Hefty prices were being paid for barely profitable businesses in Scandinavia and the UK. Even the more established players were making bad calls which would come to light when the crunch started. This was of course not isolated to

Iceland: most deals done in 2006 and 2007 would turn out to be bad ones, for the buyers at least.

It was probably a bad sign when a couple of the Icelandic business-men began to show interest in football clubs again. Obviously the memory of Stoke City had faded. One of the deals went through, when Bjorgolfur Gudmundsson acquired West Ham United in November 2006. The other deal in which I was involved didn't happen. In June 2007 I had got a whiff that Jon Asgeir was interested in acquiring Newcastle United from Mike Ashley. We got involved, and as I knew the seller and buyer well, I followed the progress my colleagues in the Investment Banking and Capital Markets division were making. Mike had not been minded to sell at the time, but didn't reject the possibility of accepting the right bid.

A local Newcastle businessman was involved with Jon Asgeir and he mainly managed the discussions with Mike. As it progressed Mike felt he was getting mixed messages and got irritated to the point where he didn't want to take it further. When that happened in July, I was in Sardinia on holiday, at the same time as Mike was there. After discus-sions with Jon Asgeir, Mike arranged a private jet for us to fly over to St Tropez where Jon Asgeir was holidaying. When we landed Jon Asgeir characteristically didn't answer his phone. We had limited time as Mike needed to fly back that day. Eventually I managed to track down Jon Asgeir by getting hold of other people who were with him. We sat down, and were able to shake on a deal and fly back to Sardinia before night fell. At this meeting Mike stressed that if the deal leaked, he would back out immediately. On the way back he told me the reason he was progressing with the deal with Jon Asgeir was because I vouched for him. He pointed the finger at me and said 'I am not putting my trust in Kaupthing, I trust you!' That made me slightly uncomfortable.

A few weeks later, Jon Asgeir flew to Iceland on his private jet with one of his closest business partners Palmi Haraldsson. They both ex-ited the plane in Reykjavik airport dressed in Newcastle shirts. When they went through customs in the tiny airport they spoke loudly about the deal, and one of the customs officer alerted the newspapers. First reports claimed that Jon Asgeir's shirt had had 'Owner' written on the back, but the customs officer turned out to be dyslexic. It simply said 'Owen.' Amazingly, Haraldsson, although not admitting to a deal, was quoted in the paper saying 'Newcastle is a great club, with a great manager and I have been a fan for a long time.' I hadn't known that Haraldsson was involved with Jon Asgeir, and Mike had never even heard of him! The news went straight to *The Times* and the deal was dead in the water. Fortunately for Jon Asgeir, unfortunately for Mike as it turned out.

***

In July, just as the credit crunch was rearing its ugly head, I attended a dinner hosted by the business magazine *Euromoney*, and accepted an award on behalf of Kaupthing which had been chosen the best bank in the Nordic region. It was a good example of how far we had come. A couple of years earlier no one would have considered us. And the position of the bank at the time was much stronger than people would think. Our liquidity position was very strong, and the loan portfolio was immensely robust. Mindful of the mini crisis of 2006, we had slowed down our growth and had become increasingly conservative. The media picked up on the high-profile deals we did, the ones with football clubs or high-street chains, but they were a relatively small part of the loan portfolio. The more sizeable part of the loan portfolio were secured loans, for instance Icelandic mortgages and traditional loans to mid-size companies in Denmark.

In 2006 the parent bank stopped doing participations in the market for large leverage loans which, up until then, had been a big source of growth for us. Therefore it did not participate in any of the aggressive, covenant-lite structures of 2006 and 2007, where downright retail deals, like Alliance Boots, were being structured and marketed as non-cyclical, recession-proof health care assets. At that time we were solely investing in assets that were originated and syndicated by our own Investment

Banking team, and we were being quite successful in distributing those assets to the market. There were still a few leverage loans on our balance sheet that were larger than we would have wanted, but those were modestly leveraged and way within the market standard. Those were therefore not a big worry.

The retail and corporate portfolios in Iceland also looked good. Kaupthing had not been aggressive in the domestic market for years and had nowhere near the same market position as our competitors. Landsbanki had been very aggressive in that market and had channelled a large part of their foreign borrowings into the Icelandic corporate sector. At its peak their market share in corporate lending was close to 40 percent – twice ours. We didn't fight aggressively for market share, as the Icelandic corporates were even more in debt than we were witnessing abroad. On the retail side, the picture was even rosier. Although we had initiated the private competition with the House Financing Fund, as house prices rose rapidly we had later pulled back. By the middle of 2007 our mortgage lending portfolio had a loan to value of less than 60 percent. Importantly, despite heavy pressure, we never solicited mortgage lending in foreign currency against our retail clients. The constant raising of interest rates by the Central Bank had fuelled a demand for loans in other currencies where rates were substantially lower. We were, generally speaking, sceptical about the strength of the krona and the volatility associated with the carry traders the high rates had attracted. A large part of the balance sheet of the group was in the various subsidiaries, mainly in the Danish FIH and in KSF. The asset quality at KSF was good, and FIH probably even better. They had traditionally had first priority pledge over the businesses they lent to, while the other Danish commercial banks ranked behind. The other smaller subsidiaries in Scandinavia and Luxembourg also had a fairly robust loan portfolios.

Unlike most of the international banking sector, Iceland didn't have much subprime exposure. What got us into trouble were our loans against securities. This was the big difference in asset quality between

Icelandic banks and the rest of the world: less subprime, more securities. In particular, lending to the various investment companies would prove to be similarly lethal as subprime lending for the American banks. When the credit crunch began, the position was considerably different from how it looked when the banks crashed. In the summer of 2007 most of the largest investment companies, which held strategic positions in the Icelandic banks, were actually being financed by institutions such as Citigroup, Barclays, Commerzbank and Morgan Stanley.

Our lending against securities in the Icelandic market was not aggressive at the time. We presented an overview of our positions against investment companies for our Icelandic board in mid-year 2007, and it did present a picture of almost all of our clients, large and small. Almost all loans had a security coverage ratio of more than 200 percent, and for some of the largest ones the security coverage ratio even went above 1000 percent. So, in general, we felt we were in a strong position by the summer of 2007 and probably better than a lot of our peers. Little did we know that the credit crunch in front of us would practically wipe out most of our largest clients as well as almost the whole of the Iceland Stock Exchange and lead to an enormous deterioration in our loan portfolio.

As strange as it may seem, there were many reasons to believe that the Icelandic banks might come out of the crunch considerably better-off than most financial institutions. UBS in late July published an extensive Credit Analyser, where they speculated in one of their headlines whether the Icelandic banks were a safe haven in the turmoil, pointing to the fact that CDS spreads were rising less on the Icelandic banks than others. One obvious reason was that the toxic subprime assets were almost non-existent in the Icelandic banks. Glitnir and Landsbanki had none, but unfortunately we had invested part of our liquidity in structures that included subprime debt. That was done through an entity we had set up in London called New Bond Street Asset Management. They had managed part of the bank's liquidity and placed in what was considered very conservative securities with credit ratings from A to

AAA. As it turned out, many of those did not merit the high ratings and we needed to write off hundreds of millions of euros when we closed down the positions by the end of 2007. Still the amounts were small compared to the hundreds of billions that were being written down in the international banking system. The Icelandic banks, particularly us, had also tended to have quite high capital ratios. Our aim was to have a Capital Adequacy ratio of no less than 11 percent, and it usually stood at 12 percent, while the large international banks were much more leveraged and maintained the same ratios at closer to the minimum 8 percent. After the Geyser crisis, all the banks had strengthened their liquidity policy, and Kaupthing was indeed very liquid when the storm began to blow up in the middle of 2007.

There were weaknesses, of course. In particular the Icelandic banks' relatively high proportion of wholesale funding (bonds) versus deposits became a big liability. Landsbanki was an exception, with the success of Icesave in the UK. As the crisis dragged on it became practically impossible for any financial institution to issue bonds. The only source of liquidity became the central banks who eventually flooded the market with cash to avoid a complete collapse of the banking sector. The banking sector in Iceland, however, had grown to such a size, that a small and ill-prepared Central Bank could do very little to help. As this became more evident the hyenas looking for the weak animals in the banking herd began to turn to Iceland.

Early in the crisis we made a tragic mistake, which increased attention on the Icelandic banks. For almost two years our focus had been on consolidation, during which we had made no acquisitions. We had looked at a few, but always walked away. The most interesting of the opportunities we looked at was the acquisition of the Nordic investment banking giant Carnegie. They had incurred heavy trading losses and their shares were suffering in the spring of 2007. We saw an opportunity to buy on the cheap a business that could consolidate our Nordic operations and create a strong franchise there. After detailed negotiations with the board and key members of staff we eventually aborted the transaction. It was becoming clear that the troubles they had gone through was resulting in a deterioration of the franchise. There was a lack of loyalty amongst key staff and thus a big risk of people leaving.

Shortly after we aborted the Carnegie transaction, a tempting opportunity arose in the form of the corporate bank NIBC. To simplify, NIBC was a Dutch version of our Danish FIH. This acquisition would further establish us as one of the leading banks for small and medium sized businesses in Europe. It would be by far the largest acquisition in Icelandic corporate history, the total value of the bank, a colossal €3 billion, leading to the balance sheet of Kaupthing doubling in size. One of the attractions to us was that the consortium that owned NIBC, led by the well-known American banking investor J.C. Flowers & Co. would take a large part of the consideration in the form of shares in Kaupthing. The deal hadn't closed when the crisis hit, although no one knew then how enormous it would be. Kaupthing had the option to walk away in light of the market conditions, and seriously considered it. Unfortunately it was decided to renegotiate the deal, rather than walk away, and on 15 August the acquisition was announced. Importantly it was subject to approval of the Icelandic FSA, which was expected to be forthcoming in the last quarter of 2007.

By acquiring NIBC, we were further adding to our main weakness, the wholesale funding. The Dutch bank had no deposits at all, and was therefore wholly funded through securities issuance into the capital markets. A market that was now closing. The market had already picked up on this prior to the announcement of the deal, and this fact coupled with a big subprime exposure had lifted NIBC's CDS spread to almost 10.00 percent – a gigantic spread. Kaupthing negotiated the deal such that the subprime assets were mainly left with the shareholders of NIBC. The belief was that the CDS spreads for NIBC would come rapidly down because of that when the deal was announced. It did. The market began to view Kaupthing and NIBC as the same risk – the NIBC spreads came down but the Kaupthing ones went up. By the end of August our CDS spread had gone above 1.00 percent for the first time since the Geyser crisis. We were the highest of the three banks, but their spreads were also being pushed up. As the end of the year approached the spreads kept climbing, and although that was true across the board of financial institutions, the Icelandic banks stood out uncomfortably. It gradually became clear that acquiring NIBC was a big mistake, also because we needed to raise equity to partly fund the purchase, and by year end our shareholders were less than keen on using their shrinking cash piles. As we considered our options, Hreidar came up with the idea that, instead of Kaupthing acquiring NIBC, we would do a reverse transaction where NIBC acquired us, and the headquarters of the bank would move to Holland. In the end that idea was aborted, but looking back it is tempting to think that this approach could have saved the bank. In the end it was up to the governments and central banks of practically every country to rescue their banks, and unlike the Icelandic one, the Dutch would have been able to do just that. In early 2008, the Icelandic FSA indicated to us and J.C. Flowers that they were not likely to approve the takeover in light of the market conditions. The parties agreed to abort the deal, and in the circumstances we were relieved. But the damage was done.

The CDSs kept on rising. One of the major factors was a matter of supply and demand, rather than serious concerns about the banks. Many of the original buyers of our bonds were funds and conduits, that themselves were now running into problems. Investors were withdrawing money out of the funds, and they became forced to sell their assets. We had issued so many bonds in recent years, creating a significant supply of our bonds, and now demand for them was becoming scarce. Those that had cash, but didn't want our exposure, could buy the bonds at a discount and then buy a protection in the CDS market. That lifted our spreads, which in turn made other bondholders concerned. The rising spreads also attracted the attention of the media and the hedge funds, resulting in further rise to the spreads and we were back in the vicious circle we experienced in 2006. And this time around, the world was not flush with cash.

To further our problems, the Icelandic banks, not least us, had many high-profile clients who began to run into trouble. Their troubles in turn intensified the media focus on the banks. The Icelandic banks were also bundled together, although the CDS spreads differed to begin with. Eventually the situation reached the point that any bad news on one of the banks affected the other two. Not only that but any negative news of any Icelandic business or other known clients of ours resulted in negative discussion and higher CDS spreads for the banks. As the crisis dragged on, the feeling grew that we were all bundled together in a small dingy in the Atlantic while the perfect storm raged. If one fell overboard, the whole boat would rock, increasing the chances of others sharing the same fate.

***

What had exposed to us the full effect of the looming credit crunch were two deals that we were involved in with Robert Tchenguiz. In July 2007, Robert was on top of the world. He was immensely cash rich, and had all but exited his massive stakes in two of the UK's blue chip businesses. If he had done so successfully, he would have been one of the biggest 'winners' of the crunch. He would have cashed out over a billion pounds, and cut his exposure to the falling market almost completely. He would have been a hero. But just as he was slipping through the closing door, the winds of fortune changed and slammed the door in his face.

We were one of a few banks that had financed a 20 percent stake-building for his R20 vehicle in the pub operator Mitchells & Butlers (M&B). The thinking behind the deal was a good example of Robert's innovative mind. M&B had an enormous portfolio of properties from which it operated its pubs. While the company as a whole was seemingly trading at reasonably high multiples of just over 8 times EBITDA, Robert realised that in the current market, the property portfolio was considerably more valuable than the share price implied. By splitting the business into two, a property company (a real estate investment trust) and an operating company, the value of the two businesses would be significantly greater than the market capitalisation of M&B as a stand-alone, integrated business. Property companies were valued at around 20 times EBITDA or rent and that equalled the total market value of the entire company. M&B eventually decided to split out its property assets into a joint venture with Robert's R20 investment vehicle, and to borrow against them. The idea was then for the company to pay the funds out to its shareholders. The amount was staggering, over a billion pounds. If successful, R20 would get paid out in dividend almost the whole of what it had invested in M&B, and still own a 20 percent stake in the operating company, and 50 percent of the property company in a joint venture with M&B.

In early summer it seemed he had clinched the deal. The board had agreed the transaction, and UK banks were lining up to provide the financing. Credit approved term sheets had been negotiated and agreed, and M&B had even entered into enormous interest rate and inflation swap agreements to hedge the loans, at the insistence of the banks. And then the crunch hit. The banks suddenly realised that all credit markets were closing because of the subprime problems, and they wouldn't be able to sell down their loans, as they intended to. They pulled their hand and left M&B with the huge exposed swap position. As the company scrambled in co-operation with R20 to find other sources of financing the swaps began to fall in value. Eventually when it became clear that the credit markets were closed for the foreseeable future, and the company decided to close the swaps, the losses were over £350 million. The stock got a triple whammy. The company had realised an enormous loss on the swaps, the prospect of a big dividend had disappeared, and the market now saw R20 as a short-term shareholder who would need to sell out. The share price dropped like a stone.

Before that, when it looked like his M&B play was working out, R20 began to build a stake in Sainsbury's, one of UK's biggest supermarket chains. Again Robert saw the attraction in the enormous property portfolio. As he began to accumulate a stake that would eventually reach 10 percent, another big player began to do the same. A fund called Delta Two, backed by the Qatari royal family and managed by a former employee of Robert's, Paul Taylor, began to accumulate shares as well. Taylor had seen the same opportunity as R20, and in a matter of months had built up a 25 percent stake in the enormous retailer. In the middle of July, Delta Two submitted a takeover bid for the whole of Sainsbury's. The size of the deal was enormous, over £12 billion. Very few buyers could finance such a large takeover, but the fund was backed by the Qatar Investment Authority, one of the largest sovereign wealth funds in the world. For them, banks were willing to take out their wallet, despite the growing credit crisis. A few weeks later they had agreed a price with the board and were allowed to conduct a quick due diligence exercise. Again it looked like R20 was about to exit successfully and cash out hundreds of millions. But it was as if the Almighty had it in for them. In early November Delta Two announced that they were withdrawing their bid. The shares dropped over 20 percent in one day and eventually dropped to less than half of the proposed takeover price. The official reason for their withdrawal was that 'the required funding and cost of capital has increased significantly, which has adversely affected the investment case.' Other reasons were rumoured to be behind the decision, a rift between Taylor and the QIA or that the banks had withdrawn because of the increasingly difficult market conditions. Whatever the reason, by November R20 was left holding the two large positions, with both exit strategies in the dustbin.

Anyone holding shares in listed companies felt the pain when stock markets rapidly declined as the extent of the credit crunch became gradually clearer. That included practically all the large investment companies in Iceland. They had enjoyed an extended time of rising share prices which, coupled with considerable amount of leverage, had resulted in great appreciation of their share price. Like the US investment trusts in 1929, they would now feel the less pleasant effects of bullish growth and heavy leverage.

Although everyone was feeling losses, it was FL Group which immediately ran into trouble. After their considerable success with the stake-building in Easyjet, and the disposal of Icelandair, they had focused their attention on four main investments, apart from their stake in Glitnir. One was the leveraged buyout of a Dutch company called Refresco, one of the largest juice manufacturers in Europe. We had advised them and Coca-Cola Iceland on the takeover, underwritten the debt and subsequently sold it down. This proved to be a successful transaction, which performed well through the looming economic downturn. The other three, however, were a disaster. Two were positions in listed blue chip companies. They had accumulated around three percent share in the German Bank, Commerzbank, and seven percent share in the struggling American Airlines. They soon realised that a bank and an airline were not what you wanted to own. Financial stocks were plummeting, as the extent of losses became known, and Commerzbank was no exception. Airline stocks were also dropping like a stone, as for a period of time oil prices skyrocketed while the economic outlook looked dimmer and dimmer. The third investment was the acquisition of a Danish low-cost airline called Sterling. The Sterling story was at best incredibly embarrassing and resulted in heavy losses for FL Group. Sterling had been bought from Palmi Haraldsson (Jon Asgeir's partner) resulting in sizeable capital gains for Haraldsson. While the company was losing money, it was sold from FL Group to another company called Northern Travel Holding for what seemed an even higher price. To many in Denmark this was a great example of Icelandic business practices – people selling a worthless asset between themselves whilst escalating the price. But this was of course also frowned upon in Iceland. The turnaround never materialised and in October 2008 Sterling went into administration. In January 2009 the economic crime department of the Icelandic Police began an investigation into the Sterling transactions on suspicion of fraud.

As the investments began to collapse in value, FL Group itself began to run into serious difficulties. It had taken on way too much debt, and was now struggling with maintaining its solvency. Baugur had taken an 18 percent stake in FL Group to further cement their relationship with Hannes's group, which turned out to be one of their worst decisions. In order to recapitalise FL Group, Baugur put in all their property assets in December 2007 and became the leading shareholder with 36 percent of the shares, and Hannes Smarason stepped down as CEO. But assets continued to drop in value, both the share investments and the properties that Baugur had contributed. The share price of FL Group further halved in value between Christmas 2007 and summer 2008, when the company was delisted.

***

Just as the New Year's champagne bottles emptied in 2008, the worldwide crisis began to escalate. Stock markets were crashing, dropping many percentages in single days. Rumours of failing financial institutions were commonplace. Northern Rock had been nationalised in September 2007 and everyone was on the lookout for the next victim. The CDS spreads of the Icelandic banks rose and rose, making us feel decidedly twitchy. The spreads had no practical meaning for us in the sense that neither we nor any other financial institutions were able to issue any bonds. But again it gave the media something to focus on, printing article after article about how risky 'the market' thought the Icelandic banks were. There was little doubt that the hedge funds were actively shorting everything Icelandic. The fund managers came to Iceland and made no attempt to hide their intention. At the trendy bar at the 101 Hotel in Reykjavik, a drunken hedge fund manager visiting with his buddies told one of our brokers, 'These guys think Iceland will be the place for the second coming of Christ, a new financial Armageddon.' And it wasn't just the funds that were negative. Moody's downgraded the Icelandic banks, and both Bear Sterns and Morgan Stanley issued very negative reports on Iceland. There were other reports that were positive, but generally the tone was not flattering. This was beginning to affect our deposits, and the parent company as well as its subsidiaries in Scandinavia were experiencing considerable withdrawals. We hadn't felt that in KSF during 2007, but by the end of the year it was evident that new deposits had slowed down considerably and some depositors were leaving. In the New Year that trend continued.

In January our CDS spreads went into orbit at over 5.00 percent. Following the announcement that we were aborting the NIBC transaction, the spreads tightened and went closer to 4.00 percent, but that was a short-term correction, as the spreads kept on rising. When a relatively small investment company called Gnupur went belly-up in January it was splashed all over the business pages of the international papers. It was a private company set up around the assets of two wealthy individuals, and run by the former CEO of Straumur Investment Bank. It had borrowed too much and fell apart when the stock market continued its crash. Why it was big international news was bizarre, the only explanation being that we were now under constant scrutiny in the media and market spotlight. This further pushed the feeling that the failure of one large institution in Iceland, whether it was a bank or one of the big investment companies, might prompt the market to attack the others – thus creating a domino effect.

Kaupthing had taken various actions to counter the new world of liquidity shortage. Although it should have been done earlier, we had got ourselves out of the NIBC transaction. From the autumn of 2007 there was practically a freeze on the balance sheet. Also, we had started our own internet deposit platform, Kaupthing Edge. In late 2006 and early 2007 we had opened Kaupthing Edge in most of the Scandinavian markets and a couple of the European countries. The biggest market, however, was the UK, and the group was keen on building a platform there. In the spring of 2007 KSF was finalising an agreement with one of the building societies in the UK to outsource the operations of the internet bank to them. This would have meant that Kaupthing Edge would have been up and running in the UK before the end of the summer. Just as we were about to sign the agreement, they backed out. The building society did the outsourcing for Landsbanki as well, and they had become their biggest clients. When Landsbanki found out they were signing with us, they blocked the deal. This was a big mistake; as they failed to acknowledge that we were in the same boat. There was a limited availability of outsourcing parties, and at the beginning of November we were still scrambling to find an outsourcing partner. Hreidar had then lost patience and called me and asked whether KSF could do this in-house. After some investigation and analysis, we concluded we could set it up ourselves and in February KSF launched Kaupthing Edge.

We opted to take the deposits into KSF rather than a branch of the parent company like Landsbanki did with Icesave. We had permission from the FSA to do either. There was some debate about this internally, as in many ways it was more convenient for the group to take the funds into the parent company. The problem was the deposit guarantee schemes. Depositors into Icesave were counting on a guarantee for deposits up to £35,000 (that would increase to £50,000 in early October). They did have a guarantee, but it wasn't a full guarantee from the UK compensation scheme. Rather it was a split guarantee between the Icelandic deposit compensation fund, which guaranteed the first £16,000 and the UK scheme that guaranteed the remaining amount. The issue with this arrangement was that the deposits of Icesave had reached billions of pounds, while the Icelandic fund only had €100 million worth of assets in it. That was typical of a guarantee funds anywhere – they usually only have a very small portion of what they guarantee in available cash. If they need to, they will raise more liquidity from banks, who are the contributors to the fund. It didn't take an Einstein to see that this route wouldn't be as straightforward if Landsbanki had problems. The Icelandic fund would then in theory go to the other banks and ask them to provide liquidity to the fund. The financing need, however, was so enormous that there was no way Kaupthing and Glitnir would cough up the money. This meant that the fund would have to go the Icelandic government for support, but again for them the amounts in question were huge. I was adamant that we should keep the deposits in KSF. To me the Icesave model was not sustainable, and I was always surprised that Landsbanki had been able to run it without interference from either the UK or the Icelandic FSA when the amounts became so large. It was difficult to see how a tiny population like Iceland's could back up those amounts and we always expected that at some point in time the FSA would block further expansion of deposit gathering on the back of a guarantee from an Icelandic guarantee fund. Thus we decided to take deposits into KSF.

In February, when I saw that the media attention was beginning to affect our deposit base, I took some tough action. I decided to shrink the balance sheet by more than a billion pounds. We closed one of our banking divisions and wound down £350 million of loans in a matter of months. Two other divisions were merged. We placed the whole of the Asset Finance business, a total of £700 million of assets, up for sale. This was likely to result in the loss of 200 jobs. Richard Pyman, head of our Asset Finance department, was heartbroken and so was I. But I still felt that we had no choice – the well-being of the bank had to come first.

The media bashing went on and on. Every week there were articles on the Icelandic banks. It wasn't that there was any specific news – we weren't defaulting on our debt or incurring large losses. The underlying trend again were the high CDS spreads – the market's indication that we were likely to fall. This was incredibly frustrating as no one knew exactly what was behind the rises. How much volume was behind the trades? Who was shorting the CDSs, concerned bondholders or avaricious hedge funds?

We weren't the only ones under pressure. Bear Sterns was being hunted relentlessly, their CDSs and their shares being shorted in enormous quantities. Eventually, on 17 March, the Federal Reserve Bank of New York stepped in, and mediated a sale of the business to JP Morgan Chase. The hedge funds had claimed their first victim. The search for the next one began. Iceland stayed in the firing line, and HBOS was singled out in the UK. A couple of days after the Bear Sterns takeover, after intense rumours that the Bank of England was bailing it out, the share price of HBOS fell almost 20 percent within the day. This prompted announcements from the Bank of England and the FSA aimed at quashing the rumour. The market was jittery and we bore the brunt of that. In the run-up to Easter, as in the Geyser crisis, the krona was also being shorted, which resulted in more and more media coverage on the dire straits of the Icelandic economy and its financial system. By the end of March our CDSs exceeded 10.00 percent.

Despite the performance of Kaupthing Edge, and the winding down of our loan books, the frenzy had a very negative effect on KSF's liquidity. Our wholesale depositors began to leave in their numbers, and our counterparties for securities financing withdrew a part of their funding. We had established a liquidity swap arrangement with the parent company; we now drew upon over £300 million to make sure we were liquid. We also informed the FSA that we were operating under code Red of the Treasury contingency plan. I was beginning to feel very uncomfortable, particularly when two UK newspapers printed articles with headlines saying that British savers were withdrawing funds from Icesave and Kaupthing Edge. This was practically the equivalent of saying there was a run on the bank. For Kaupthing Edge at least, this wasn't true – even during the worst of the Easter crisis, we had internet deposits coming in, not going out. We could demonstrate this to the papers, and with the threat of legal action, they both published a correction the size of a classified ad. On top of this it became evident that many of the big lenders to Iceland were jumping ship. We also believed that some of our counterparties were shorting Kaupthing shares for some of this period. But then just when it looked like it couldn't get any worse, it stopped.

There was a considerable PR effort on the part of the Icelandic banks and the government. In an interview with the *FT* Sigurdur Einarsson named four hedge funds he claimed were attacking Iceland. Truth be told he could not be sure they had done anything, but it was intended as a deterrent. He also announced that Kaupthing was considering a lawsuit against Bear Sterns, who he claimed had aided some of their hedge fund clients. Both Oddsson, on behalf of the Central Bank, and Haarde speaking for the government, came out publicly to complain about what they saw as a hedge fund attack on the country and its banks. Oddsson warned that 'unscrupulous dealers' wouldn't succeed in breaking down the financial system. Haarde went further, and threatened that the government would look into setting a 'bear trap' for the greedy hedge funds. The idea of the bear trap had been floated by a journalist at the *New York Times* who cited the example of Hong Kong, where hedge funds, aggressively shorting both the HK dollar and the stock market in 1998, incurred huge losses when the Hong Kong Monetary Authority bought stocks aggressively. The Hong Kong government had followed the advice of American president Teddy Roosevelt, and had spoken softly, but carried a big stick. Unfortunately Haarde spoke loudly, but there was never any sight of a stick. For the time being though, the loud words made a difference, mainly because at the time everyone believed that the Central Bank and government were able to quickly boost the currency reserves of the country. Iceland had practically no debt, and it was assumed that the country had many friends.

Whether it was the threats of law suits, bear traps or the fact that at the same time the world's central banks had begun flooding the markets with liquidity, the attacks ceased. The media attention declined, and the CDS spreads dropped dramatically down to almost 4.00 percent. Despite this, we realised that words needed to be followed by actions for another attack not to happen. Shortly following the end of the Easter crisis, Sigurdur wrote a letter to the Prime Minister, and sent a copy to the Governor of the Central bank, stressing the need for the government to bolster the country's currency reserves by up to €10 billion. Work commenced on raising the currency reserves. The Treasury, advised by the Central Bank and working with JP Morgan, looked to raise funds via a bonds issue in the London market, while the Central Bank began negotiating with a number of central banks to install swap lines which could be used to sell kronur for foreign currency.

When the Treasury did a roadshow in London, the reaction wasn't bad, but the pricing reflected the prevalent climate and scepticism regarding Iceland. Apparently the Treasury was offered close to three billion euros at a price of 1.75 percent margin over LIBOR rates. For a AAA government it was of course a high price, but given the conditions it was understandable. Unfortunately it was decided that this was not acceptable and the offer was rejected. This was a big mistake. Three billion euros would have made a very big difference in dealing with the crisis ahead. Also, a bond offering of this size would have restored confidence in the government. The Treasury's thinking was that the market would look at it as a sign of desperation if they accepted such a high pricing, but in my opinion the opposite was true. As we saw in the Geyser crisis, the key thing was to show that you had access to funds; pricing was a secondary issue. Later JP Morgan and the Central Bank would blame each other for why the offering was not taken.

As for the swap agreements, the central banks of Sweden, Norway and Denmark each signed an agreement with Iceland where they would swap the equivalent of €500 million each for kronur at the request of the Icelandic Central Bank. This was helpful, but what we needed was to get a sign of support from the big three, the Bank of England, European Central Bank, and the US Federal Reserve. Information about dealings with these three is unclear, but what is in no doubt is that all assistance was rejected. Later the Central Bank would disclose that initially the reaction to help had been positive, but that by late April 'the friendly attitude had turned and the three central banks rejected the plea for help. It was obvious that these foreign central banks were acting in collaboration.' This reaction was a major shock to the government and

Central Bank officials. It was dawning on people that we were being left out in the cold, just when we needed help the most.

The attitude of the big central banks can be explained in various ways. I believe that one of the reasons was the internet deposit taking of Icesave and Kaupthing Edge. By this time, the two Icelandic banks had accumulated almost £10 billion of retail deposits in the UK and Europe. I am fairly confident that this annoyed the big banks in these countries no end. They had the large costs associated with their branch network and would never have been able to compete with us on pricing. In my opinion a fundamental change was happening in retail deposit taking via the internet. People made a lot of the fact that we paid high interest rates to attract the deposits, interpreting this as a sign of desperation. But we didn't have the cost associated with taking deposits, such as operating high street branches, like the big clearers had. And we needed to replace bond funding with deposit funding. For most of 2008 we were paying somewhere between 0 percent and 1.00 percent margin over LIBOR for deposits. Our cost for issuing bonds, even in the good times was at similar levels, and for us it was also possible with increased liquidity to buy back our own bonds at discounts of around 20 percent. The £10 billion that was deposited into Kaupthing Edge and Icesave came from somewhere and that place was the big clearing banks. And they didn't like it.

There was also the matter of size. I always believed that if Iceland ran into trouble it would be easy to get assistance from friendly nations. This was based not least on the fact that, despite the relative size of the banking system in Iceland, the absolute size was of course very small. For friendly nations to lend a helping hand would not be difficult. But in the end it was probably true that the small size was a reason not to lend a helping hand. Iceland as such was not too big to fail. The effect of Iceland collapsing would never bring the world economy down. And, I suspect, to many this tiny nation should never even have been an issue on the world financial stage.

As the government was struggling, Kaupthing's position began to improve. The liquidity of the bank was strengthening by the day. In fact it was an amazing achievement how it had turned the liquidity situation around. When it became evident that the wholesale markets were closed to all financial institutions, we had been singled out for understandable reasons. We couldn't raise money by issuing bonds, and in a world where the only source of money for banks was the central banks, ours was so small it couldn't offer adequate support. Because of this belief we had sustained relentless attacks that had an immense effect on our liquidity. We lost many billions of pounds of deposits at both group level and at KSF level. What was underestimated was how quickly we had reacted, by selling assets and rolling out Kaupthing Edge. If we had not suffered the constant withdrawals, the group's liquidity position would have been close to £5 billion at the end of September, with a continuing liquidity of more than half a billion coming in every month. But the continuous attacks were constantly draining liquidity. While we were making good progress in so many areas of funding in the first part of 2008, the outflows countered that. We were like a jeep with its wheels spinning in the mud. Every time we thought we were getting out, we sunk back into the dirt. It wasn't until summer that the tires began to get a grip. But then the jeep was quickly out of the mire and our liquidity position was improving by the day, in particular in KSF, but also at group level. In total the group was receiving almost €800 million of new deposits a month in the summer. Kaupthing's deposit to loan ratio had gone from 36 percent at the end of the first quarter to over 50 percent at the end of September. We were forecasting that the ratio would exceed 60 percent at the end of 2008 with further improvements in 2009.

The profitability of the group was also intact for the first two quarters of 2008, and the equity base was still strong thanks to our hedges against the weakening of the krona. A couple of years earlier, the board of Kaupthing had concluded that one of the biggest risks to the bank was the possible and inevitable deterioration of the currency. The bank's equity was in kronur while 70 percent of the assets were in foreign currencies. This meant that in the event of a sharp devaluation, the equity ratios of the bank would deteriorate to such an extent that it might become problematic. Kaupthing, thus, had hedged the Icelandic krona in an amount equal to its equity, effectively converting the equity base into euros. As the krona crashed, the capital of the bank was preserved and profitability maintained. The weakening krona resulted in very high inflation, which further added to the bank's profits. Kaupthing, like the other Icelandic banks, had much more index-linked assets than liabilities. High inflation improved the profitability materially. In the first half year of 2008 we made profits of over £200 million which was a good performance given the market conditions.

What was still bound to happen was a deterioration of assets, as the falling krona caused problems for clients in Iceland. There were also other underlying problems. One of the large mistakes made by Kaupthing during the crisis was not to cut down the stock market positions of its best clients more aggressively. When they began to deteriorate, the bank continued to support them. There were two likely reasons for this. One was the fact that historically that is what we had always done. Kaupthing was not a fair-weather bank, and through almost 15 years of banking, the lesson had been that if you stood by your good clients, provided the underlying assets were strong, you would come out of it stronger when the markets turned. Unfortunately this crisis was different from anything people had experienced, and the markets never turned. Some shares went to price levels we would never have imagined. And in a majority of cases it wasn't because the companies were not performing; on the contrary. The issue was that, when liquidity is not available, it doesn't matter how cheap a stock is relative to its underlying value, it can always go lower.

The other likely reason for supporting big clients was this overwhelming feeling that everyone was in the same small dingy. The Icelandic banks were so haunted by hedge funds and the media, that they became scared to death of the reaction if any of the big players in Iceland was seen to be collapsing. The damage done when the small

Gnupur fell in January was incredible. What would happen if Baugur collapsed? Because of this scare, the international banks that had been funding share purchases for many of the big shareholders in the banks were able to throw their problems onto the Icelandic banks. In the first quarter of 2008, when the likes of Citigroup and Morgan Stanley began to withdraw their funding to the investment companies, the Icelandic banks were pulled into the situation. They began to refinance loans from the international banks to the investment companies, which I suspect they would not have done otherwise.

Despite this, there was a feeling of optimism in Kaupthing as the summer progressed. With the liquidity position improving day by day, people began to focus on other issues. Some saw opportunities in the big discounts that the bank's bonds were trading at. Despite some of the problems we were facing, we firmly believed that we were making good progress to get out of the crisis. Buying Kaupthing bonds at a discount was believed to be a great trade. The group did a bit of it and also financed purchases for clients. When the bank collapsed this would be heavily criticised.

Another thing people began to work actively on was to find an international strategic investor for the bank. Although the capital ratios were still high, it was important to further strengthen the capital, as the outlook was not rosy in terms of expected asset deterioration. With all asset classes in a worldwide downward spiral, practically every bank in the world was doing the same, and like the others Kaupthing mainly looked towards the Middle East, principally to Qatar. The first approach was to an investment bank called QInvest, which we had helped to finance the Shard of Glass project. One of our people on the property side in KSF, Mike Samuels, knew the chairman well, and initiated the discussions which also involved the son of the Prime Minister. The intention was that they would buy a 20 percent stake in the bank for close to €1 billion. I was pulled out of holiday in February to fly to Qatar with Mike, Sigurdur and Henrik Gustafsson. When we met the chairman, Mike, who had known him for 15 years, greeted him by kissing him on both cheeks. I was right behind Mike, and had to make a split second decision whether it was customary for people to greet in this way, even if they didn't know each other. It wasn't. When faced with quick decisions like this, I have an almost perfect record in making the wrong one, and this was no exception. As I leaned forward and placed two sloppy kisses on the unexpected chairman, I could practically feel Sigurdur and Henrik cringing behind me.

Whether it was the kiss or something else, the interest of QInvest faded, but instead we began discussions with the much larger Qatari Investment Authority (QIA), one of the most respected sovereign wealth funds in the world. Having them on board was a major coup. After lengthy discussions and due diligence, they submitted an offer to invest half a billion euros into the bank, but at a discount to the current share price. After some consideration, it was concluded that this was not acceptable. By then we were becoming very optimistic, as it turned out mistakenly so, and not taking the offer was probably a mistake, although it is unclear whether it would have made a difference in the coming turmoil. The third Qatari attempt was successful, when in mid September Sheikh Al-Thani, the brother of the Emir of Qatar, bought a five percent stake. This further increased the optimism within the bank, and when I heard the news, I began to speculate that Kaupthing would be the bank to 'beat' the credit crunch.

With almost a billion euros of cash coming in every month through Kaupthing Edge, Kaupthing was on the right track. We had come up with a restructuring plan that would be the first step for Kaupthing to move its headquarters out of Iceland. The idea was to have FIH managing the Scandinavian operations, and for KSF to take over all other international operations, including Luxembourg. The next step was to move the headquarters of the bank to the UK. On 18 September I met the FSA to present the plan, which got positive feedback. Any step to get Kaupthing out of Iceland would be favourably met. A week earlier KSF had changed its formal liquidity position from amber to green, reflecting the improved cash position.

We had some concerns, but things were actually looking bright. But then, unknown to me, there were fundamental problems in the financial system that would soon wash onto our shores.

Chapter Ten

The Perfect Storm

Monday 15 September 2008, London

I was flipping through a draft presentation for a Kaupthinking seminar in Paris at the end of the month. My presentation was called 'Beating the Credit Crunch' and detailed how KSF had, over the previous nine months, managed to sail through the immense funding difficulties.

With perfect hubris, it was then that I heard the news. The mighty Lehman Brothers had gone into administration and US authorities weren't going to bail them out. Still, though, I wasn't too concerned about KSF. We didn't have any exposure to Lehman or any trading relationship with them so I wasn't expecting any losses. Our liquidity position was strong and had been improving rapidly thanks to a series of measures we had taken at the end of 2007 and early 2008. Cash liquidity was higher than ever during almost three years of working as CEO of Kaupthing Singer & Friedlander, and was getting stronger every week.

We had just sold our insurance premium finance business for over £100 million, and were in the final steps of selling the remaining part of our Asset Finance business, which would generate an additional £600 million of liquidity. By this time Kaupthing Edge was generating over £100 million in new deposits every week. For a bank of our size, with around £3.5 billion of lending, this was a huge influx of funds. We had practically no long-term debt to repay. Amidst all the turmoil, we were in an enviable situation.

Yet the demise of Lehman wreaked havoc in the financial system. Soon we would begin to feel it. It started with the news that the acquirer of our asset finance business, a subsidiary of RBS, had pulled out of the acquisition after two months of preparation and only a week before scheduled closing. Our liquidity position wouldn't improve by that £600 million we had expected. This was the brunt of our blow from Lehman's fall and we felt two other significant developments over the coming days.

One of our business segments was securities financing, where we financed clients taking equity stakes and in turn financed ourselves with various other banks. This was either done through so-called contracts for differences (CFDs) or instruments called repurchase agreements, popularly referred to as repos. Although technically different, you might say both were a way of financing listed securities. One of the biggest players in that market had been Lehman. Their downfall had a massive impact on the number of banks who had been Lehman's counterparties. These other banks had a big mess on their hands and were not too keen to jump into new deals while they were sorting through the wreckage.

This had a chain reaction in the market. Soon we started to feel some resistance when renewing repo contracts. This wasn't due to any concern counterparties had with us and it was believed (wrongly!) that the market would be back to normal sooner rather than later as the mess would be sorted out. Because we experienced all this slowly, we weren't too concerned.

Meanwhile, on the deposit side of the business things were also changing fast. We had been steadily pulling in Internet deposits since we launched Kaupthing Edge in early February. When Lehman fell and HBOS was rescued by Lloyds the following day, we saw a peculiar development in our depositor base. Where we once had a fairly steady rate of new depositors, around 700 to 800 a day, we suddenly began to see the number of new clients jump to 1500 to 2000 a day. At the same time, there was a noticeable, although relatively small, outflow of deposits where balances were in excess of the £35,000 guaranteed by the UK government. It was clear to me that the confidence in the UK banking system as a whole was deteriorating. In response, savers were starting to spread their bets, putting amounts less than £35,000 into a number of different institutions. Although I suspected that diminishing confidence in banks could not be good news, in the short run we were obviously benefitting from this trend. We suddenly saw our pipeline of deposits go from an estimated £75–100 million a week to around £150 million.

So, despite some of the negative effects from the demise of Lehman, it initially appeared that in the medium term we were going to benefit from a liquidity standpoint. What I didn't fully appreciate was the effect that the Lehman collapse was having on other institutions, in particular the other Icelandic banks. That would become very clear in the next two weeks.

Friday 26 September 2008, London

Thordis and I were drinking coffee, about to board the Orient Express to Venice for her birthday, when I got an indication that something more serious was wrong. The phone rang. Charlie Brook-Partridge who ran our Contracts for Differences (CFD) business was on the line. He was upset when he told me that Deutsche Bank, our main counterparty in CFD trading, had demanded significantly higher haircuts from us if they were to continue trading with us. This was a roundabout way of telling us they were going to lend us less funds against the same security.

Around Easter the same thing had happened, when we had been bombarded with negative press. This time, though, there was nothing happening in relation to the bank and Deutsche knew that our liquidity position had steadily improved. Something had changed but we didn't know what. We continued to debate the new arrangements with Deutsche through Friday, but it was no use. The Germans weren't budging. It wasn't until Sunday morning that I finally got to the bottom of Deutsche's misgivings. Our head of Treasury in Iceland, Gudni Adalsteinsson, called and simply told me, 'Glitnir is in trouble.'

I hadn't realised that Glitnir was in such hot water, but the news didn't come completely as a bolt from the blue. While Landsbanki and Kaupthing had built up online deposit programmes in Europe, Glitnir hadn't. They had done some securitisations, and were working on asset sales, but they were proving difficult. The bank was now struggling to repay bonds maturing in October. Their options were limited to say the least. On Thursday 25 September they had finally asked the Central Bank of Iceland to front them €600 million against various collateral so they could repay the maturing bonds.

For a bank to seek assistance from a Central Bank is a measure of last resort. For Glitnir, with the Baugur-controlled FL Group as the main shareholder, it seemed even worse than this. Jon Asgeir, through the board and CEO of Glitnir, had to come cap in hand to his old nemesis Oddsson and ask for help. When Thorsteinn Baldvinsson, the chairman of the bank, told Jon Asgeir that he was going to seek the assistance of the Central Bank, Jon Asgeir told him 'this is not a good idea.'

Oddsson was never one to shy away from tough decisions. However, despite the governor being a shrewd man, his knowledge of global markets was limited and so his ability to predict market reactions was handicapped though, of course, he had advisors. This was key. Any action taken with Glitnir would be scrutinised and any sign of weakness could undermine the entire Icelandic banking system. Given the relationship history, it was also difficult to know if he could take an objective stance. After having been at war with Jon Asgeir for almost a decade, destiny and the credit crunch had placed Oddsson in a position where he could effectively bankrupt Jon Asgeir's business empire, Baugur. Jon

Asgeir had already taken a number of hits to his large portfolio of assets and if his holdings in Glitnir, one of his largest stakes, were wiped out or seriously damaged, it was difficult to see how Baugur could survive.

Glitnir's fate wasn't solely in Oddsson's hands. The other key decision makers were Prime Minister Geir Haarde and Finance Minister Arni Mathiesen. The leader of the Social Democrats, Ingibjorg Gisladottir, was less involved as she had been rushed into emergency surgery in New York with a brain tumour. Given his past political clout, though, logic suggests that Oddsson must have been in charge. Haarde and Mathiesen had served under Oddsson during his stint as chairman of their party and as Prime Minister for most of 14 years. In this situation, the sheer force of his personality came to the fore.

On the morning of that same day the CEOs of the three big banks in Iceland had met with the FSA in Iceland to discuss the global markets and the banks' situation. Nothing had been revealed at this meeting but Hreidar got the feeling that something was not quite right. Confidentially, he asked Larus Welding, the CEO of Glitnir, 'Are you having any problems? You have to tell me if that is the case.' Larus didn't answer, but gradually during Saturday it became evident that trouble was brewing.

On Sunday afternoon, Hreidar was called upon to meet with Prime Minister Haarde and his economic advisor. He was joined by Adalsteinsson, our head of Treasury. They snuck into the Prime Minister's office through the back door to avoid the journalists who had caught wind of what was happening and had set up camp outside the building. The situation became clearer. The Prime Minister asked them, if the government helped out Glitnir, whether Kaupthing would ask for similar assistance. Hreidar told him that Kaupthing was not contemplating asking for any assistance, and when he left the meeting his impression was that the government would support Glitnir.

Later that day Hreidar was asked by board members of Glitnir whether Kaupthing would consider buying Glitnir's operations in Scandinavia for €600 million. They were obviously exploring avenues beyond central bank support. By that time Hreidar had become concerned about Glitnir's situation. He couldn't see that €600 million in funding would be the end to its problems given the repayment schedule in the coming months. His enthusiasm was limited.

Late that same afternoon he received a phone call from Oddsson. The governor asked him if it was correct that Kaupthing was buying Glitnir's Scandinavian operations. Hreidar declined. Oddsson's comment was, 'that's a pity – I had bought tickets to the cinema tonight'. Hreidar responded, 'sorry, but you're not going to make the cinema – you'll have to sort this out yourself!' Sigurdur and Hreidar became convinced that the government and the Central Bank were working towards a secured facility for Glitnir. The possibility that Glitnir might be nationalised didn't occur to them.

Monday 29 September 2008, London

I was just about to kick off a management offsite at Browns Hotel, when news reached us that Glitnir had effectively been nationalised. My head of Treasury told us that his desk was receiving numerous phone calls from clients asking what this meant for KSF. With my stomach churning, I decided to cancel the offsite. It was more important for people to be in the office, at least until we found out more.

The government and the Central Bank had decided the previous evening to decline to provide Glitnir with secured debt funding. Instead, they decided to take 75 percent of the shares in Glitnir in exchange for €600 million in capital. Sigurdur and Hreidar learned of this development late in the evening and quickly came to the conclusion that this was likely to have a disastrous effect on the whole Icelandic banking system. This route exposed the weaknesses of both Glitnir and the Central Bank and, in turn, would undermine confidence in the other Icelandic banks. If Glitnir was in dire need for cash at this point, it would struggle immensely over the next 12 months to scrape together the €2000 million to repay debts coming due. Sigurdur was so concerned that he called the Prime Minister after midnight and asked him not to go down the route they had planned. Haarde replied, 'the decision has been made, it won't be changed.'

In most other countries the fact that the government was a 75 percent shareholder would have created confidence in the bank. However, Iceland's total currency reserves were only around €2500 million at the time. Additionally, foreign exchange swap lines totalling €1500 million had been set up with three of the Nordic central banks in equal amounts. As would later be revealed, even these low figures were exaggerated. Part of the currency reserves were short-term bills that were due and payable in October and the lines with the Nordic central banks were not committed.

Despite this, the government and the Central Bank thought their actions would be well received. The official line was that this action would provide stability for the Icelandic banking system. Comments allegedly made by Oddsson to key managers of Glitnir on Monday morning imply that he sincerely believed this action would be well received by the capital markets. He apparently voiced his view that the CDS spreads on Glitnir would come down to the same level as the Icelandic government, and he expected the Icelandic krona to strengthen following the announcements. At a press conference explaining the transaction he also said that, even though the shareholders were looking at a 75 percent dilution, that would probably be countered by the fact that the share price would most likely strengthen as a response.

It quickly became evident that the nationalisation was not well received at all. Following a press conference on Monday morning where the Central Bank and Glitnir announced the government's actions, Larus Welding, the CEO of Glitnir, organised a conference call for international investors. Audibly shaken by the events, he failed miserably to build any confidence among the investors. After the meeting, most analysts were negative regarding the 'rescue', and one of the French banks published a report where they argued that the CDS spreads on

the Icelandic government should go up to the same levels as Glitnir's
– not the reverse, as Oddsson had predicted. The CDS spreads on all
the banks skyrocketed and the krona weakened dramatically. Given the
reaction, the government and the Central Bank quickly realised things
had started to deteriorate.

Tuesday 30 September 2008, London

The effects of the foolhardy nationalisation were beginning to be felt.
On Tuesday morning Fitch became the first rating agency to respond.
It downgraded all the Icelandic banks immediately, doubtful that the
government's actions would maintain the stability of the Icelandic
financial system. Both Kaupthing and KSF were downgraded to BBB,
which meant that the banks were on the edge of being sub-investment
grade. Although what I would call a fully fledged bank run only
commenced the week after, the ripples were spreading quickly from
Reykjavik to London.

Watching a wildebeest being hunted by hyenas is a terrifying sight.
Hyenas hunt in packs and single out the prey that has fallen behind.
They gradually drain enough blood until it starts slowing down. The
pack bites and eats the terrified animal as it stands immobile. They
essentially eat it alive. For those who haven't experienced it, and fortunately few have, a bank run has a similar feeling to it. As the news
about the Glitnir collapse began to spread we felt the gnawing at our
heels. Although it was slow in the beginning we could still feel that we
were beginning to suffer small wounds in all areas of funding – retail
deposits, wholesale deposits and securities financing.

Deutsche Bank had taken the first bite the week before when they
increased their haircuts. When that happened, Charlie Brook-Partridge
had quickly contacted a few of the other banks in the market that had
been keen to do more securities financing with us. That Friday, the
initial reaction was very positive. Charlie was actually confident that
he could replace the Deutsche financing with even better terms than

we had had previously. On Monday afternoon, when we were in the process of finalising the financing deals, the tone began to change. They had learned of the Glitnir nationalisation and wanted to understand better what it actually meant for Kaupthing and KSF. Later that week, we had still managed to place a part of the portfolio of stocks with some of the banks, but the haircuts were then getting higher and the amounts lower.

The deposit base also began to show some signs that clients were getting more nervous. We were still getting large inflows of deposits through the Internet with Kaupthing Edge, but the outgoings markedly increased during the week Glitnir was nationalised. Instead of having net positive inflows of £100–150 million, the week ended with close to £50 million net outflow. The wholesale deposit base was even worse. One big client withdrew £100 million on the Tuesday, which was a sizeable amount for us. In general it was also getting much more problematic to roll over deposits. Deposits were leaking out and new deposits were pretty much impossible to attract. As the week progressed, it became hard to deny that the failed Glitnir nationalisation was undermining market confidence in us, the Kaupthing group, and the Icelandic banking system as a whole.

Most disturbingly, from our point of view, on the Wednesday we began to get indications that the parent company was having liquidity problems. Apparently, they were getting squeezed all over the place in the same way as we were and liquidity was being drained out of the group's Treasury unit. The direct consequence was that it would be tough for us to draw on back-up facilities and other lines we had with them, if needed.

It was beginning to look like KSF's liquidity would become worse, rather than better. The cash liquidity had dropped by a few hundred million pounds, so instead of being comfortably over a billion pounds we were suddenly looking at numbers closer to £700 million.

I began to formulate a plan to improve the liquidity by around £1 billion before the end of the following week. We informed our colleagues in Iceland and Luxembourg of the increased margins we were imposing on them in our securities financing unit. If they didn't find it acceptable they would need to scale down their positions. The message I got from the parent company was that they wanted to go down that route. This would generate a few hundred million pounds, if successfully executed.

Additionally, we would sell the bulk of our leverage finance portfolio in the secondary market that existed for those kind of loans, and a few other measures that should enable us to improve our liquidity position. I believed if this worked out we should be comfortably over a billion pounds in liquidity within the next 7–10 days, barring any further deteriorating development.

The next week would be filled with deteriorating developments, but the next twist in the tale came in the form of the Financial Services Authority.

***

Since taking over Singer & Friedlander in 2005, we had enjoyed a very good relationship with the FSA. A few months prior to our takeover of the bank, the FSA had written a very negative report on the systems and controls at Singer following their semi-annual 'Arrow' visits to the bank. They required the bank to hire KPMG to write a report, which would then be the basis for improvements in the bank's control environment. When we took over Singer it had something of a negative image with the FSA. I am sure they were a bit concerned that, on top of all that, it was being bought by an unknown Icelandic bank, and a 37-year-old Icelander was coming in to run it.

Yet, relatively quickly, we managed to build up confidence as they saw the measures we took early on to strengthen the bank. So when the FSA conducted their Arrow visit half a year after the takeover they were pleasantly surprised by the development of the bank and we got a lot of credit for what we had done in a short period of time. Further down the line, they had also been impressed with how we had handled the funding difficulties that arose from being the subsidiary of an Icelandic bank in the midst of a global credit crunch. They were obviously the recipients of regular liquidity reports so they witnessed the positive development of our liquidity situation over the spring and summer in 2008. I also made it a rule of mine always to be very open and proactive with them, so if there were any important developments on our end I would aim to present that to them early on.

In the weeks prior to Glitnir running into trouble we were in frequent contact with the FSA. They had conducted their Arrow visit, a specific treasury review and a credit review in the summer months – all resulting in what we considered positive feedback. Less than two weeks before, I had met with them to discuss the big strategic changes within the Kaupthing group and how it would affect KSF.

I had requested to see some senior people at the FSA, but at the time we must have been low on the priority list, and I only presented the plan to the usual relationship team. At the time they were busy in dealing with the big clearers and what concern they had about Icelandic banks seemed very much focused on Landsbanki and Icesave.

I called our relationship people at the FSA after the announcement of the Glitnir nationalisation was announced and informed them that we were being very alert because of the development in Iceland and the possible affect on KSF. We were already submitting daily reports on liquidity, so they were already up to speed, but we wanted to make it clear that we were concerned. Following that conversation and a further call after the downgrade of our credit rating by Fitch, they asked for a meeting with us on the Wednesday afternoon.

Again it was only the two main relationship people that attended. At this meeting we went through the current situation and recent developments. The following morning they requested another meeting. This time the relationship team was accompanied by a 'swat team' of liquidity specialists. This team was made up of Americans, ex-SEC people who were considerably more aggressive than the people we had met so far. The team leader was a big guy called Matt, aggressive but razor sharp in understanding every detail of the situation. I suddenly felt like I was in a bad cop movie as he shouted 'if you can't give me the correct answers I am going to lose it!' In typical British fashion the relationship team stayed behind after the swat team left and were very apologetic about the aggressiveness of the Americans. I told them they didn't need to be, I understood that they were concerned.

Thursday 2 October 2008, the FSA, Canary Wharf, London

In the evening, we were summoned to Canary Wharf. We met a large group of people, including many of their senior people, led by June Walker[1], who would be our main contact in the coming days. She made it clear that the FSA was now very concerned. The sudden shift in tone began to ring alarm bells. At the end of the meeting, it was clear that we were at the FSA's mercy. They had by this time become extremely worried about what was happening in Iceland and the effect that might have on us. The signs of increased liquidity shrinkage further alarmed them.

Friday 3 October 2008, London

Early in the morning a team from the FSA arrived to monitor our operations. The news that they were there spread quickly, especially as they made little endeavour to cover up their identity, writing 'FSA' in big letters in the visitors' book. Staff became increasingly nervous.

I was in regular dialogue with Walker, trying to figure out what exactly their intention was. At the same time I was in constant contact with Iceland to understand what their position was and what support they could offer. It became apparent that the liquidity position of the parent company was further deteriorating, and it was clear it would be very difficult for them to honour the liquidity arrangement we had

---

1 Not her real name

in place and our calls for increased margins. In the afternoon, as our deteriorating liquidity position became clearer, it was evident that we needed to be able to draw at least £80 million from Iceland for us not to be in breach of our liquidity ratios. Walker made it clear that if that didn't arrive they would close the shop. Despite Kaupthing being in a tight spot, they obliged and transferred £100 million to KSF.

In the following hours and days, we worked hard to save KSF. Mixed messages came from the FSA and the UK Treasury. On one hand I felt that I had a very co-operative relationship with the FSA. Their only priority was KSF so they naturally wanted us to draw on the lines we had with Iceland. It was, however, evident that Iceland couldn't oblige, so I was focusing all my effort on convincing Walker that I could execute the plan we had already been preparing to generate liquidity with minimal support from the parent company. What was confusing was that, while I was getting positive signals from Walker and her people on our plan, her superiors were being very aggressive with the Icelandic FSA. Essentially they said that if £1.5 billion was not forthcoming to KSF from the parent bank on Monday, the FSA would close down the bank. This message was repeated by the UK Treasury through conversations between Alistair Darling and Geir Haarde the Icelandic Prime Minister.

We worked around the clock preparing a plan to get this £1.5 billion. Colleagues in Iceland kept telling us that the UK FSA was telling the Icelandic FSA that, if we didn't have this money by Monday, we would almost certainly be closed down. The work was done in collaboration with the FSA, but at times I couldn't help feeling that the plan was doomed. Eventually Walker called to let me know the plan was OK. For the first time in days, I felt relieved and cautiously optimistic.

Crucially, we needed to wind down the securities financing book quickly and efficiently. Some of the stakes in the book were quite chunky, but mostly very good companies with relatively liquid shares. If the market was decent, you should be able to offload a large portion of the shares in the first couple of days. I went to bed late Sunday evening, praying for a good market in the morning.

Sunday 5 October 2008, Reykjavik

Back in Iceland, our colleagues had been working hard over the weekend trying to persuade the government to abandon the doomed route of nationalisation. Sigurdur, Hreidar and some of my other colleagues in Iceland met with both the Prime Minister and the Central Bank in the days that followed the nationalisation of Glitnir. They tried to convince them that the nationalisation of Glitnir was a disaster and they needed to unravel it at all cost. They argued that, even though Glitnir was the smallest of the banks, it was the one most difficult to save. They had a total of €2500 million in bonds to repay through to the end of 2009, with €1200 million of that falling due in the next four months. On top of that, they had very few options in terms of creating new liquidity and would thus have to rely on the government as its biggest shareholder. In comparison, the figure for Landsbanki was only around €850 million through to the end of 2009. Kaupthing had significant repayments, but unlike Glitnir we were generating considerable amounts of liquidity to fund the repayments.

Currency reserves in Iceland were only a fraction of the amount necessary to refinance. The market knew this, and faith in the Icelandic banks hit rock bottom. Our suggestion was that Kaupthing would take over Glitnir and its assets be split between Kaupthing and Landsbanki, with the support of the government. This solution was presented to Geir Haarde and his advisors on the Friday. The government was, however, very reluctant to unravel the Glitnir transaction, citing both reputational loss and the possibility of litigation. Still, Sigurdur and Hreidar pressed on and during Saturday they had meetings with the CEO and some board members of Landsbanki. They agreed that the only plausible solution would be for the government to renege on the Glitnir takeover and that Landsbanki and Kaupthing would take over Glitnir. In Hreidar's mind it was crucial for Kaupthing's survival to protect Landsbanki, as our retail deposits would suffer greatly if Landsbanki and Icesave were to run into trouble. We were all in the same boat.

In further meetings with the government, the Icelandic FSA and their advisors that followed, Hreidar gave a long and emotional speech, begging them to accept this solution; the only one that could save the country from bankruptcy and thereby ensure a brighter future for all of their children. The message fell on stony ground.

With the benefit of hindsight, at this stage we were probably too late. Iceland's biggest problem throughout the crunch was a lack of trust; the internecine fighting in a small country, full of jealousy, pride and long-held grudges. People only joined forces when we had stepped off the precipice. The CEOs of the three banks didn't particularly like each other and didn't divulge much information. The relationship between Hreidar and Sigurjon of Landsbanki was particularly bad. The governor of the Central Bank didn't trust any of the CEOs and they certainly didn't trust him. To top it all Oddsson wasn't particularly fond of the Chairman of the Board of the FSA and was at daggers drawn with Bjorgvin Sigurdsson, the Minister of Banking. When openness was most needed, meetings were conducted like poker games.

After the meeting with the government, the rest of the Sunday was spent waiting for something to happen. Journalists waited patiently outside the Prime Minister Office and people in Iceland sat in their homes, checking the internet for news. At close to midnight Geir Haarde stepped out of the office and journalists immediately swarmed round him. Like a policeman at a murder scene telling curious passersby 'there is nothing to see,' he told them that the conclusion was that there was no reason for a government action package.

Monday 6 October 2008, London

The worst day in the stock exchange's history, save for the crash in October 1987. The FTSE 100 dropped by almost eight percent. Moving any sizeable amount of shares was nigh on impossible. On top of that the secondary market for leverage debt collapsed. As liquidity evaporated, it turned out that banks across the board were in dire straits.

I hadn't realised how bad it was, probably because, save for our association with Iceland, we had been doing well. That was not the case with most other banks, who had not been as quick in disposing of assets and finding new funding channels as we had. As they scrambled to generate liquidity, the market for secondary loans had become flooded.

The week before, when I had started contemplating selling the leverage loans, the loan desk estimated that we could sell around £200 million worth. They believed this could happen relatively quickly, in a matter of days. On the Monday the price had dropped by 35% from a few days earlier. Even if you wanted to sell at these prices, it was questionable whether you actually could.

That wasn't the only problem. After Glitnir was nationalised, the UK media began to hound the Icelandic banks again, having mostly left us alone since Easter. The weekend papers had been horrendous, with massive speculation about the problems of the Icelandic banking sector. On Sunday afternoon Icesave closed its website. They cited 'technical difficulties', but many people, Kaupthing included, suspected more. It turned out that the FSA had closed down their operations due to lack of liquidity. Kaupthing Edge was fundamentally different from Icesave, in the sense that our deposits were fully guaranteed by the UK government, whilst Icesave was jointly guaranteed by Iceland and the UK, but we were still the closest comparison. This began to have an effect on our depositors. Over the weekend, the money began to pour out. This continued on Monday, when the Icesave website remained closed.

At the same time many wholesale depositors were calling demanding their money back. Even though we wouldn't break deposits (i.e. release funds before maturity), maturing deposits were haemorrhaging out. And it wasn't only on the deposit side we were suffering. Our counterparties in pretty much all parts of our business were closing lines. CFD and equity repo lines were closed down and many brokers were refusing to deal with our Capital Markets desk. Our clearing bank, Barclays, refused to repo Treasury Bills for us until the FSA called in a favour. They still closed staff's corporate credit cards – cards were declined when people tried to pay for client lunches.

We were being snapped at from all directions and blood was leaking everywhere. We were still running, but barely so, and the pack of hyenas was growing bigger.

The Monday evening and night was spent with people from Barclays who were looking to acquire KSF. This had been initiated by the FSA and originally I believed this would not be a bad thing, given the situation we were in. If Kaupthing was to survive in any form it was essential that neither of the big subsidiaries, KSF or FIH in Denmark, would go into administration, so a sale was not something we ruled out. We agreed to work with Barclays through the night to enable them to evaluate what they were willing to pay for the business. I assumed that their interest was primarily for the Asset Management business, or more likely Kaupthing Edge. The amounts the internet platform had been generating in new deposits were so large, they would even be meaningful for a bank the size of Barclays.

As we went through the night it became clear that Barclays were not talking about the sale of shares in KSF, and had limited interest in any operation, whether it be Brokerage, Asset Management or Treasury. What they were aiming for was to do a quick asset purchase at a big discount. This would of course have thrown KSF into administration and thus led to the immediate downfall of Kaupthing. If this route had been taken, the UK Treasury would have been the biggest creditor in the administration, since they guaranteed the bulk of private client deposits. Thus any discount given to Barclays would be to a very large extent be borne by the Treasury. The price discussion therefore didn't involve Kaupthing at all, rather it was a discussion between Barclays and the UK Treasury with the involvement of FSA. In the end they couldn't agree. Barclays had offered to buy the assets with a 50–75 percent discount, a ludicrously low price for what was essentially a robust loan portfolio. The Treasury didn't agree to the plan and Barclays went away empty handed during the early hours of Tuesday.

Monday 6 October 2008, Reykjavik

The desperate scenes taking place were almost identical to the panic engulfing us in the UK. Credit lines and settlement lines with international banks were being cut all over the place and deposits were being withdrawn. The panic had also extended to the public. Long queues formed outside branches of all the banks as even Icelanders queued up to take out cash and stow it under their pillows. One of our private banking clients in Iceland withdrew more than a million pounds in cash from the bank. He practically needed wheelbarrows to get it all away. The police got concerned about this development and warned people against keeping too much cash as they risked tempting burglars to their homes. The banks were almost running out of cash. Getting currency was not possible. Fights erupted in one of the bank branches, when Polish workers were refused as they tried to exchange their salaries into euros.

Trading on the Iceland Stock Exchange was halted due to all the uncertainty. By then it was clear to the government that Landsbanki had run out of liquidity. They must also have come to the conclusion that their takeover of Glitnir was dead in the water and they couldn't support it. Kaupthing seemed to have a fighting chance, although we were in a difficult spot. Not only was our liquidity being drained, but the collapse of Glitnir and Landsbanki would directly and indirectly result in substantial asset deterioration and wipe out a big part of our equity. So capital had become an issue as well.

After it became clear that Landsbanki wouldn't survive, Hreidar and Sigurdur's approach to the government took a different course. Now the plan was for Kaupthing to take over Glitnir in such a way that it would recapitalise the bank – this time without the involvement of Landsbanki. It would be done in arrangements similar to those that had been used when Washington Mutual in the US was placed into receivership. There the banking subsidiaries were immediately sold out of the receivership to JP Morgan and creditors left behind to claim their funds from the remaining assets. This solution was aggressive, but it was the only way to prevent a total collapse of the banking system. Gradually, the government seemed to be coming round to the idea.

Of course this didn't solve the liquidity issue for Kaupthing; cash continued to drain out. Through pressure from the Prime Minister, the Central Bank agreed on the Monday to lend €500 million against the shares in FIH, our Danish subsidiary. This was a tremendous relief at the time, a sign that the government was focusing its support on us. But the next step taken by the government would change all the rules.

It is said that everyone of a particular age in America remembers where they were when they heard that John F. Kennedy had been killed in 1963. Icelanders of my generation will remember where they were when they heard Geir Haarde's address to the Icelandic nation on national TV on the Monday afternoon. Everyone was aware of the crisis, so it wasn't difficult to guess what he would be talking about. Factually, he described the difficulties facing the banks, and the extreme measures that would be needed to ensure that the nation wasn't bankrupted. He also seemed to despair, making emotional pleas that people go and be with their families and comfort their children. When he finished, exclaiming 'God save Iceland,' every single person on this little island in the Atlantic Ocean stared at the TV screen like rabbits staring into the headlights of an approaching truck.

The extreme measures came in the form of new legislation on financial institutions that would become known as the 'emergency law'. The key components were that the Icelandic FSA was given powers to take over financial institutions in trouble with wide discretion, and deposits were given priority over bonds and other claims. In a separate declaration, the Icelandic government guaranteed all deposits in Icelandic banks in Iceland.

In practice the Icelandic FSA could take over a bank and effectively split it into two banks, usually referred to as 'new bank' and 'old bank'. The new bank would be best described as an Icelandic savings bank. It would take over all deposits of Icelanders and all domestic loans and assets. The government guaranteed the deposits of this new entity and committed to inject equity into it. This would be an operating entity, servicing Icelandic customers through its branch network.

The old bank, run by a Resolution Committee formed by the FSA, would take over all other assets and liabilities and would not be operational as such. The main assets were non-Icelandic loans and other international assets, in addition to some Icelandic assets that were 'loss likely'. This entity was immediately in administration and the main creditors were mainly international bond holders.

The legislation had been worked on day and night during the weekend and up until it was put through parliament on Monday afternoon. Both the law and the way it was implemented was ruthless towards most international creditors. Deposits were given priority over bonds and other claims. Understandably, the bond holders were furious.

It's commonly thought that deposits generally rank higher as claims than bonds, but in fact they always rank equally. Deposits, however, are usually guaranteed by deposit funds or even directly by governments. In case of a bankruptcy the cost of compensating depositors against losses are then borne by the fund or the government. The difference in Iceland was that the bond holders would in fact absorb the cost of saving the depositors. Put bluntly, the bondholders were getting screwed.

On the back of this legislation the Icelandic FSA took over Landsbanki on the Monday evening and then Glitnir the day after. After this, Kaupthing was the only hope that something might rise from the ashes of the Icelandic banking system. Although it was squeezed it was now getting support from the Central Bank. The subsidiaries were feeling the heat too, but in Scandinavia they were getting support from local authorities. Kaupthing Luxembourg and Kaupthing Singer & Friedlander in the Isle of Man were struggling as depositors rushed to take out money, but they were not big enough to cause the whole group to fall. KSF had become the key to survival. If it did not survive, clauses in the parent company's loan agreements, which stipulated that the administration of FIH or KSF was an event of default, would be triggered. That would be the end of Kaupthing.

Tuesday 7 October 2008, London

On the Tuesday morning, after events in Iceland became clear, yet more liquidity poured out. Lines with other financial institutions were cut to such a level that both our asset management business and capital market units couldn't operate in a normal fashion, unable to settle trades. By the middle of the day, my hopes of survival were diminishing every minute as the only news I got was bad news. Then suddenly there appeared to be a ray of hope from the East.

In a surprise announcement, the Central Bank of Iceland claimed that Russia had agreed to extend a four billion euro facility to Iceland. The press statement was very specific, saying that the term of the loan would be 3–4 years and interest would be 0.30–0.50 percent over LIBOR. If true, this would increase the likelihood of our survival dramatically. The Central Bank would be in a position to support Kaupthing with liquidity and, suddenly, we were eyeing a renewed chance of survival.

Unfortunately the Central Bank had completely jumped the gun. Later in the day they sent out a correction where it was emphasised that Russia had only shown willingness to entertain discussions to consider a possible loan to Iceland. The offer was as firm as jelly, and in the end nothing happened. In the meantime, some interesting stories spread about Russia's interest in lending money to Iceland. The most popular opinion was that, in doing so, they were planning to take over the old US naval base in Keflavik, Iceland, which the US had deserted a few years earlier.

Another possible lifeline showed itself later in the afternoon. By that time, after we realised no Russian money was likely to appear any time soon, we had all but given up on saving KSF as a fully owned subsidiary of Kaupthing. The focus shifted to finding some way of disposing of KSF so it wouldn't fall into administration and effect the downfall of the whole Kaupthing group. At the time we still believed that some form of survival would be possible for Kaupthing with the assistance of the Icelandic government, if we could avoid KSF going into administration. Hreidar picked up the phone and called Ravi Sinha at J.C. Flowers. His suggestion was that NIBC would acquire KSF for £50 million, less than 10 percent of its equity value. A meeting was set up late in the evening with Ravi and three of the key executives of NIBC to go through a presentation of KSF and its financials. Ravi had been positive about the likelihood of doing a quick deal on the phone with Hreidar. I, though, was quite sceptical. The management of NIBC would have to make a quick decision on a big acquisition with limited information, so their support was not obvious. I went through the presentation and hoped for the best. In some ways, it seemed like it could be a good transaction for NIBC. There were various synergies, and the change of ownership should have stopped the outflow of deposits and even started bringing money back in – important for NIBC, which had no real deposit platform. After hours of presentations and discussions it became evident that they wouldn't be able to conclude a deal quickly enough. We were fast running out of options.

What could save KSF and give Kaupthing a fighting chance was support from the UK authorities. Although KSF was a subsidiary of an

Icelandic Bank it was a UK entity. In Sweden, the Central Bank had stepped in to support Kaupthing there and the Danish authorities had supported FIH in the same manner as it had supported other sizeable Danish banks. The way the UK authorities would handle KSF was key to any possibility of survival. If the will was there, they could very easily step in and save the bank from administration. They had done that previously in various forms with Northern Rock, Bradford & Bingley and HBOS.

Diplomatic relations between the UK and Iceland, however, were a ticking time bomb. Developments in Iceland had been closely monitored by the Treasury and the FSA for a long time. Until the final week, the spotlight had been focused not on KSF, but on Landsbanki and Icesave. By the middle of 2008 they had accumulated £4.5 billion of deposits in the UK, more than 60 percent of Iceland's GDP.

There had been a dialogue for some months between Landsbanki, the FSA and Icelandic FSA in Iceland to try and convert the branch into a UK entity. By the end of September those discussions had come to nothing and all of Icesave's deposits were jointly guaranteed by the UK and the Icelandic fund. When Glitnir stumbled and concerns about the Icelandic banks grew, the issue of the deposit guarantees suddenly became a focus point for the UK Treasury and the FSA. There had been a meeting some weeks earlier between Alistair Darling and Sigurdsson, the Minister of Banking, where it seems that the UK Chancellor got some assurances that the Icelandic government would back up the deposit guarantee fund. However, when the emergency legislation was put in place in Iceland the awareness of UK authorities was raised and they became suspicious that Iceland was not going to back up the fund. The declaration said clearly that only deposits in Iceland were directly guaranteed by the government, but that didn't apply to deposits in overseas branches. The legislation, followed by conversations between Alistair Darling and Arni Mathiesen on Tuesday, and probably comments made by David Oddsson on Icelandic television on the Monday evening, was interpreted by the UK government in such a way that the Icelandic government was not going to compensate depositors in Icesave. This would result in a diplomatic war between Britain and Iceland over the following days.

To be fair it was never completely clear whether the intention of the Icelandic government was to back up the guarantee fund or not. Reading transcripts of the conversation between Arni Mathiesen and Alistair Darling, Mathiesen doesn't clearly say that Iceland will guarantee the deposits, but neither does he say clearly that it won't. On Icelandic television Oddsson said that the authorities would not pay the foreign debt of the Icelandic banks, but he wasn't talking explicitly about Icesave and could have been referring to the fact that foreign bond holders were being left behind in the 'old banks'. What I suspect was the reason for the vagueness was that it was unclear what the liability on Icesave would be after assets of Landsbanki had been liquidated. If after the sale of assets the liability that should be borne by Iceland was £500 million, would they have shouldered that liability? Very likely. If it was £4 billion, would they have accepted it? Almost definitely not, if they could avoid it. What was clear was that the Icelandic government had no ability to pay out in cash the billions of pounds it needed to immediately pay out the depositors in Icesave. They would at least have to borrow it initially from the UK government and pay it back over a long period of time.

The government's responsibility to pay up was far from obvious. The fund in Iceland did not have an implicit government guarantee and the agreement on the European Economic Area, which the fund is based on, only stipulates that governments should establish a guarantee fund holding cash the equivalent of one percent of deposits. This the Icelandic government did, so it was fulfilling its duty according to the agreement. One would also have to ask, if deposits were the explicit responsibility of the government, why establish a special fund?

Wednesday 8 October 2008, London

The British government was furious when it became apparent that Iceland wouldn't or couldn't back up the fund. In a television interview Alistair Darling said: '…it really is extraordinary when you get a country like Iceland which is basically defaulting on its obligations and we are going to pursue them.'

They didn't take long to act. The Anti-Terrorism, Crime and Security Act was brutally used to freeze the assets of Landsbanki and the Icelandic Central Bank in the UK. Fury raged across the Atlantic. The British public was furious at Iceland and its banks, which they viewed as stealing deposits from British savers. The public in Iceland in turn was appalled that the UK had used a law, established to fight terrorists, against a small, friendly nation in dire straits. Later people filled the internet with picture of ordinary Icelanders, often children, usually holding up signs reading something like: 'We are not terrorists Mr. Brown!'

So, it became clear that the UK authorities were far from minded to assist Kaupthing and KSF. We suggested a number of things that would have saved KSF and possibly Kaupthing, at least in some form. I asked the deputy head of the FSA whether the Treasury or Bank of England could provide us with liquidity against our Asset Finance loan book, which in a securitised form had been approved as eligible security in repo transactions with the Bank of England. The answer was no. Sigurdur and Hreidar sent a letter to Hector Sants, the head of the FSA, where they requested that KSF be included in the £50 billion government recapitalisation scheme that was being set up for UK financial institutions. There was no answer. It's clear that action could have been taken, 700 jobs could have been saved, and the deposits of individuals, local authorities, charities and businesses safeguarded. Instead, the government chose to distance themselves from KSF, portraying it as an 'Icelandic bank' in the media. In an environment where governments and central banks had gone from being the lender of last resort to the lender of only resort, we were caught between two governments: one that couldn't help, and another that didn't want to.

***

June Walker called me on Wednesday morning saying we needed £300 million of liquidity from Iceland if they were to allow us to continue to operate. When I spoke to Hreidar, he was adamant that Kaupthing could provide us with more liquidity, although they were in a very tight situation. A couple of hours later, news of the sale of Kaupthing Edge to ING appeared on TV and the Chancellor of the Exchequer announced prematurely that KSF was in administration.

We set up a teleconference with the FSA at midday. There we voiced our dissatisfaction that the Treasury had sold Kaupthing Edge while we were still in discussions with the FSA about further liquidity injections from the parent company. The trust had gone and Hreidar informed them that there would be no funds coming from Iceland. We asked again about the possibility of KSF being included in the new recapitalisation scheme. The answer from Hector Sants was brief: 'Those funds are not for you.' The FSA wanted to place KSF into administration and requested that the board cooperate during that process. Without other options, we duly agreed.

Years ago, I read an article on why men don't cry. One of Iceland's best footballers was asked this question. He responded that it was because crying was a sign that you had given up. A man would only cry if he had explored, without success, all avenues of sorting out or fixing whatever problem or issue he was dealing with. And that's exactly how I was feeling as I sat by myself in the office. It was all over. No solutions, no one to call, no brilliant ideas. For the first time that week, a lump rose in my throat. I wanted to get out of the office, out of the building and go home. But I couldn't. I had to wait for the administrators and help in their meeting with the management of the bank. Our relationship team from the FSA also wanted to come personally and give me the administration order.

I spent the next four hours holding back the tears. When colleagues came to see how I was doing I just stared down the floor. Not because I was angry or upset, I just knew I would burst into tears if I opened my mouth. Neither could I call my wife, my parents, my kids – I knew I would break down in seconds when I heard their voices. I couldn't even keep face when our contacts at the FSA showed up and delivered the administration order. My voice cracked and my eyes went moist so I quickly said goodbye to them and hurried back to the office.

In the afternoon I went home. My 13-year-old daughter Margret and 3-year-old son Atli were there and immediately as I saw them, I broke down and cried uncontrollably. My daughter, who knew what had happened, broke down as well and cried in my arms. Atli stared big eyed at us sobbing and repeatedly asked me what was wrong. For the next weeks he regularly reminded people of the time when dad had suffered an accident at work.

By the evening, I almost felt relieved that it was over. I convinced myself that things in Iceland couldn't be so bad as the hype suggested.

Unfortunately, the nightmare was just beginning.

Chapter Eleven

The Hangover

My BlackBerry woke me on the morning of 9 October. I had two new e-mails. One from Kaupthing, Singer & Friedlander on the Isle of Man, saying they were in administration, and another from Kaupthing Luxembourg, who had suffered the same fate. Those were practically the only e-mails I received that day. It was as if the world had ground to a halt or was, at any rate, ignoring me. Even the spam offering me Viagra stopped.

As I lay in bed, reality gradually began to sink in. My world had been turned upside down. I was now unemployed and Kaupthing had been taken over by the FSA in Iceland. The whole banking system of my homeland had crashed, and although it wasn't clear how bad a shape the country was in, it was clearly in a mess. Its reputation was in ruins, and a political war was brewing with the UK and others.

My personal finances were in tatters. In the havoc of the last two weeks I had completely forgotten about them. Despite being far from frugal, I had still inherited some of my mother's ability to prepare for the worst, and didn't spend more than I earned. In August, however, I had placed my funds on deposit in the bank and also bought some Kaupthing bonds. This was really a combination of optimism, because we were doing very well at the time, and romantic attachment, since I felt that I should put my money where my mouth was. But now pretty much all of my funds were trapped and, thanks to the emergency law, my Kaupthing bonds were practically worthless.

In the week that followed I didn't want to get up in the morning. I'd lie in bed almost until noon. When I pushed myself to go out for a run, I had to give up after a mile and walk back to the house. At the gym I was half-heartedly lifting a fraction of the weights I normally do. Only the fact that I had to go back to the bank for the grim job of assisting the administrators meant that I forced myself to shave. Gradually, though, I managed to pull myself out of the gloom. Not because things got better – they didn't – but, as I said before, if you can get used to singing to billionaires on a yacht, you can also adapt to the opposite, unemployment and opprobrium.

***

Ordinary people in Iceland were also in a state of utter shock after the financial meltdown had struck the country like a tsunami. The global credit crunch had now claimed its first national victim, not just a bank or another insurance company this time, but an entire economy. The country's entire banking system had collapsed like a house of cards within the space of a week. The fairy tale was over and Icelanders felt the accusing eyes of the world upon them.

News networks from around the globe suddenly turned their cameras and microphones on our island. The crash, it seemed, was a sensation and Iceland was prime-time news. Discredited doom-mongers, who had warned of Iceland's imminent demise, found themselves being reinstated and swiftly sending their crumpled suits to the dry cleaners. Now they could gleefully wag their fingers on chat shows and say 'I told you so.' They had prophesised that Iceland would face its day of financial reckoning, and here it was, live on TV. Iceland hadn't enjoyed this amount of international media coverage since the Reagan–Gorbachev Summit of 1986, although 'enjoyed' was not the appropriate word. Terrifying as this may have been to the local population, for macroeconomists and theorists Iceland's meltdown suddenly became a fascinating case study and laboratory. Observers swooped in like vultures, salivating at the prospect of being able to capture the implosion of a modern western economy at first hand. But for the people on the ground, who had suddenly been catapulted into this new uncertain reality, this was, of course, no academic exercise. The all-pervasive mood among the population was one of confusion and disorientation. Many pushed themselves through the motions of business as usual in a state of numbed stupor, secretly nurturing the hope that this might all still turn out to be a short-lived misunderstanding.

Only days after the bank crash, none other than Sir Philip Green flew in to Reykjavik Airport on his private jet, looking to buy up some of the UK assets of Baugur, which were now effectively controlled by the failed banks. The UK newspapers reported that he might be spending up to £2 billion to buy the various high-street companies that were controlled by the banks. No one who knew Green believed those numbers, and they were nowhere close to reality. The newly formed resolution committees of the banks weren't sure if he was joking when he offered between 10 and 15 percent of the book value of the various assets. His offers quickly leaked to the local press, and people felt even more humiliated.

Green wasn't the only one – the hotels in Reykjavik were full of various fund managers, offering pittances for the international assets of the banks. They knew that many of the companies that were owned by Icelanders or funded by the Icelandic banks were under intense pressure from other creditors and suppliers. Many top companies almost went bankrupt when their credit insurance was cancelled and suppliers stopped extending credit to them. Eager buyers for the businesses played the scare card: if the banks didn't sell quickly the Icelandic ownership would result in bankruptcy. There was no hesitation in trying to empty the wallet of this wounded nation as it lay on the floor. Fortunately, the resolution committees of the banks took a deep breath and few fire sales were conducted. They supported the companies and maintained value.

Iceland's greatest vulnerability was, of course, the krona, the smallest floating national currency in the world. The bank crash had, in fact, been partially caused by a currency crisis. Kaupthing didn't actually run out of liquidity – it had almost 100 billion Icelandic krona when it ceded control to the FSA. But they couldn't be converted into other currencies. The government's main task in the days immediately following the collapse consisted of trying to keep the banks' payment systems operational in order to avoid panic. In the drama of those early days, it felt as if the national economy had been rushed into intensive care and was now breathing on a life-support machine. Fortunately, the heart was still beating, but foreign banks were refusing to trade the krona. No one wanted to touch it with a barge poll.

The Central Bank became Iceland's sole lifeline to the outside world – i.e. the only entity that could trade currency. But it soon became clear that the bank's IT system was a relic from the Stone Age and dealers had to run between floors brandishing yellow slips of paper every time they needed to settle trades. The bank was also struggling because it didn't have enough experienced foreign exchange staff. Eventually some of the foreign exchange brokers who had worked for the now defunct commercial banks were seconded to the CBI.

Although the situation was often exaggerated in the foreign media, Icelanders began to fear shortages of various imported goods, but these were mainly fed by rumours. One day it was reported that fuel was on the point of running out on the island and, on the next, that there had been a stampede for the pasta on the shelves in the supermarkets. Relatives and friends from abroad started phoning home to make sure no one was starving. People feared that Iceland was about to slip into the old Eastern bloc scenario of black and white movies, rations, endless queues and food shortages. Foreign journalists called their colleagues in Iceland, and excitedly asked 'what do you see when you look out the window!?' expecting an angry mob pillaging a supermarket.

The situation was a far cry from the drama portrayed by the international media, but some Icelanders travelling abroad at the time did get into some very awkward predicaments. Because of the payment problems, their credit cards stopped working for a few days, and became about as valuable as Monopoly money. Students who had been using Icelandic credit cards were suddenly unable to buy food and other basic necessities. Two years earlier Iceland had been the wealthiest nation in the world; now no one would accept our cards and currency. Some Danes took particular pleasure in the misfortune of their former colony. In Copenhagen, two girls were thrown out of a store. Not because their credit cards didn't work, but simply because they were Icelandic. The Danish gutter press, *Ekstra Bladet*, organised a mock collection for the 'poverty-stricken Icelanders' outside the offices of the Baugur-owned magazine. They were collecting money, they said, for the land of tycoons where everyone drove around in Range Rovers and wore golden Rolexes.

Meanwhile, across the water in the UK, there was less mocking and more anger. Icelanders living in England slipped on dark sunglasses and kept a low profile. Some pretended to be Finnish. The Icesave scandal had hit the front pages of the national tabloids with headlines like 'Give us our money back'. About 300,000 Britons held Icesave accounts and were now very anxious about the fate of their savings.

Until that moment, Icelanders were used to being admired – a plucky little country that punched above its weight. No one could feel threatened by this small nation, the world admired it like a poodle performing tricks. Even an international conflict like the Cod War with Britain felt more like a puppy that was biting at one's leg. The UK couldn't really use force against such a small country – that would have been like kicking the poodle in front of everyone. But now it was different. The poodle had turned into a vicious little mongrel, which had bitten the hardworking savers in many countries. And it now looked like the whole thing had been a scam. Most people's instinct now was to kick the nasty creature, and for Icelanders to face that kind of an attitude was shocking.

***

Shock quickly turned to anger. There was little interest in explaining the Icelandic crash in the context of the global credit crunch. As economic links were temporarily severed with the outside world, much of the population narrowed its focus to finding the culprits at home. Entrepreneurs, bankers, politicians and governors – no one was spared in the blame game. The only option for those that were blamed was to point the finger at someone else. Thus began a massive Old Maid card game. Whoever held the queen of spades became the focus point of the media and got a pummelling until they in turn managed to pass the card on to someone else, and so on.

The spotlight fell on Glitnir first. It had been the first bank to get into trouble, triggering off the series of events that precipitated the collapse of the banking system. But it didn't take long for the Icelandic public and the media to turn their anger at Landsbanki. When Landsbanki had expanded Icesave in the UK, and negativity about the Icelandic banks began to mount, I was quite surprised to see how stable their deposit base was and that it was growing. People were obviously counting on the guarantees of the UK and Icelandic deposit insurance fund.

After the collapse, it quickly became clear that the governments of the UK and Netherlands, the two countries where Icesave had raised a total of around £5 billion in deposits, were not going to allow Iceland to slip away without paying the bill. It suddenly dawned on people that Icesave had effectively pledged the nation as collateral. But no one knew how great the damage would be and, more importantly, how much of the bill would have to be footed by the public. The former heads of Landsbanki stuttered reassurances, saying they were hopeful that the bank's assets would be sufficient to cover the Icesave deposits, but others estimated the losses at over £2 billion. For weeks on end, the only topic of conversation seemed to be Icesave or 'Iceslave', as it was now half jokingly referred to.

Initially, Kaupthing was spared the blame. To many, we were a victim of the collapse and had been dragged down with the rest of the system. People were confused about what had happened in the UK and many people, including members of parliament, thought that Kaupthing had been taken over on the basis of the terrorist law. We weren't spared for long. Eventually, we probably came in for some of the most stinging criticism. The media began regularly to publish negative news on Kaupthing shortly after the collapse.

In the minds of the public and the media, loans to wealthy entrepreneurs now read 'gifts to criminals.' A news article shockingly described how it had been 'discovered' that KSF had lent £300 million for the acquisition of yachts and private jets, as if that were some kind of a criminal activity. Actually that had been one of Singer & Friedlander's market niches for years. When details from the Kaupthing loan book were consistently leaked to the media, a criticism of large loans to key clients mounted. Kaupthing had made the mistake of continuing to support its key clients because it was of the opinion that the underlying assets were strong, even if the market disarray had caused them to fall in value. That had been a big mistake, both for the bank and the clients. Rather then cutting their losses, many of these clients had piled on all their cash and assets as security, which they subsequently lost and were practically wiped out. But the consensus was that we had somehow been ploughing money to them so they could get them to offshore accounts in the Caribbean where piles of cash were waiting for these crooked businessmen to pick up. This was not the case and, as far as I know, Kaupthing certainly did not assist anyone in 'cashing out' after the credit crunch hit.

Offshore accounts were a popular subject in the media and, in the minds of the public, having an account in offshore regions essentially proved you were a criminal. This was ludicrous. The offshore structures were, as far as I know, tax planning, and as long as people were not involved in tax evasion, there is nothing illegal about that. People may debate the ethics of avoiding or trying to minimise taxes, and I have a lot of sympathy for those arguments, but it's legal and a fact of life. In my six years of work in the UK, I don't recall ever being involved in a deal that was not set up in some kind of offshore structure. Whether they were Icelandic or UK entrepreneurs, private equity funds or blue chip UK companies, everyone had offshore companies. In a government study, conducted in the US in 2008, 83 of the 100 largest public companies in the US had tax haven subsidiaries, mainly in the Caribbean. A lot of the offshore companies set up by clients of the Icelandic banks were in the British Virgin Islands, and Tortola became synonymous with offshore 'scam'. Olafur Olafsson, who is nicknamed Oli, was now called 'TortOli' by his critics.

In his book on the stock market crash of 1929, the celebrated economist John Kenneth Galbraith describes how after the crash a generation of Americans were told:

> 'sometimes with amusement, sometimes with indignation, often with outrage, of the banking practices of the late twenties. In fact, many of these practices were made ludicrous only by the depression. Loans which would have been perfectly good were made to look perfectly foolish by the collapse of the borrower's prices or the markets for his goods or the value of the collateral he had posted. The most responsible bankers – those who saw that their debtors were victims of circumstances far beyond their control and sought to help – were often made to look the worst. The bankers yielded, as did others, to the blithe, optimistic, and immoral mood of the times but probably not more so. A depression such as that of 1929–32, were it to begin as this is written (in 1954), would also be damaging to many currently impeccable banking reputations.'

There are many things that indicate that the Icelandic bankers will endure the same fate. Although there are undoubtedly cases of bad banking and unjustified mistakes made by the bank's officials, there are a large number of loan decisions that made sense when they were made, but look very bad because of the enormous crash. The severity of the global credit crunch resulted in enormous asset deterioration, which was reflected in the heavy loan losses of the international banking sector as a whole. Practically all banking systems went bankrupt and needed to be bailed out. In Iceland this was exacerbated by the fact that almost 90 percent of the stock market was wiped out with the bank crash, and the currency more than halved in value. Many transactions and loans made by the banks looked very questionable and were scrutinised.

What looked especially suspicious after the crash was the exposure the banks had towards some of their key shareholders. Unusually, the biggest shareholders in the banks were also the biggest clients. The shareholders were essentially conglomerates, so there was a significant amount of risk diversification in the overall lending, but the amounts were very large. This was a situation specific to Iceland, and one of the key weaknesses of the system. It originated from the controversial privatisation of Landsbanki and Bunadarbanki, which legitimised this structure, and further developed in later years in all of the three banks. In most cases the shareholders had been clients of the banks before they became shareholders, rather than vice versa. A suspicion of favourable treatment towards these shareholders was still understandably widespread.

***

In the hunt for a culprit, politicians pointed the finger of blame at the banks. The politicians were more than happy to throw the blame at the banks once the hunt for the culprits commenced. In the immediate aftermath of the crash, the government and the Prime Minister, Geir Haarde, pointed the finger at Britain – they had slammed those horrible anti-terrorist laws on Landsbanki and the Central Bank of Iceland. They had caused Kaupthing's demise. It struck a patriotic chord in Icelanders' shaken hearts and seemed to win Haarde unanimous support. 'Those bloody Brits', people muttered in Reykjavik bars, 'it's a good job we won the Cod War'.

But it wasn't that simple, and gradually the tone changed. Haarde and the government were in a sticky position. They didn't look too good. After all, the system had collapsed on their watch. The Prime Minister therefore issued a stern warning to resist any personal recriminations or finger-pointing, emphasising that this was a catastrophe that was afflicting the international financial system as a whole. Wise words, but Haarde didn't practice what he preached for long. As soon as the government's work started to come under attack, he was one of the first to blame the directors of the banks and the 'Viking' entrepreneurs who had built empires for themselves abroad. They were the ones who had brought this upon the nation, he said, categorically denying that either he or his government had played any part in it. By the time he finally issued an apology, he had narrowed his responsibility to that of having not ensured distributed proprietorship when the banks were privatised. He then added that they had actually wanted to do that, but the other party in the coalition at the time had pushed them to sell the banks to strategic investors. Not much of an apology really.

In the game of pass the buck, the heads of the commercial banks placed a lot of their blame on the doorstep of the Central Bank, claiming it had failed to live up to its function as the 'bank of banks'. Banks in other European countries had received assistance and found shelter in their respective central banks, but the Central Bank of Iceland had not acted as a lender of last resort. On the contrary, they said, it had worked directly against the interests of its banks. Governor Oddsson, not one to take criticism lying down, pointed out that the banks had grown far too big for a country of this size and that it was preposterous to have expected the Central Bank to have accumulated sufficient currency reserves to support them. The Central Bank had fulfilled his supervisory role, he said, and issued the due warnings, which others had failed to act upon – the 'others' in this case being the commercial banks, the government and the Financial Supervisory Authority. Oddsson also claimed that he had told the heads of government in the summer of 2008 that he believed the banks' chances of surviving the looming difficulties were next to nil.

That was a surprising claim in light of the Central Bank's actions during the period in which Oddsson claimed he was convinced the banks would be going down. One of the most questionable actions they took in the months prior to the downfall of the banks related to the Glacier Bonds. Banks, like Toronto Dominion, which had entered into swaps with the issuers of the Glacier Bonds, like Rabobank, had hedged their own positions with short-term swaps with the Icelandic banks, which they regularly rolled over. In the swaps Toronto Dominion was getting paid interest in Icelandic kronur and paying interest in euros. In February 2008, Glitnir and Landsbanki stopped rolling over the swaps and, after a while, so did Kaupthing. This resulted in banks like Toronto Dominion having to physically hold Icelandic kronur, which they needed to place on deposit with Icelandic banks. This increased their risk considerably, as they were now subject to big credit risk on the Icelandic banks. Toronto Dominion had a very good relationship with the Central Bank, mainly through their Chief Strategist, Beat Siegenthaler – often referred to as 'Up-Beat' in Iceland because of his initial bullish view of the krona. Through this relationship, they managed to persuade the Central Bank to begin issuing certificates of deposit to the market. The result was that Toronto Dominion, other foreign banks and numerous others who had deposits in the Icelandic banks withdrew them, and bought the certificates of deposit. Over a few months, more than a billion pounds worth of kronur were thus drained out of the banks and placed with the Central Bank. To reverse the flow of money, the Central Bank entered into repurchasing agreements with small investment banks and securities houses. These small entities bought unsecured bonds from the big banks, repo-ed them to the Central Bank and took a margin. This was referred to as the 'love letter' trades. Thus, kronur were transferred from the Central Bank back to the banks.

This was a horrible mistake. Effectively the Central Bank had transferred the credit risk on the Icelandic banks from the likes of Toronto Dominion and taken it on themselves. When the banks crashed, the bonds that the Central Bank had taken as security through the repo agreements were worth a fraction of their nominal value, mainly because of the emergency law that placed deposits ahead of bonds. When Oddsson explained the emergency law on television on 6 October, he said that the government was not going to pay the debts of 'reckless men'. He wasn't correct. The Icelandic government ended up paying the bill for two banks, Landsbanki and the Central Bank, which effectively went bankrupt when the banks fell. The Central Bank lost almost two billion pounds when the banks crashed.

The entire male species was another easy target for some commentators. One claimed that some kind of 'biggest penis competition' had been taking place in the banks, which were all driven by men, who were of the same age, wore the same suits and came from the same universities. These men lacked a 'risk awareness' that women, on the other hand, had plenty of. Things would have worked out better, they claimed, if women had been in power. Some journalists pointed out that one of the few financials that was coming out of the crash practically unscathed was Audur Capital, a female run and oriented investment bank. The fact is, however, that the company only received its Icelandic FSA licence in April 2008. Even men would have struggled to bankrupt the business within five months. Many of the comments were incredibly sexist. An associate professor at Reykjavik University said in *The Times* that the logic of microlending is perfectly applicable to Iceland. She quoted the propagator of microlending Mohammed Younis in saying: 'I don't want to lend to men, they take unnecessary risks, they get drunk and they don't give the money back. If I lend to women they use it sensibly and they pay it back.' Another Icelandic business woman in a *Daily Mail* interview said, 'male values are about risk-taking, short-term gain and a focus on the individual; female values tend towards risk-awareness, the long term and team goals.' For us at Kaupthing, whose biggest losses had, to a large extent, originated from the female-run New Bond Street Asset Management, these theories rang a little hollow.

In this general mayhem of accusations and counter accusations, the public understandably grew increasingly confused and simmered with rage. It all looked like one big slanging match. Bankers and entrepreneurs who had previously been held on a pedestal by the media were now being toppled and denigrated as traitors to the nation. Men who were being hailed as business geniuses just a few months earlier were now being accused of daylight robbery. People longed for 'change', but were often at pains to define what that change entailed. Slogans like 'rebirth' and 'new values' became the order of the day.

***

Gradually, as anger mounted, people took the fight to the streets of Iceland in what became known as the 'cookware rebellion'. Large crowds gathered on a daily basis in cacophonous protests. But unlike the French revolutionaries of yore, who had armed themselves with pitchforks, muskets and swords, modern Icelanders opted for a milder and slightly quainter arsenal – of Ikea pots and pans. They wanted change – almost any kind of change. Although the occasional bank flag was burned, the demonstrations were aimed mainly at Haarde's government and the governor Oddsson. For the first time in the history of Iceland, authority figures had to be escorted by bodyguards. Both Oddsson and Haarde had people from the special forces of the police close by their side for protection.

The crowd demonstrating seemed to be a mixture of 'normal' people, anarchists, college students and supporters of the non-government parties. There was a strong political undertone and an MP for the Left-Green party was spotted in parliament giving directions to the demonstrators outside. Some of those demonstrating were very young and seemed to be there mostly for the atmosphere. A news reporter asked a 13-year-old, who was throwing stones at the police, why he was doing it. 'I'm so angry!' he answered. Then he smiled cheekily and said 'yeah, right!' Petty criminals, and the 'usual suspects' known to the police, were ecstatic when it dawned on them that it was now acceptable to throw things at their tormentors. They suddenly appeared in the front row of the demonstration throwing stones, fruit and even urine at the line of police special forces.

Outside the House of Parliament and the Prime Minister's office, windows were broken, fires were lit, and things were thrown at special forces. On one occasion, a large Christmas tree, a gift from the city of Oslo, was set alight. People were carrying various signs, most of them calling for the government to resign or Oddsson to step down. One demonstrator became famous in Iceland with a sign that people felt in its simplicity eloquently described all the anger and confusion that had gripped the nation. It simply read 'Damn, fucking, fuck!'

For the most part, and by any international standards, the demonstrations were peaceful. The police used pepper spray and on one occasion tear gas. There was general support for the demonstrations, as long as they didn't get out of hand. When things looked like they might get out of control, many people expressed their objections to violence. In the final days of the rebellion, the Prime Minister's Office was attacked by demonstrators, and this time there were few policemen around. Red paint was splashed on the building, windows were broken, and people were able to invade the office. Suddenly many of the demonstrators felt enough was enough, turned around and lined up in front of the building to support the police. That brought things to a halt.

The demonstrations bore fruit, however, and at the end of January Geir Haarde's cabinet resigned en masse and a new government took over. It was the coalition of the Left-Green and Social Democrats. The government was led by Johanna Sigurdardottir, a veteran politician, famous for her strong principles and generally considered honest and trustworthy. The international press thought it more newsworthy that Sigurdardottir was the first openly gay Prime Minister in the world. As the American talk show host Conan O'Brian put it on his show, 'Iceland appointed a lesbian ex-air stewardess as its Prime Minister. Or was I just dreaming?!'

Even after the collapse of the government, the crowd was still thirsty for heads to roll and the biggest one on everyone's list was David Oddsson's. Calls for Oddsson's resignation were coming from all quarters now, not least from the new Prime Minister herself. If nothing else there was a unanimous recognition that Iceland urgently needed to restore some semblance of credibility and integrity in the eyes of the world. Characteristically, Oddsson refused to step down. An embarrassing standoff developed between the new ruling coalition and the Central Bank. Barricading himself inside his office bunker at the Central Bank's headquarters, while the crowd tirelessly chanted slogans outside, 'the father of the nation had become the madman on the roof', one well-known writer commented. But finally the government pushed through the necessary legislation to fire him and Oddsson was left with no choice but to pick up his pencils and go.

The CEOs, boards and many other key people in the three big banks had quickly been removed by this time. When the government collapsed, the Minister of Commerce made it his final task as minister to request the board of the Icelandic FSA to offer its managing director a compromise agreement, and resigned immediately afterwards. So, by February, pretty much all of the people one could think of blaming had been removed from their positions.

***

But internal worries were the least of Iceland's troubles. International relations were at an all-time low at the same time as Iceland was facing a currency crisis and desperately needed assistance. There was one obvious recourse – the International Monetary Fund. As soon as the banks collapsed, it became clear that the country would need the fund's assistance to get it back on its feet again. But initially there was a lot of opposition to that option. Pride was an important factor, of course, and a reluctance to be the first nation in the crunch to seek emergency aid. But two weeks after the crash, the government reluctantly made its move. A lot of uncertainty and nervousness surrounded the conditions the IMF might impose on its emergency aid. But there weren't any options left. The truth was that there was no foreign currency in the country to speak of. The reserves of the Central Bank were all but wiped out.

It soon became clear, though, that even countries we considered our closest friends – the Nordic countries, for example – would only assist us if the IMF got involved. There were some worthy exceptions who extended an unconditional helping hand: the tiny Faroe Islands offered a loan worth €45 million on favourable terms, and Poland surprisingly offered a $200 million loan. Unfortunately, Iceland needed much more, and that would only be forthcoming with the IMF holding our hand.

In late October, the government reached an agreement on the terms of an emergency aid programme with the IMF representatives, which included, among other things, a $2.1 billion loan from the fund. According to the plan agreed between the government and the IMF, another $2 billion was required from other sources, and subsequently Norway, Finland, Sweden and Denmark lent us that amount. The agreement with the IMF needed to be ratified by the IMF board, a procedure that was considered to be a formality. But that turned out to be a false assumption when the Icesave dispute reared its ugly head again.

Ever since the crash, a political war had raged between Iceland and the two countries where Icesave had operated, the UK and Holland. Landsbanki had conquered a big slice of the Dutch savings market and received €1.5 billion of Icesave deposits. When Landsbanki collapsed and it wasn't clear who was guaranteeing the savers, depositors became incredibly frustrated. Icesave employees in Holland received death threats and were forced into hiding. Their office in Amsterdam was immediately shut down, the sign taken away and the post box removed. No one answered the phones and the website was shut down. Not a single trace of their operation remained. It was hardly surprising that people were going crazy with despair.

Eventually the Dutch government announced that they would guarantee the deposits, as the UK had done earlier. On the other hand, neither country was happy to be left holding the Icesave bill on its own. Iceland, they insisted, was responsible for honouring these deposit guarantees under the terms of the EU directive. British actions were particularly aggressive. By enacting the terrorist laws against Landsbanki, the bank had been shot straight to the top of the UK's terrorist hit parade on a list that included Al Qaeda, the Taliban, North Korea and Zimbabwe. Not the best of company.

'This was very unpleasant,' Prime Minister Geir Haarde said with typical understatement to a journalist from *The Times*, 'and I told the British Chancellor of the Exchequer that we are not pleased with this at all.' This was the first time that these terrorist laws had been levelled at a western state, although the Central Bank and the Ministry of Finance were soon taken off the list, leaving Landsbanki to fend on its own.

The British PR machine was set in motion and made mincemeat of the Icelanders, who didn't seem to realise what was happening until it was far too late. With his head high, Gordon Brown declared at a press conference that: 'We are showing by our action that we stand by people who save' and announced that legal action was being taken against the Icelandic government to force it to honour its obligations to British Icesave deposit holders. Icelanders wouldn't be allowed to discriminate according to nationality. This went down very well with the British public. As one reporter put it, Gordon Brown had just been handed his Falklands war on a platter.

The vast sums and lack of clarity meant that Iceland wanted to go to the European Court of Justice for arbitration. Arni Mathiesen put this to the annual summit of the ministers of finance of the EU and European Free Trade Association (EFTA) on 3 November in Brussels. This was rejected, and after a good grilling by his opposite numbers, he ended up reluctantly agreeing to the formation of a five-man arbitration committee to resolve the issue. When he got back to Iceland after the meeting, his colleagues in the government felt he'd done a rotten deal. Iceland didn't stand a chance in front of that arbitration committee, they argued, immediately distancing themselves from it. It was now painfully obvious that the country had very few allies in Europe. There was unanimous consent among the European ministers of finance that this deposit guarantee issue needed to be resolved as soon as possible, as Europe's entire deposit system hung in the balance. If the European public could no longer trust banks with their deposits, the run could rapidly spread, and it would destroy confidence in the banking system as a whole, which would take a good 30–40 years to rebuild again.

When the discussions between the IMF and Iceland commenced, it created the opportunity for the British and the Dutch to exert their influence on the fund. A solution to the Icesave dispute thus suddenly became a prerequisite to the IMF loan being approved. Icelanders protested vociferously. 'We'll never bow to such pressure,' Geir Haarde declared, 'these are two separate issues.' 'Not on my life,' another Icelandic MP said, 'I'll never say yes to a loan that drags Iceland into poverty.' The IMF, its critics claimed, had been changed into a loan collector for the British and Dutch. A gun had been put to Iceland's head and honouring the Icesave obligations was the price it had to pay for its emergency aid. In the end, though, the government had no options. Whatever the legal position, it became clear that, without accepting the Icesave liability, Iceland faced an international freeze. On 16 November, an agreement in principle was reached with Holland and the UK, which paved the way for the board of the IMF to agree to the agreement with Iceland.

The fallout from the Icesave dispute was mainly left for the new government to tackle. A negotiations committee was formed in early 2009 under the leadership of Svavar Gestsson, a former politician and ambassador. After months of meetings, it was announced in early June that an agreement had been reached with Holland and the UK. Like Neville Chamberlain, a triumphant Gestsson flew to Iceland and waved his agreement with UK and Holland, which would ensure peace between Iceland and the two nations. Just like Chamberlain's, Gestsson's agreement was not the greatest. Iceland took on the full amounts owed by the Icelandic deposit fund, collectively over £3 billion. This was practically a given, as the prior government had accepted the liability to get the IMF on board. Gestsson and his crew had done well in agreeing that Iceland didn't have to start repayments to the two countries for seven years. The most important part to negotiate, however, was the interest that would begin to accumulate on the £3 billion. It was agreed that the debt would carry a 5.5 percent interest rate from day one. This was around 2.5 percent higher than the UK was funding itself with seven-year bonds. I had been hoping that the amounts would bear no interest, at least for a few years. The reason why I would have thought this was possible was, for one, that we were actually taking on liabilities that no one seemed sure were legally ours. Also, any interest calculated on the amounts for Iceland were huge, especially in light of the horrendous economic situation. Although one understands the point of view of Holland and the UK that Iceland had at least a moral obligation to take on the Icesave debt, I hoped they would be more lenient on the interest rate. In the scheme of things the interest amounts were of little consequence for the two big countries, either economically or politically. The media in Holland and Britain were unlikely to react in a hostile way whether the interest rate was 2 percent or 3 percent or 5.5 percent. When the BBC and *The Times* announced the agreement, they didn't even mention the interest rate. Because of this I found it strange that the two countries were effectively making around 2.5 percent in interest rate differential on a country that was potentially in ruins. That interest differential alone was the equivalent of £100 million for Iceland, which is around 2 percent of its GDP. It is not known how much the eventual bill to Iceland will be. That is dependent mainly on the eventual recovery of the Landsbanki assets and how quickly those assets are realised. According to the assumptions the negotiations committee used, it is likely that Iceland's liability will end up in the region of £1.5 billion, close to 30 percent of GDP. The equivalent number for the UK would have been £300 billion.

***

So how bad are things in Iceland? It is not an easy question to answer – months after the banks fell there are still many unknowns.

By the summer of 2009, unemployment had rocketed, reaching nine percent, a big change for a country used to one or two percent. Inflation was at around 10 percent, but was gradually coming down. The currency crisis the country was facing had an enormous effect on people. Faith in the krona evaporated after the collapse and large amounts of funds were eager to flee the country. Glacier bond holders were, of course, eager to convert their krona into foreign currency, but that was not possible. To prevent a flight of capital out of the country, currency restrictions were imposed – all the glacier bonds in the country had been clamped until further notice. These restrictions were imposed to comply with one of the first conditions that the IMF had set for its emergency aid. This led to a duel market in the krona. On one hand there was the Central Bank's official exchange rate and, on the other, the offshore rate, which was considerably lower. Even the Central Bank rate clearly reflected the demise of the currency. You now needed 220 kronur to buy a pound, compared to 107 kronur just two years earlier.

In fact, the biggest effect of the crash for most people was the sinking currency. Their purchasing power was destroyed and the cost of travelling abroad has doubled in just two years. Many homes and companies that had borrowed in foreign currency saw their debts double overnight. Fortunately, though, most home mortgages were denominated in Icelandic krona. The weak currency still had some effect there, as it caused higher inflation, which increased the size of the inflation linked mortgages considerably.

One of the topics on everyone's lips was government debt. Was it 30 percent of GDP or 300 percent? So many conflicting numbers were mentioned that it was difficult to keep track. Measuring a government's debt is a notoriously difficult task, as there are many interpretations on what constitutes debt. Do you count in future pension liabilities? Should you add the liabilities of government-owned limited liability companies such as the energy companies? The most cited numbers were around 100 percent of GDP, which is high by any international standards, but not insanely high. The position of Italy and the UK is fairly similar. There was a lot of confusion on what direct effect the crash would have on government debt. Many people thought that because the government had taken over the banks, the loan losses incurred by the banks would be taken over by the state, but that was not the case. Although there were mixed feelings about the effectiveness of the emergency law, it had achieved a number of important things. The bill had been left with the bond holders of the banks and the Icelandic government initially eschewing responsibility for the banks' debt. When the law was put in place, the government and the governor of the Central Bank clearly hoped that no debt would fall directly on the state. This failed in regards to the Icesave obligation and the technical bankruptcy of the Central Bank because of the 'love letter' trades. Also, a decision was taken shortly after the crash, to protect the money market funds managed by the banks. The funds, which in normal circumstances should be very safe, had lost very large amounts of money in the crash. These funds were denominated in ISK and the only issuers in ISK were Icelandic so the funds were some of the worst sufferers of the systemic risk of Iceland. They held considerable sums of bank notes, which were now worth a fraction of their original value. Some of the funds had also been quite aggressive in buying bonds issued by the leveraged investment companies, which were now on the brink of collapsing. The government allegedly spent almost £1 billion to buy out some of the worst assets to protect the savers in the funds. The largest part of it was presumably spent on the money market fund managed by Landsbanki as it was by far the largest money market fund, and the one with the smallest proportion invested in deposits. These three liabilities, amounting to an estimated £4 billion, were the bulk of the direct obligations taken over by the government in the wake of the crash. Through the IMF scheme, Iceland has access to a total of almost $5 billion of loans, but these have not been drawn and should not result in an increase of net debt. There is an obligation to place equity in the new banks, but if the split from the old banks is done correctly, the shares in the bank should be worth what is paid for them and should therefore not result in increased net debt. There are also discussions on creditors taking over New Glitnir and New Kaupthing, which would reduce the government's contribution. What will, however, increase the debt burden of the government is the budget deficit, estimated this year at almost 15 percent of GDP, which is likely to accumulate considerable debt in the next few years.

Individuals and companies are also heavily indebted. Many were too leveraged to begin with, and with the fall of the currency and high inflation, that debt burden has increased significantly. Importantly the Central Bank hasn't felt able to lower interest rates by any measure after the crash, so households and firms are crumbling under the high interest costs. If the transfer of loans from the old banks to the new banks is done as planned, however, this situation might change for the better. The new banks will take over the loans of these households at a 'fair value.' That will mean a considerable discount from the nominal values of the loans, although it is not yet clear by how much. The discount should mean that the new banks will be able to write off a significant part of the loans to the private sector. The execution of this will be of paramount importance.

The fall of the Icelandic billionaires was dramatic following the banking crash. FL Group went into administration the day that Glitnir was nationalised. That subsequently meant that Baugur's assets did not match its debts. After months of attempts to agree a financial restructuring with its debtors, Landsbanki, the largest creditor to Baugur, pulled the plug on the company and it was placed in administration in early 2009. Landsbanki still made an arrangement with Jon Asgeir to assist them in realising value from the various companies they now controlled. Most others are still attempting to salvage something from their fallen business empires. The banks formed a large part of the assets of both Exista and Bjorgolfur Thor, so they are suffering huge losses. The Gudmundsson brothers are in the middle of a financial restructuring of Exista and Bakkavor – not an easy task with a weak financial position and hostile Icelandic creditors. Following the crash, they have lost the good will that was formerly their most prized asset. Bjorgolfur Thor lost his other banking asset at the beginning of 2009 when Straumur was also taken over by the Icelandic FSA. He is rumoured to be attempting a sale of his Actavis business, which is struggling with the heavy debt burden from Deutsche Bank. Most other former business moguls are struggling in a similar way. The destruction of assets was of such magnitude and the leverage of most investment companies at such high levels, that most people's equity was wiped out. This is in stark contrast to the position held by the large investment companies and their owners a couple of years earlier. Rather than deleverage following the early successful investments that were made between 2000 and 2006, the investments grew and so did the leverage. Eventually it all came crumbling down as asset prices plummeted.

Although the quality of the Icelandic entrepreneurs and businesses varied, many being sub par investors or operators, quite a few undeniably had a lot of skills. Jon Asgeir identified ahead of anyone three of the most lucrative takeovers in the UK in the last decade – Arcadia, Somerfield and Big Food Group. These deals created billions of pounds in equity value, although as fate and the Icelandic authorities would have it, Jon Asgeir only managed to close one of these. The Bakkavor brothers created one of the largest producers of fresh food in Europe, having started out of their garage in Reykjavik. Few people would rank ahead of Bjorgolfur Thor in successful telecom investments in Eastern Europe, and building one of Russia's largest breweries from scratch was no mean task. In the end however, they had extended too far and the very thing that had brought them to the heights of international finance, leverage, also brought them brutally back to earth. The nouveau riche Icelandic businessmen were entrepreneurs at heart and the idea of wealth preservation and the attendant caution that often characterises old money was not at the top of their mind.

Kaupthing, like the other two big banks, was split into 'New Kaupthing', which is fully operational in Iceland today, and 'Old Kaupthing'. All the Scandinavian subsidiaries were saved from administration through various measures. In July 2009 Kaupthing Luxembourg was sold to the Rowland family from the UK, resulting in all depositors being fully paid out and other creditors receiving over 85 percent of their claims. The recovery for unsecured creditors in KSF is likely to be in the area of 70–80 percent over the next two or three years. The only retail depositors that lost money depositing with Kaupthing were the ones in KSF Isle of Man. The recovery there, however, is likely to be very high – higher than in KSF – but the time it takes to get the money to people has of course caused distress amongst savers. We were also fortunate in the way we structured the deposit taking platform, so no bills are being placed on the Icelandic government because of Kaupthing Edge.

So what does the future hold for Iceland? It's a nation weighed down by debt, with unemployment on a scale never seen before, and with its international standing badly bruised. Financial glory has turned into shame and condemnation. The main debate is now on whether our future will be within or outside the European Union.

But as Icelanders have always done in difficult situations, I hope we'll find ways to work our way out of it. We don't hold the best cards, but the future will depend on how we play them.

Epilogue

I decided to write this book years ago, when the credit crunch and the crash of the Icelandic banking system were still unthinkable nightmares. At that time we were on top of the world – Iceland had finally come to be known for more than geysers and Bjork. People were talking about the Icelandic entrepreneurs and how they were affecting the business world. For a nation of 300,000 people stuck on a rock in the middle of the Atlantic to have such a big effect was a fairytale worth documenting. Then it all turned sour.

Not just in Iceland, but across the world, it became apparent that the severity of the credit crunch mangled the frameworks in which banks were all meant to operate. The worst-case scenarios drawn up by financial institutions were mere hiccups compared with the abyss, which they all eventually faced. Stress tests were not stressful enough. Liquidity rules had never entertained the idea that, for more than two years, banks would have practically no access to wholesale funding or interbank lending. Essentially, almost every single banking system in the world went bankrupt, and had to be bailed out by a national government – the difference for Iceland was that we just couldn't be bailed out.

In the context of Iceland, the overriding issue, which made us so much more exposed than others, was the size of the banking system compared to the national economy. With a tiny, volatile currency, and a government dwarfed by the size of the banks the country had spawned, it should have been obvious how vulnerable we were. Iceland was operating in one of the largest banking crises in history without a lender of last resort. Ironically, within two years it's highly likely that Kaupthing would have moved out of Iceland entirely, and then might well not have met the fate that it did.

We all turned a blind eye to the teetering imbalance between the banking system and the economy of Iceland. Not just the banks, but politicians and ratings agencies too. In January 2007, just months before the system started to crumble, Moody's gave Kaupthing an AAA rating, making us as creditworthy as the US government.

One of the reason for the size of the system was the high leverage used by many investment companies, which enabled them to provide a huge amount of capital to the banking sector. This wasn't sustainable and when the high leverage caused the investment companies to run into trouble, the problem was exposed.

As in other historic crashes, this one has been followed by the hunt for scapegoats – one person or a particular group. Was it the 'Viking entrepreneurs' or the bankers, the government, the regulators or the Central Bank? The truth is that Iceland's downfall was caused by numerous factors, both domestic and external where various parties, including all the above, should accept its participation in what caused the tragic downfall. It is ironic that many of our most outspoken critics were the main culprits behind the subprime crisis and had lost all their capital many times over before a shortage of liquidity caused the collapse of the Icelandic banking system.

And there was a lot of hubris involved. We had gotten so far by our own efforts and hard work, that we assumed that graft alone would see us through all difficulties we might face. We massively underestimated the systemic risk. In the end, we were hounded on all sides and there were people who had bet so much against Iceland that its failure was almost inevitable. Hedge funds, analysts and even business journalists all wanted to see their predictions come true. 'I told you so' really did play a part in killing a national economy.

In Iceland, and much of the rest of the world, the average man or woman on the street now thinks every banker is stupid, dishonest and overpaid; a risk junkie who should go to jail for the colossal vandalism we've caused. Being perceived like that doesn't feel great.

As a group, I don't think the Icelandic bankers were stupid, dishonest or both – although there may be individuals who were. If we had been a bit more stupid, we wouldn't have been able to get as far as we got, though in hindsight that might have been better all round. In many ways Kaupthing's reaction to the credit crunch was exemplary. Selling assets, driving down loan books, and revolutionising our deposit taking. Only a few weeks before we went into administration it looked like we were pulling out of the difficulties. But looking back, many of the decisions Kaupthing made in the last months before the downfall weren't the best ones – we should have aborted NIBC transaction, and the bank's decision to stand behind key clients rather than forcing them to aggressively sell down assets exposed it to far too much market risk. But then hindsight truly is a wonderful thing, and given the conditions in the global markets it is questionable whether anything we did in the last year of our survival would have changed anything. What hurt most was the assumption in the aftermath that we had taken decisions purely to enrich ourselves or fool the market. No one is above criticism, but everyone I knew at the bank put the future of the bank and our clients at the heart of everything we did.

For me personally it was incredibly sad to witness the collapse of KSF. The fantastic work of my colleagues in winding down loan books, selling assets, diversifying our deposit base and preserving asset quality had brought us to an enviable position in the fall of 2008. This had been achieved without any support from the Bank of England and without pledging a pound of the bank's loan book, which would have reduced the recovery of unsecured creditors. All this came to nothing as events in Iceland sucked us into the abyss. While the bulk of the UK banking system was bailed out, we were left out in the cold. It felt like we had been in a race where most of our competitors were carried over the finishing line, while KSF was tripped before reaching it.

This doesn't mean that we didn't make mistakes, and after all that has happened it's difficult to hold your head high. Large amounts of money have been lost and people's lives have been turned upside down. Some depositors are struggling to recover their hard-earned money. People in Iceland who behaved sensibly are still facing ruin as their loans have doubled in value while their homes have declined. It is impossible not to feel bad because of what has happened. I still honestly believe that I tried to act sensibly and with integrity throughout my years at Kaupthing. Of course, there are decisions I regret making and things that I regret not doing.

Now, finally, I have written this book, not to make excuses, but just to tell it like it was.

Acknowledgements

I would like to thank Ellen Hallsworth, Commissioning Editor, and her colleagues at John Wiley & Sons for their help and guidance in putting this book together. I am forever grateful to my friend and colleague Jonas Sigurgeirsson, who spent almost as much time on the book as I did, and whose support and hard work was invaluable in getting me to the finishing line. Brian Fitzgibbons read through various parts of the book. Bjarki Diego, Thordur Palsson and Helgi Bjorn Kristinsson brainstormed with me on the overall content of the book, and I am thankful for their help.

Many other people read over parts of the book at various stages of its creation and I extend my appreciation to them. At the end of the day, though, the content and any possible errors are my responsibility.

I would also like to thank my wife Thordis and the kids for accepting that I spent so much time after the collapse of Kaupthing on writing this book, as I felt it was something I needed to do. Finally I would like to thank all the people I worked with at Kaupthing during my 14 years there, it was a privilege to get to know so many great people.

Index